AFFIRMATIVE ACTION:
A PSYCHOLOGICAL PERSPECTIVE

AFFIRMATIVE ACTION:
A PSYCHOLOGICAL PERSPECTIVE

DENNIS DOVERSPIKE

MARY ANNE TAYLOR

WINFRED ARTHUR, JR.

NOVA SCIENCE PUBLISHERS, INC.
Huntington, NY

Editorial Production: Susan Boriotti
Office Manager: Annette Hellinger
Graphics: Frank Grucci and Jennifer Lucas
Information Editor: Tatiana Shohov
Book Production: Patrick Davin, Cathy DiGregory, Donna Dennis, Jennifer Kuenzig,
  Christine Mathosian, Tammy Sauter and Lynette Van Helden
Circulation: Lisa DiGangi and Michael Pazy Mino

Library of Congress Cataloging-in-Publication Data

Doverspike, Dennis.
  Affirmative action: a psychological perspective / Dennis Doverspike, Mary Anne Taylor,
  Winfred Arthur.
    p.cm.
  Includes index.
  ISBN 1-56072-762-4.
    1. Affirmative action programs. I. Taylor, Mary Anne. II. Arthur, Winfred. III. Title.

HF5549.5.A34 D68 1999
331.313'3—dc21

                                                                          99-055

Copyright © 2000 by Nova Science Publishers, Inc.
        227 Main Street, Suite 100
        Huntington, New York 11743
        Tele. 631-424-6682   Fax 631-424-4666
        E Mail Novascil@aol.com

Printed in the United States of America

CONTENTS

PREFACE

As we were in the initial stages of putting this book together, a question we heard frequently from students, friends and relatives was "what does psychology have to do with affirmative action?" Unfortunately, in our opinion, questioning the relevance of psychology to an issue such as affirmative action is not an uncommon query, even perhaps among many people within the field of psychology. When most people, both within and outside the field, make an association between psychology and affirmative action, it is in terms of the debate over racial differences in performance on intelligence tests. Thus, our decision to write this book was based upon what we saw as a need to demonstrate and highlight the substantive contribution that psychology can make in terms of improving our understanding of why it is that people respond to affirmative action with a variety of reactions and emotions.

As this book was being written, interest in affirmative action in the United States was probably at a low point. Federal efforts seemed lost in the controversy over President Clinton's race initiative. At the state level, the best publicized initiatives, including those in California, Washington, and Texas, were those which called for strict limitations on the application of affirmative action. Within the professional human resource management literature, more press seemed to be devoted to generalized diversity efforts than to affirmative action. Finally, within the academic community, it seemed that fewer research articles and theoretical articles were being published on affirmative action, although related issues, such as reducing adverse impact on tests, did receive some increased attention. Despite the apparent waning of interest, we were of the opinion that the time was right for a book devoted to a discussion of the psychological aspects of affirmative action.

As the title suggests, our primary goal is to discuss empirical research and theoretical work on affirmative action from a psychological perspective. The intended audience for this book is primarily academics, including undergraduate and graduate students, and social science researchers. These researchers may come from a variety of backgrounds, including sociology, political science, and public administration, but we would expect that the primary audience would be psychologists. While our intended audience is academic, we have strived to achieve a writing style and a level of complexity in terms of discussion of content which would make this book accessible to nonacademics and students, as well as seasoned researchers. This blending of writing styles is a difficult task, especially to those more accustomed to scientific discourse, and so we can only hope that the resulting product of our endeavors is a book which can be read by a range of individuals from a variety of backgrounds and academic fields.

Based on the frequent calls we receive from the media when affirmative action becomes a topic of interest to the press, we would also expect that the book might appeal to a wider audience including those interested in the political aspects of the affirmative action debate. Finally, we would hope that practitioners involved in developing affirmative action or diversity programs would also find parts of this book to be of interest and useful in the design of these interventions.

Our primary context in writing this book was affirmative action in the United States. However, because most of the issues discussed in this book are not limited by geographical boundaries, we have also included a chapter specifically devoted to international issues.

A discussion of affirmative action cannot completely ignore legal and political issues. However, this book is not intended to be a legal guide nor a review of the legal or political debate on affirmative action. We would further caution the reader that we are not lawyers and do not intend to represent ourselves as presenting legal advice. We strongly recommend that anyone involved in research or practical issues concerned with affirmative action be aware of any applicable laws and regulations and seek legal guidance when appropriate. Many laws and regulations which apply to affirmative action vary by state.

In this book, we have taken the opportunity to present research from a number of published studies we have conducted and also from a number of unpublished studies. Therefore, we would like to thank all of the graduate students, undergraduate students, and other faculty, who have collaborated with us on research over the years. We would also like to thank the many undergraduates who have served as research participants in our studies.

The following individuals deserve a special note of thanks for helping to review sections of the book: Alana Blumental, Ida Doverspike, Rosanna Miguel-Feruito, and Diane Monaghan. Finally, we would like to thank our respective universities for their financial support. In particular, Dennis Doverspike, University of Akron, and Winfred Arthur, Jr., Texas A&M University, were able to work on portions of this book during sabbaticals from their respective universities.

Chapter 1

INTRODUCTION

Why is psychological research applicable to the affirmative action debate (i.e., should organizations engage in affirmative action based on protected group status in the awarding of opportunities and should the government encourage organizations to engage in affirmative action)? Affirmative action, despite its initial apparent simplicity, is actually quite a complex issue. Most people appear to have little actual knowledge of affirmative action or the complex issues involved in monitoring and implementing affirmative action. As a result, when asked about affirmative action, people's reactions often reflect: 1) the likelihood of personal benefit or loss; 2) their general opinion or attitude toward affirmative action; and 3) their definition of affirmative action (e.g., do they view it as requiring quotas?). However, attitudes toward affirmative action are often malleable and can be changed by simple communications or by a reframing of the question. Thus, when we ask people about affirmative action, we are basically collecting data on an attitude which can be changed under certain, known conditions. The topics of attitudes and attitude change are, of course, the province of psychology, and it is for that reason that psychological theories and research can make a contribution to the affirmative action debate.

In this book, we consider the question of the relative merits of affirmative action from a psychological perspective. Because that question is complex, the answer, too, is necessarily complex. Nevertheless, psychological research conducted over the past 30 years does provide us with some answers. In this book, we explore the series of solutions that the body of psychological literature offers for those interested in the past and future of affirmative action and diversity policies.

The purpose of this book is to provide a review of the research on affirmative action in a format which is accessible to readers and also useable by those both within and outside the field of psychology. By doing so, it is hoped that the results of the research conducted by many dedicated researchers will finally come to inform the debate on affirmative action (Nacoste, 1996).

Consistent with our stated purpose, this book does not try to list every study ever conducted on affirmative action nor does it try to present detail on every study ever published (for an excellent study-by-study review of the literature see Kravitz et al., 1997). Rather, we have tried to organize the relevant research in a manner which, we hope, will illustrate how and why psychological research can be used by those involved in the public debate over affirmative action. We have often featured our own research efforts, we would hope not out of conceit, but because it is the research with which we are most familiar and because this book has given us an opportunity to present previously unpublished research. We believe the results of this research can be used not only as a source of information in the affirmative action debate, but also as a starting point in increasing our understanding of how attitudes toward affirmative action can be changed.

In this first chapter, we introduce the basic issues surrounding affirmative action and define what is meant by affirmative action. We will also lay out a brief history of the debate in the United States and, finally, discuss the basic nature of a psychological approach to affirmative action.

THE BASIC ISSUE

Throughout the history of the United States, racial minorities and women have encountered social and legal barriers which have effectively, and often intentionally, blocked their participation in education and employment. Until the second half of the 20th century, many forms of what today are considered to be illegal discrimination were not only legal, but viewed as offering protection to women or minorities. In some case, practices which today might be viewed as discriminatory were mandated by the United States Government or by state governments (Wilson, 1998).

In terms of employment and education opportunities, the turning point was the passage of the Civil Rights Act of 1964. Until that point, education and employment opportunities were often openly segregated by race and sex. As might be expected, the Civil Rights Act of 1964 did not result in immediate changes. While this in part reflected resistance to social change and discriminatory attitudes on the part of the White majority, it was also partially a result of the slow process by which any piece of government legislation is interpreted by the courts through accompanying legal decisions. For example, the pivotal employment case, *Griggs v. Duke Power Company*, was not decided by the Supreme Court until 1971.

In response to what was seen as a need to facilitate progress toward the goals of the Civil Rights Act of 1964, the use of affirmative action procedures was proposed as a temporary solution. In the next section, we will further explore the operational definition of affirmative action; however, we can adapt here the general, working definition that *"affirmative action refers to policies or procedures which attempt to increase the representation of an underrepresented, protected group (primarily minority or female but may include other groups such as the aged) in education or employment through the consideration in decision making of applicant race, sex, or other protected group status."* It should also be noted that affirmative action can be court-mandated or involuntary. However, most of the concern with research and opinion on affirmative action has been directed at so-called voluntary affirmative action, as opposed to court-ordered affirmative action.

Affirmative action is often differentiated from equal opportunity. Equal opportunity is defined here as *"treating individuals in a similar fashion regardless of membership in a protected group."* Equal opportunity is sometimes associated with the concept of race-neutral decision making. Thus, affirmative action is seen as an active process while equal opportunity is interpreted as being a passive process.

The purpose of affirmative action is viewed as being to:

1. Correct or remediate the effects of past discrimination.
2. Promote diversity in government and private organizations.
3. Promote inclusion and representation in occupations.
4. Improve the economic standing of minorities and women (Crosby, 1994; Shaw, 1988; Vasquez, 1999; White House, 1995).

While the intended purposes of affirmative action are admirable, the effective implementation of affirmative action requires the identification of people based upon their race and sex. Thus, the paradox -- a procedure where the intent is the elimination of decision making based upon race and sex has the effect of requiring the identification of people based upon their race and sex and, in many cases, further requires that decisions be made, at least in part, based upon a person's race or sex. It is this conflict between what would appear to be the purpose of civil rights legislation, ensuring equal opportunity for all regardless of race or sex, and the possible consequences of affirmative action policies, requiring that decisions be made upon the basis of race or sex, which creates such an interesting psychological and political dilemma. Thus, the arguments against affirmative action include that it:

1. Leads to decisions based upon race and sex and possible reverse discrimination.
2. Violates the basic rule of distributing opportunities on the basis of merit without regard to race and sex.
3. Leads to anger, hostility and resistance on the part of nonbeneficiaries (i.e., primarily White males).
4. Can result in psychological harm to the intended beneficiaries due to the effect of affirmative action on self-assessments and evaluations by others (please note, some of the authors cited here are proponents of affirmative action and their articles rebut arguments against the use of affirmative action; Burstein, 1985; Eastland & Bennett, 1979; Glasser, 1988; Gottfredson, 1994; Shaw, 1988).

DEFINING AFFIRMATIVE ACTION

The debate over the relative merits and fairness of affirmative action policies involves consideration of a series of highly complex, interrelated, sometimes ambiguous questions, creating a type of meta-question. Thus, there is no single, simple affirmative action question. It is not simply a question of deciding whether affirmative action is equitable or not. Nor is it simply a matter of deciding whether affirmative action is legal or not. It is not possible to arrive at a single answer or a single solution in the affirmative action debate. Further complicating matters, the very act of defining affirmative action is itself a part of the political debate.

As we have already expressed our view that the affirmative action debate really involves a series of complicated issues or a meta-question, any attempt to define affirmative action is a difficult, ambiguous endeavor. However, a first step toward a definition of affirmative action can be attempted by outlining the multidimensional nature of the affirmative action question as it has been approached in the psychological literature. That is, affirmative action can be defined by looking at the variations in operationalization and use of the term "affirmative action." By doing so, a basic structure can be developed for understanding psychological approaches to the affirmative action debate.

Earlier, the following meta-definition of affirmative action was offered: *"Affirmative action refers to policies or procedures which attempt to increase the representation of an underrepresented, protected group (primarily minority or female but may include other groups such as the aged) in education or employment through the consideration in decision making of applicant race, sex, or other protected group status."* While the preceding can serve as a working definition, as a starting point for discussion, it is too broad to be useful in most psychological research. The obvious exception to the previous statement would be research (i.e., opinion survey or field survey research), where the purpose is to determine the respondent's personal definition or the meaning an individual assigns to the construct of affirmative action. As a result of the difficulties associated with defining affirmative action, in most of the psychological literature the definition is either limited by the use of specific instructions or through the scenarios provided to the study's participants.

Based on the psychological and legal literatures, there appear to be three basic dimensions which can be used or manipulated by the researcher, by either their inclusion or omission, in order to specify the operational definition of affirmative action. The three basic dimensions are:

1. The relative emphasis on merit or the type of affirmative action.
2. The protected group(s) involved.
3. Type of opportunity (e.g., education or employment).

By manipulating these three variables, the operational definition of affirmative action can be changed. For example, a survey could ask for a respondent's opinion regarding the use of sex-based, hard quotas by state governments for University admissions. Likewise, opinions could be gathered on race-based, soft quotas by private companies for hiring purposes.

Emphasis on Merit - Type of Affirmative Action

One of the major factors which can be manipulated in defining affirmative action is the relative emphasis on merit or the type or nature of the affirmative action. Taylor-Carter, Doverspike, and Cook (1995) refer to this as part of the policy context. In the psychological literature, there are basically five types or levels of affirmative action (Ledvinka & Scarpello, 1991; Seligman, 1975):

1. Recruitment - specific actions aimed at the recruitment of protected group members.
2. Removing discriminatory obstacles - taking action, including special training programs, to identify employment policies which cause problems and remove or revise those policies.
3. Soft Preferential Treatment - operationalized in terms of selecting or choosing the protected group member. When the protected group member and the majority (nonprotected group) applicant are equally qualified (or, in some cases, simply meet some minimum standards), the protected group member is chosen.
4. Hard Preferential Treatment - operationalized in terms of selecting or choosing a protected group member simply as a result of their protected group status. This may also be referred to as reverse discrimination. Some examples of typical procedures which can be classified as hard preferential treatment include the use of quotas or race norming.
5. Diversity - a relatively new entry to the list, diversity efforts are directed at increasing the multicultural nature of the workforce.

Protected Group

Affirmative action policies are aimed at particular, identifiable groups. Although affirmative action policies could be aimed at other groups (e.g., older adults), most of the research and popular attention has been focused on race and sex. Thus, in terms of protected groups, the major distinction would be between sex-based affirmative action and race-based affirmative action.

It is much easier to define sex than it is race or ethnicity. Although one can find some authors willing to dispute the definition of sexual categories, fundamentally it is a biological question that can be resolved in terms of a basic dichotomous decision as to whether the person is male or female.

Attempts to define the race or ethnicity of applicants or candidates have met with more controversy than those involving definitions of sex. For purposes of equal opportunity and affirmative action, race is viewed as a political construct and is not intended to have anthropological nor scientific meaning (Sawyer, 1998; Wallman, 1998; Williams, 1998).

Historically, the preferred means of collecting racial identification has been self-report (i.e., individuals are asked to fill out a form on which they check the most appropriate racial or ethnic category). The four categories used for the self-report of race, and the fifth category for ethnicity, are:

1. American Indian or Alaskan Native.
2. Asian or Pacific Islander.
3. Black.
4. White.
5. Hispanic.

The racial categories were the product of the United States Office of Management and Budget (Wallman, 1998; Williams, 1998) and were designed to simplify the reporting burden and also serve the purpose of enforcing civil rights law. The categories were not intended to be interpreted as making any type of political, social, or scientific statement (Sawyer, 1998; Wallman, 1998).

However, the use of the five racial categories has been the subject of controversy. The categories do not cover all possible ethnic or racial minority groups (e.g., Arabs and Hawaiian Natives). By their nature, the categories only require a single choice and, therefore, do not allow for a multiracial identification. Changes to these categories have been considered including adding a multiracial category, adding various Asian subcategories, and changing Black to African American (Phinney, 1996; Wallman, 1998; Williams, 1998).

Type of Opportunity

Although affirmative action can occur in other situations (e.g., awarding of contracts), most research deals with either affirmative action in education or employment. Of course, the boundaries can sometimes become blurred which is the case in research directed at internships, assistantships, or student employment. The distinction between public and private organizations is important in the legal literature (Robinson, Paolillo, & Reithel, 1998), but does not appear to have been a major area of concern in the psychological research literature.

HISTORY

In 1961, during the administration of President Kennedy, Executive Order 10925 was issued which used the term "affirmative action" (Bruno, 1998a; Wilson, 1998). It was after Kennedy's death, that the Civil Rights Act of 1964 was finally passed, effectively ending overt past practices of race and sex discrimination.

As a result of the Civil Rights Act of 1964, the Equal Employment Opportunity Commission (EEOC) was established and granted the authority to issue guidelines related to discrimination in employment decision and testing. One of the guidelines provided by the EEOC was the 80% rule of thumb approach to adverse impact (EEOC, 1978). Note that adverse impact refers to a theory or type of discrimination in which a neutral device has a discriminatory impact on a protected group. The 80% rule of thumb stipulates that one method of calculating adverse impact is to compare the selection rate for the minority group to the selection rate for the majority group. The selection rate is defined as the number selected divided by the number of applicants. If the minority selection rate is less than 80% of the rate for the majority group, then this can be considered evidence of adverse impact. From the affirmative action perspective, what is critical here is that adverse impact is determined by a very specific numeric ratio (EEOC, 1978).

In 1965, President Johnson issued Executive Order 11246 requiring federal contractors to take affirmative action to ensure equality of employment opportunity (Wilson, 1998). Although Executive Order 11246 prohibited discrimination on the basis of race, color, religion, sex, and national origin, it applied to only certain types of federal government contractors.

Both as Vice-President and as President, Richard Nixon played a critical role in advancing the theory and practice of affirmative action at the federal level. It was the Nixon administration that issued guidelines and a revised executive order which described the use of goals and timetables as a means for achieving equal opportunity (Wilson, 1998). During the Johnson Administration, the Office of Federal Contract Compliance (OFCCP) had started a policy of monitoring affirmative action efforts of federal contractors and under the Nixon administration the role of the OFCCP was expanded (Bruno, 1998a).

The OFCCP, which is part of the Department of Labor, has what might be regarded as an administrative definition of affirmative action. Under OFCCP regulations, organizations must maintain an affirmative action plan which contains information on their plan and how it is maintained, reporting and internal auditing systems, support for community action programs, and compliance with nondiscrimination guidelines. In addition, organizations must conduct an analysis to identify underrepresentation including a workforce analysis, availability analysis, utilization analysis, a statement of goals, and a statement of progress toward goals. This integrated analysis of underrepresentation is carried out based on an Eight-Factor Computation Method.

The eight factors are:

1. The percentage of the protected group in the population in the labor area surrounding the facility.
2. The percentage of the protected group among unemployed in the labor area surrounding the facility.
3. The percentage of the protected group in the total work force in the immediate labor area.
4. The percentage of the protected group among those having the requisite skills in the immediate labor area.
5. The percentage of the protected group among those having the requisite skills in a reasonable recruitment area.

6. The percentage of the protected group among those considered to be promotable or transferable within the facility.
7. The percentage of the protected group at institutions providing training in the requisite skills.
8. The percentage of the protected group among those at the facility whom the contractor could train in the requisite skills.

Once raw statistics are calculated for each of the eight factors, the raw statistics are multiplied by a weighting factor. This gives a percentage for each of the eight factors. The percentages are added together to arrive at a final availability percentage which represents the percentage of that protected group hypothetically available for employment. The actual percentages are then compared to these final availability percentages. This comparison of percentages is referred to as the utilization analysis. If underutilization exists, the company can set goals in order to attempt to reach full utilization. There is also a set of problem areas which are supposed to be reviewed as part of the affirmative action plan.

This administrative definition of affirmative action as offered by the OFCCP is quite different from the type of definitions of affirmative action used in psychological research. The OFCCP can conduct affirmative action compliance reviews, which can include an analysis of an organization's employment data and the Affirmative Action Plan. Based on the review, the OFCCP may suggest possible remedial actions including termination of status as a federal contractor.

Fast-forwarding to the 1990s and returning to the impact of legislation on affirmative action, Section 106 of the Civil Rights Act of 1991 appeared to prohibit race norming and restrict various types of affirmative action. Thus, as a result of Section 106, it is considered an unlawful employment practice to adjust or otherwise alter scores on employment tests on the basis of race, color, religion, sex, or national origin.

In 1995, as a result of the continuing debate over affirmative action, President Clinton requested a review of all federal affirmative action programs (White House, 1995). This report concluded that affirmative action programs had worked in the sense that they had advanced equal opportunity and had fostered inclusion (White House, 1995). While the White House report identified areas where improvements could be made, overall, Federal affirmative action programs were judged to be fair. Fairness was defined in terms of:

1. Avoiding quotas.
2. Consideration of race neutral options.
3. Flexibility.
4. Limited in time.
5. Did not unduly burden nonbeneficiaries (White House, 1995).

Consistent with the goals of the Clinton national initiative on race, the Clinton administration's view could be seen as one which was generally favorable to the continuation of affirmative action until a better alternative could be found (Bruno, 1998b).

Although our discussion has concentrated on employment issues, affirmative action has also been an issue in situations involving education and minority contacting (Bruno, 1998b; Dale, 1998b; Eddy, 1998). It could be argued that the first use of the term "affirmative action" occurred in the context of the discussion of an "affirmative duty" in education cases (Dale, 1998a; Dale, 1998b). Furthermore, a number of the major, defining court cases have involved education.

In terms of affirmative action, most of the research has been concerned with questions involving race or sex. However, questions concerning affirmative action could be extended to other groups, especially those groups covered by anti-discrimination legislation.

Age discrimination is not covered by the Civil Rights Act, but it is covered by the Age Discrimination in Employment Act of 1967 (ADEA), which protects individuals 40 years of age and older (Jones, 1998). Physical or mental disabilities are covered by the Americans with Disabilities Act of 1990 (ADA) and by the Vocational Rehabilitation Act of 1973, which forbid discrimination on the basis of disabilities. Vietnam-era veterans are covered by the Vietnam Veterans Readjustment Assistance Act of 1974, which requires employers to take affirmative action to hire and promote Vietnam-era veterans.

The California Initiative

In 1996, California voters approved a controversial measure known as Proposition 209 or the California Civil Rights Initiative. Aimed at banning both discrimination and preferential treatment, this proposition would appear to have the effect of eliminating, or at least severely limiting, affirmative action in California State employment, contracting, and education. An interesting feature of the debate over this initiative, however, was the argument concerning the meaning of the preferential treatment clause and whether it constituted anti-affirmative action (Bruno, 1998c; Dale, 1998a).

Washington State Initiative

In November of 1998, Washington State voters approved a measure similar to California's Proposition 209. This measure, referred to as Initiative 200, was designed to prohibit granting preferential treatment to individuals or groups based on race, sex, color, ethnicity, or national origin in public employment, public education, and public contracting. In both the California and Washington votes, one of the main issues involved the wording of the initiative, in particular whether both initiatives would ban all affirmative action or merely the strongest forms of preferential treatment.

Court Cases

Although we have purposely tried to stay away from a discussion of legal issues, no discussion of the history of affirmative action in the United States would be complete without some discussion of court cases. The problem with any discussion of court cases, even a historical one, is regardless of the recency of the written text, a new decision may be issued or a new law passed, that not only changes the future, but also changes the way past court decisions are viewed and interpreted. In addition, most of the pivotal court cases dealing with affirmative action were decided before the passage of the Civil Rights Act of 1991. As noted previously, the Civil Rights Act of 1991 contained language which could be interpreted as limiting certain strategies aimed at increasing participation of underrepresented groups.

One of the early critical court cases was *Regents University of California v. Bakke* (1978) in which the Supreme Court struck down a medical school plan that set aside slots in an educational program for minorities. The *Bakke* decision has been interpreted as prohibiting setting aside a specific number of positions, although allowing for the use of race as one of many factors involved in the selection process. One interpretation could be that while *Bakke* prohibited the strict use of quotas, it did allow for "tipping" or the use of race when the qualifications of the two individuals were otherwise equivalent (Dale, 1998a).

In *Steelworkers v. Weber* (1979), a voluntary affirmative action plan was upheld for employment purposes. The agreement to initiate the voluntary plan had been reached between Kaiser Aluminum and a union, the United Steelworkers of America. The Supreme Court allowed the plan to stand based on the reasoning that is was a temporary measure adapted in the face of a large discrepancy in the percentage of Whites and Blacks in skilled craft positions. Furthermore, the plan did not result in White employees enduring an unfair burden (Bruno, 1998a).

In *Johnson v. Transportation Agency, Santa Clara County, California* (1987), the Supreme Court ruled that an affirmative action plan could consider the use of sex in selection. The hiring of a qualified woman was allowed even though a male who scored slightly higher was rejected. Although there was no proof of discrimination, the finding of a large sex imbalance was seen to offer a sufficient rational (Bruno, 1998a; Moore & Hass, 1990).

At the federal level, the most critical case to date involved the decision of the Supreme Court in *Adarand Constructors, Inc. v. Peña* (1995). This decision would appear to require that federal affirmative action programs be subject to the standard of "strict scrutiny," a standard which would require more detailed statistical analyses, clearer proof of past discrimination and of a compelling governmental interest, and a more narrow tailoring of the program than had previously been the case (Dale, 1998a).

At present, the case law on affirmative action can be summarized as follows:

1. The organization must identify a specific problem involving past discrimination or underrepresentation.
2. The affirmative action plan should have a narrow focus aimed at the specific problem.
3. The affirmative action plan should be limited in time so that once the specific problem is resolved, the plan is terminated.
4. The rights of nonminorities or males must also be considered.

The aforementioned, four principles based on case law would appear to be compatible with and similar to the fairness principles described in Clinton's Presidential Report on Affirmative Action (White House, 1995).

PSYCHOLOGICAL APPROACH TO THE PROBLEM

Psychological research on affirmative action has typically centered around the issue of attitudes. Attitudes have been used both as criterion variables and as mediating variables between initial conditions (i.e., independent variables) and final criterion variables. As a result of a limited knowledge of affirmative action, people's reactions are often dependent upon two general classes of independent variables, the characteristics of people and the characteristics of the organization, including the type of affirmative action implemented by the organization. In an earlier article (Taylor-Carter et al., 1995), we developed a model for explaining resistance to affirmative action which was based on these two main factors, the evaluator perspective and the context in which the affirmative action policy was embedded. The evaluator perspective referred to attitudes, beliefs and values relevant to the outcomes arising from affirmative action policies. Policy context referred to the specific type of affirmative action policy used and the organizational setting associated with a particular affirmative action policy.

A simpler version of the above model, and one perhaps more applicable to the debate over affirmative action, can be offered by considering the issue as basically being one of communication. That is, from a practical perspective, the question of greatest interest is one of how can a party in the debate communicate their message to an intended recipient of their message. In this context, we can recast our two main factors into characteristics of the message and characteristics of the target of the message. (Note: From a communication perspective, the characteristics of the sender would also seem to be critical. However, the issue of the sender of the message has been largely ignored or considered to be part of the characteristics of the message).

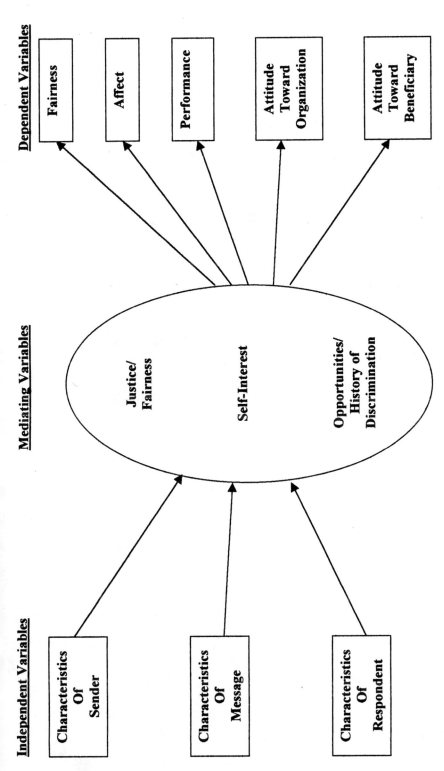

Independent Variables

Characteristics Of Sender

Characteristics Of Message

Characteristics Of Respondent

Mediating Variables

Justice/ Fairness

Self-Interest

Opportunities/ History of Discrimination

Dependent Variables

Fairness

Affect

Performance

Attitude Toward Organization

Attitude Toward Beneficiary

Figure 1. Model of the Psychological Processes Involved in Affirmative Action

Thus, a simple psychological model which serves as a framework for much of the literature on affirmative action can be developed (see Figure 1). At this point, we do not pretend to suggest that we are offering a model intended to be interpreted as proposing strict cause and effect relationships or any type of path or causal model. Rather, the model presented here is intended to be a conceptual model or a very general model offered as a way of organizing and making sense of the available literature. While it may be possible to derive testable hypotheses from this model, the intent is to have the model serve as an organizational aide rather than as a strict statement of a psychological theory.

At the independent variable end of the model, there are three broad classes of variables which include characteristics of the sender of the message, characteristics of the message, and characteristics of the respondent, target or subject. Differences in these three broad classes of variables then determine or cause differences in mediating variables. We acknowledge that not all studies include mediator variables. Further, a mediator in one study could very well be used as a criterion variable in another. Having said that, there are some common mediators including perceptions of justice/fairness, self-interest, and perceptions of the number of available opportunities open to the group and the role of the past history of discrimination in limiting the number of opportunities.

As noted above, one researcher's mediator variable can be another researcher's dependent variable. However, of the variables mentioned above, the one which seems to cause the greatest confusion is perceptions of fairness. Given that the trend in recent research has been to treat fairness as a separate concept from attitude, we have included perceptions of justice-fairness as a mediating variable and also included fairness as a dependent or criterion variable.

Through effects on the mediator variables, the three broad classes of independent variables then determine or cause differences in attitudes or occasionally performance, which serve as the dependent or criterion variables. Examples of some common criterion variables include judgements of fairness (see discussion above of fairness as a mediator), affect, performance, attitudes toward the organization, and judgments of characteristics of the recipient or beneficiary of affirmative action.

The dependent variable of judgments of the characteristics of the recipient also deserves special notice, because a topic of great interest in the psychological research has been whether affirmative action may actually do harm to the intended beneficiaries by affecting judgments of their own ability, motivation, or performance. Specifically, judgments of competence have often been included as a dependent variable. Of course, the judgements of others, of nonbeneficiaries, concerning the characteristics of recipients may also be affected by the presence of affirmative action policies and has also been a topic which has attracted research interest.

ORGANIZATION OF THE BOOK

Given this general framework, there are a number of theories and research methodologies which can be applied to the study of the psychology of affirmative action. In Chapters 2 and 3, we discuss the basic theories relevant to understanding affirmative action and the accompanying research. This includes various justice theories in Chapter 2 and theories related to attitudes and attitude change and also individual differences in personal traits in Chapter 3. Of course, within this book we could not give complete coverage to all of these theories, but we do hope to provide enough of an overview to illustrate their importance to the affirmative action debate.

In Chapter 4, we present the basic methods used in affirmative action research. The four major methods used are the opinion survey, the correlational study, the paper-person scenario, and the assigned leader paradigm.

Following the basic model of the psychological processes presented in Chapter 1, Chapter 5 reviews research relevant to the characteristics of the sender and of the message. As previously indicated, because properties of the sender are often confounded with the manipulation of the message, there is insufficient research on sender characteristics to present it as a separate section. In Chapter 6, research on the characteristics of the respondent or target of the message is presented. The questions of possible mediating mechanisms are discussed in Chapter 7. Due to its importance and its unique nature, the question of whether affirmative action may harm the intended beneficiaries is addressed in Chapter 8.

The review of the literature contained in Chapters 5 through 8 was based on an extensive and exhaustive search conducted in order to identify studies that had examined psychological reactions, specifically attitudes. We commenced with a search of the electronic databases *PsycINFO*,

ABI/INFORM, and *Business Insite* using "affirmative action" and "equal opportunity" as the primary key words. The electronic search was supplemented with a manual search of the current literature including the programs of several academic and professional conferences. Although we completed an exhaustive search, our intent in this book is not to provide a study by study recapitulation (see Kravitz et al., 1997), but rather to integrate the research within an overall model of the applicable psychological processes.

The implementation of affirmative action also affects the organization and its systems. Chapter 9 looks at some alternative methods of increasing minority and female representation. The affirmative action debate is not limited to the United States, and in Chapter 10 we provide a brief discussion of research and experiences from other countries. In Chapter 11, we present suggestions for implementation based on psychological theory and research on affirmative action. Final conclusions, including research recommendations, are offered in Chapter 12.

REFERENCES

Adarand Constructors, Inc. v. Peña, 115 S. Ct. 2097 (1995).

Bruno, A. (1998a). Affirmative action in employment. In S. N. Colamery (Ed.), *Affirmative action: Catalyst or albatross* (pp. 59-109). Commack, NY: Nova.

Bruno, A. (1998b). Affirmative action: Recent congressional and presidential activity. In S. N. Colamery (Ed.), *Affirmative action: Catalyst or albatross* (pp. 35-40). Commack, NY: Nova.

Bruno, A. (1998c). California Civil Rights Initiative. In S. N. Colamery (Ed.), *Affirmative action: Catalyst or albatross* (pp. 53-57). Commack, NY: Nova.

Burstein, P. (1985). On equal employment opportunity and affirmative action. In C. B. Marrett & C. Leggon (Eds.), *Research in race and ethnic relations* (Vol. 4, pp. 91-112). Greenwich, CT: JAI Press.

Crosby, F. J. (1994). Understanding affirmative action. *Basic and Applied Social Psychology, 15,* 13-41.

Dale, C. V. (1998a). Affirmative action law: A brief introduction. In S. N. Colamery (Ed.), *Affirmative action: Catalyst or albatross* (pp. 1-7). Commack, NY: Nova.

Dale, C. V. (1998b). Minority and small disadvantaged business contracting: Legal and constitutional developments. In S. N. Colamery (Ed.), *Affirmative action: Catalyst or albatross* (pp. 121-134). Commack, NY: Nova.

Eastland, T. & Bennett, W. J. (1979). *Counting by race: Equality from the founding fathers to Bakke and Weber.* New York, NY: Basic.

Eddy, M. (1998). Minority and women-owned business programs of the federal government. In S. N. Colamery (Ed.), *Affirmative action: Catalyst or albatross* (pp. 147-163). Commack, NY: Nova.

Equal Employment Opportunity Commission (1978). Uniform guidelines on employee selection procedures. *Federal Register, 43*, 38290-38309.

Glasser, I. (1988). Affirmative action and the legacy of racial injustice. In P. A. Katz & D. A. Taylor (Eds.), *Eliminating racism: Profiles in controversy* (pp. 341-357). New York: Plenum Press.

Gottfredson, L. S. (1994, November). From the ashes of affirmative action. *The World & I,* pp. 365-377.

Griggs V. Duke Power Company, 401 U.S. 424 (1971).

Johnson v. Transportation Agency, Santa Clara County, California, 480 U.S. 616 (1987).

Jones, K. D. (1998). The age discrimination in employment act (ADEA): Overview and current legal developments. In S. N. Colamery (Ed.), *Affirmative action: Catalyst or albatross* (pp. 241-259). Commack, NY: Nova.

Kravitz, D. A., Harrison, D. A., Turner, M. A., Levine, E. L. Chaves, W., Brannick, M. T., Denning, D. L., Russell, C. J., & Conrad, M. A. (1997). *Affirmative action: A review of psychological and behavioral research.* Bowling Green, OH: Society for Industrial and Organizational Psychology.

Ledvinka, J., & Scarpello, V. G. (1991). *Federal regulation of personnel and human resource management.* Boston, MA: PWS-Kent.

Moore, D. P. & Hass, M.. (1990). When affirmative action cloaks management bias in selection and promotion decisions. *Academy of Management Executive, 4,* 84-90.

Nacoste, R. W. (1996). Social psychology and the affirmative action debate. *Journal of Social and Clinical Psychology, 15,* 261-282.

Phinney, J. S. (1996). When we talk about American ethnic groups, what do we mean? *American Psychologist, 51,* 918-927.

Regents University of California v. Bakke, 438 U.S. 265 (1978).

Robinson, R. K., Paolillo, J. G. P., & Reithel, B. J. (1998). Race-based preferential treatment programs: Raising the bar for establishing compelling government interests. *Public Personnel Management, 27,* 349 -360.

Sawyer, T. C. (1988). Measuring race and ethnicity: Meeting public policy goals. *American Statistician, 52(1),* 34-35.

Seligman, D. (1975). How "equal opportunity" turned into employment quotas. In K. N. Wexley & G. A. Yukl (Eds.), (pp.470-479). *Organizational Behavior and Industrial Psychology.* New York, NY: Oxford Press.

Shaw, B. (1988). Affirmative action: An ethical evaluation. *Journal of Business Ethics, 7,* 763-770.

Steelworkers v. Weber, 443 U.S. 193 (1979).

Taylor-Carter, M. A., Doverspike, D., & Cook, K. (1995). Understanding resistance to sex and race-based affirmative action: A review of research findings. *Human Resources Management Review, 5,* 129-157.

Vasquez, M. J. T. (1999). President's message reaffirming affirmative action. *Psychology of Women, 26(1),* 1-4.

Wallman, K. K. (1998). Data on race and ethnicity: Revising the Federal Standard. *The American Statistician, 52(1),* 31 - 33.

Williams, J. D. (1998). Race and ethnicity: Possible revision of OMB's classifications. In S. N. Colamery (Ed.), *Affirmative action: Catalyst or albatross* (pp.227-240). Commack, NY: Nova.

Wilson, R. (1998). Affirmative action: Yesterday, today and beyond. In S. N. Colamery (Ed.), *Affirmative action: Catalyst or albatross* (pp. 10-33). Commack, NY: Nova.

White House (1995). *Affirmative action review: Report to the President.* [On-line], Available: www.whitehouse.gov/WH/EOP/OP/html/aa/aa-index.

Chapter 2

THEORETICAL PERSPECTIVES - JUSTICE THEORIES

The testing of theories and associated hypotheses is at the heart of the psychological approach to the study of affirmative action. Theory should inform and direct research as well as serve as the basis for program design and implementation. Yet, much of the research on affirmative action has been atheoretical, or at least minimalist in terms of theoretical underpinnings. This is not surprising, in the sense that affirmative action research has often been rather utilitarian in nature and oriented toward asking simple, practical questions. However, while not surprising, the lack of emphasis on theory is disappointing from a psychological perspective, in that there are a number of attitude or social judgment theories which could serve as a guide for research and as a framework for integrating research results.

In this chapter and the next, we will review theories which we find to be particularly relevant to affirmative action research. In this chapter, we will concentrate on what are referred to as justice theories. These theories shed light on how individuals perceive the justice of different forms of affirmative action. Justice theories can be divided into three major types - outcome (or distributive justice), procedural justice, and interactional justice. Following the discussion of justice theories, three other theoretical perspectives which have been applied to affirmative action will be discussed in the next chapter (see Chapter 3).

OUTCOME JUSTICE

Focusing on the results of a policy, or the shift in the actual distribution of resources, entails using theories of distributive justice. Distributive justice focuses on the outcomes arising from the implementation of a policy (Folger & Greenberg, 1985) and, therefore, we have chosen to use here the more general term "outcome justice." There are two main theories which help to explain how the justice or fairness of outcomes are evaluated. The outcome theories we will review are equity theory and referent cognitions theory.

Equity Theory

Perhaps the best-known perspective on outcome justice is equity theory (Adams, 1965). The concept of equity comes very close to the popular concept of reward based upon merit. According to equity theory, a person engages in a type of cognitive mathematics where they compare the ratio of their inputs or efforts into a class, job or organization to the value of the outcomes which they receive. According to the theory, the person then compares their input/outcome ratio to that of employees, students or other organizational members whom they view as being comparable to themselves. Inputs include such components as ability, effort, performance, and attendance. Outcomes include tangible resources such as pay, in the case of workers, or grades, in the case of students. Less tangible outcomes may also occur such as praise or positive interactions with peers. An important component of this theory is the assumption that these calculations are not necessarily rational reflections of reality. Rather, the assessment of inputs and outcomes is based on one's purely subjective assessments.

Once an individual has identified their inputs and outcomes and the inputs and outcomes of a comparative other, they can then calculate an input to outcome ratio for both themselves and the referent. An individual will experience equity if their input to outcome ratio is equal to the input to outcome ratio of the comparative other. The existence of inequity in the ratios will result in tension, with the resolution of that tension partially depending upon whether the person views themselves as under compensated, or over compensated, as compared to the referent other. However, a weakness of equity theory, and, in fairness, most of the justice theories, is that it is difficult to predict exactly how individuals will attempt to restore equity.

While there are a number of permutations of the input/outcome comparison, two are particularly relevant to affirmative action. The first situation would occur with soft preferential treatment where a majority group member's merit (i.e., inputs) are equivalent to that of a minority, but only the minority is given the opportunity (i.e., outcome). The second situation would occur with hard preferential treatment where a majority group member's inputs exceed that of a minority group member and the minority is given the opportunity. In both cases, equity theory would predict that the minority would be over rewarded relative to the majority group member, and the outcome would be viewed as unfair from a distributive justice perspective. From the perspective of the majority group member, they have been under compensated and would have to reduce this perceived inequity. From the perspective of the minority group member, perceptions of inequity would depend on whether they believed past discrimination had limited their opportunities. If they did believe this, the opportunity would be viewed as fair compensation for past inequities, and feelings of overcompensation would be less likely to occur. However, it they did not believe that past discrimination had limited their opportunities or advancement, they would feel overcompensated and would have to reduce this inequity.

Equity theory would also predict that hard preferential treatment would be viewed as less fair than soft preferential treatment, since hard preferential treatment more strongly violates acceptable input/outcome comparisons. While equity theory has not been used as a theoretical foundation for most research in affirmative action, empirical data does reveal this predicted pattern of fairness perceptions. Affirmative action evokes the most negative reactions when hard preferential treatment is used (see Chapter 5, also see Arthur, Doverspike, & Fuentes, 1992; Kravitz et al., 1997; Kravitz & Platania, 1993; Nacoste, 1987; Warner & Steel, 1989).

Thus, equity theory has some utility for examining how one might view the fairness of affirmative action. However, by ignoring procedural, contextual, and individual level variables which impact on fairness perceptions, the theory does suffer from a number of weaknesses. In particular, by not considering aspects of the policies used to reach an outcome, equity theory overlooks a central component of justice perceptions (Folger & Greenberg, 1985). The same outcome may be viewed differently if the employee is allowed to voice their opinion on the unfairness of the process or if the unfair procedure is attributed to upper administration, rather than to the person implementing the policy (Tyler & Bies, 1990).

Furthermore, equity theory implies that the outcomes which are most relevant are those which are directly experienced by the individual. Is it the case that only outcomes which personally affect a person are important in fairness? Does personal self-interest alone drive fairness perceptions, so that the only outcomes viewed as unfair are those in circumstances where an individual's outcomes are unfavorable? This cynical view is not supported by the data. Research on justice shows that people may view policies as unfair even when their personal outcomes are favorable (Greenberg, 1990).

In summary, while equity theory can make some simple predictions regarding the perceived fairness of outcomes, it does not have the explanatory power of typical procedural justice approaches, nor does it allow one to make specific recommendations for enhancing the perceived justice of policies.

Referent Cognitions Theory

Referent cognitions theory (Folger, 1986) is related to equity theory in that both focus on outcomes. However, referent cognitions theory extends beyond equity theory in that it incorporates some consideration of the policies used to reach an outcome. In referent cognitions theory, one looks at dissatisfying outcomes and beliefs about the procedures which lead to the outcomes. Reactions to a policy are based on beliefs about relative outcomes which might have occurred had a different policy been used. Resentment should be maximized when people believe they would have received a more positive outcome if a fairer procedure had been used (Folger & Martin, 1986; Greenberg, 1990). Thus, referent cognitions theory incorporates some elements of procedural justice theory.

This perspective may be helpful in understanding resentment of affirmative action by nonbeneficiaries who are directly influenced by the policy. Those who are passed over for an opportunity because of a strong affirmative action policy, and believe they were more qualified, may view the policy as unfair, because it denied them an opportunity they would have received had a merit-based policy been used. While this seems a logical explanation of this type of resistance to strong affirmative action, research which uses referent cognitions theory has not been conducted in this area.

A view related to referent cognitions theory is Rutte and Messick's (1995) work on distributive justice. In their perspective, unfairness is influenced by the discrepancy between anticipated and received outcomes, and whether a negative outcome was expected. A strength of this approach is that it deals in some detail with aspects of outcomes which influence fairness judgments, such as the amount of discrepancy between outcomes and expectations and the subjective importance of the outcome to the individual. The weakness of this model is similar to that of equity theory. By focusing on the outcome, components of a "fairer" procedure are not fully developed in this approach. However, it should be noted that referent cognitions theory was intended to develop our understanding of how outcomes influence fairness perceptions, rather than to explore aspects of policies which impact justice.

PROCEDURAL JUSTICE

Procedural justice involves a consideration of the elements of the policy used to make decisions about employment resources (Greenberg, 1990). A procedural justice perspective applied to affirmative action highlights the effects of weighing factors such as minority status in making employment decisions. For instance, one could examine how shifting the relative weight given to race or merit in a selection decision influences fairness perceptions.

An early foundation for understanding procedural justice was supplied by Leventhal (1980) and Thibaut and Walker (1975) who sought to identify the aspects of policies which were most important in determining fairness perceptions. While Leventhal (1980) identified a set of components of policies central in justice judgements, Thibaut and Walker (1975) focused on the central role of control in determining justice perceptions. More recently, Nacoste (1996) has developed a procedural-interdependence model of affirmative action and conducted a program of research based on this model. Our discussion of procedural justice theories will be somewhat artificially divided so as to reflect the work of the two major, early theorists and the recent work of Nacoste (1996).

Leventhal

According to Leventhal (1980), the following components of policies used to distribute resources are critical in justice assessments: consistency, bias suppression, accuracy, correctability, representativeness, and ethicality. Clearly, some forms of affirmative action may violate the consistency aspect of fair procedures, as well as other components. Hard and soft forms of preferential treatment dictate that protected group status be used in evaluating eligibility for educational or employment opportunities. By definition, forms of preferential treatment dictate that selection decisions should not be based on merit alone, but by some joint consideration of merit and sex or race. Thus, violations of consistency are likely to occur when these policies are used and it is likely that they will be viewed as unfair (Nacoste, 1985).

A number of studies have attempted to identify the types of affirmative action which are seen as most and least fair. Studies in this area have shown that an increased emphasis on protected group status and a decreased emphasis on merit are related to perceptions of increased procedural unfairness (see Chapter 5). While inconsistency in the use of merit as a basis for selection decisions can account for the research results, Leventhal's (1980) theory was not used as a way to frame the studies; nor did researchers examine whether consistency violations accounted for the differences in attitudes toward soft and hard preferential treatment. Therefore, while Leventhal's (1980) theory may prove useful in examining reactions to affirmative action, its utility has not been fully explored in this area of research. However, related research suggests that consistency in employment policy use is an important issue in understanding perceived fairness of policies (Arvey & Sackett, 1993; Gilliland, 1993).

Arvey and Sackett (1993) pointed out that the extent to which one believes the consistency rule has been violated in affirmative action may depend on one's personal view of the importance of merit in employment decisions. When merit is viewed as the sole legitimate criterion for making employment decisions, affirmative action will be viewed negatively. When merit is viewed as one important criteria, but not the only important consideration, affirmative action may be seen as more acceptable.

Thibaut and Walker

Thibaut and Walker's (1975) work regarding procedural justice focused on the amount of control exerted by those influenced by a policy and subsequent judgments of the fairness of the policy. While this theory has not been explored in the context of affirmative action, a wealth of research on other employment policies suggests that control is a powerful influence on justice perceptions. Given the importance of this factor in justice, it is useful to closely examine the particular aspects of control which contribute to more positive assessments of policies.

One of the most important influences on perceived control over policies is voice, or the opportunity to express one's opinion on the policy. Research has revealed that the perceived procedural fairness of even unpopular policies may be enhanced when people are allowed to express their opinions on the issue (Bies & Shapiro, 1988; Tyler & Bies, 1990). While it makes sense to expect that voice will not compensate for policies viewed as extremely unfair, the fact that voice effects have such far reaching benefits should not be ignored by those who must implement controversial policies. The implications of these findings for the successful use of affirmative action will be discussed in the implementation chapter (see Chapter 11).

The second factor which is related to control is the extent to which organizational members are given a clear explanation or rationale for the implementation of affirmative action. Clear, adequate explanations for the use of the policies may be particularly important in situations where outcomes are important and the policies governing allocation decisions for the outcomes are ambiguous (Rutte & Messick, 1995). This is particularly relevant to affirmative action, since employment and educational opportunities are valued by others, and individuals often are not sure or have erroneous information concerning the nature of affirmative action policies and the nature of beneficiary qualifications (Kravitz et al., 1997; Kravitz & Platania, 1993; Kravitz, Stinson, & Mello, 1994). Research which specifically examined the importance of providing a rationale for affirmative action revealed that resistance to policies was significantly higher when no justification for the policy was provided (Murrell, Dietz-Uhler, Dovidio, Gaertner, & Drout, 1994).

Nacoste

Nacoste's (1990, 1994, 1996) theory of procedural-interdependence was based on both procedural justice theory and the theory of interdependence (Kelley & Thibaut, 1978). According to the theory, affirmative action policies affect not only the organization, the targeted protected group, and the nontargeted group or the nonbeneficiaries, but also the interdependence between the three. The main hypothesis is that it is the affirmative action procedures which affect the parties and their relationships and not general attitudes toward the ambiguous concept of affirmative action.

According to Nacoste's (1996) model, it is not only the contribution related-claims, but also the voice that individuals and groups have in decision making which predicts outcomes. Thus, Nacoste's (1996) work incorporates one of the classic views of procedural justice, that expressed opinions of a policy are a central component of justice perceptions (Thibaut & Walker, 1975). Furthermore, affirmative action procedures have procedural reverberations which affect decision makers, target group members, and nontarget group members. Procedural reverberations also have implications for the social interactions which take place between the parties. Thus, the evaluation of affirmative action by various parties in the process is a function of the procedures used to implement affirmative action, the relative emphasis of those procedures on merit versus group status, and the impact of those procedures on the affected individual's voice in social relationships and the group's voice in the organization.

Nacoste's (1996) view represents an important development in our understanding of fairness perceptions of affirmative action, since it implies that fairness views are complex and may change over the course of time. His work suggests that "snapshot" experiments, where perceptions of the policies are captured at a single point in time, represent an overly simplistic view of the psychological process involved in fairness judgments.

INTERACTIONAL JUSTICE AND COMMUNICATION THEORIES

Much of the research on procedural justice examines general reactions to policies. A new perspective, interactional justice, makes a contribution by focusing on specific situational and interpersonal factors which influence fairness (Tyler & Bies, 1990). This is a somewhat microanalytic approach to fairness in that it focuses on the interpersonal treatments individuals receive when a policy is implemented as well as whether procedures are justified or explained (Greenberg, 1990).

According to the interactional justice model, people use personal, situation-specific factors in evaluating the justice of policies. The way a policy is presented, the person presenting a policy, and the organizational context may all have a significant impact on perceived fairness of procedures. For example, the courtesy shown by a corporate recruiter can be a significant predictor of an applicant's rating of the perceived fairness of a recruiting technique and of their attitude to the company itself. Another variable which influences procedural fairness is allowing individuals to express their opinions of the policies (Bies & Shapiro, 1988). Such findings suggest that the entire context of procedures, the way in which they are used and implemented, may be as important as the actual content of the policy in predicting affective responses to such policies.

The impact of justifying policies and allowing those influenced by them to have a voice in proceedings has been investigated to a certain degree in the procedural justice literature (Folger, 1977; Greenberg & Folger, 1983), although other variables which may be situation-specific have not been as thoroughly examined in the context of procedural justice. However, the focus of the procedural justice perspective is usually on aspects of the policy rather than on the context in which it is implemented. Thus, this interactional approach to justice has not traditionally been incorporated in procedural and distributive justice theories, and represents a new direction in justice research (Greenberg, 1990).

The interactional approach to justice has the potential to broaden our views of the variables which may be important in predicting fairness and to direct our attention to critical situational variables. While this level of analysis is not typical in affirmative action research, there is a great deal of related research in the area of communication theory. Within this area, studies from the literature on persuasion allow us to predict which aspects of organizational environments may be most powerful in predicting responses to policies such as affirmative action. While it may seem unusual to consider affirmative action from this standpoint, implementing any controversial policy, such as affirmative action, is often an exercise in persuasion. We can benefit from an understanding of the variables which influence responses to such policies.

Two interrelated approaches to persuasion which have been extensively tested are the Elaboration Likelihood Model (Petty & Cacioppo, 1985) and Cognitive Response Theory (Greenwald, 1968; Petty & Cacioppo, 1979, 1981). Persuasion theories suggest that one should consider the individual-level cognitive evaluations of policies in order to understand whether they will be accepted. These approaches suggest that individual-level responses to policies are dependent on three major factors: characteristics of the recipient of the information, the source of information or the "message sender," and the actual content of the message or information conveyed (Petty & Cacioppo, 1985). These variables influence the way information about policies are processed by individuals, and this processing determines how a policy will be viewed. This explains why the same policy may be received very differently, depending on who implements it and the way in which it is presented.

A critical respondent characteristic in responses to any policy-relevant communication is the level of involvement of the recipient of information. When involvement or interest is high, people pay close attention to situational cues surrounding the message. Thus, the characteristics of the communicator and the content of the message itself are critical when the listener is involved in the issue under discussion (Petty & Cacioppo, 1981). When involvement is low, and people are disinterested in a message, it is unlikely that they will closely scrutinize these situational aspects or the information about the policy.

In most applied settings, it is probably reasonable to expect that people will believe that affirmative action holds important consequences for them (Taylor-Carter, Doverspike, & Cook, 1995). Under these conditions, respondent involvement is usually high. Thus, the characteristics of the message sender and the message itself are likely to have a significant impact on responses to the policies.

The source of the message is the conveyor of information concerning affirmative action. This can be a person or an impersonal source, such as a generic company memo. If a person conveys information about the policy, characteristics of this individual may become an important influence. According to cognitive response theory, the most persuasive individual is one who would be viewed as an expert in the area and someone who is trusted (Petty & Cacioppo, 1981). This leads us to believe that the person chosen to implement affirmative action may have an impact on how the policy is accepted. In the literature on affirmative action, we were unable to find any published work which directly examined this issue. However, one of the strongest predictors of the success of affirmative action in the field is whether it is backed by top management (Hyer, 1985; Morrison, 1992). This suggests that the source of information about affirmative action may be a powerful influence on how the policies are viewed. More research is needed in order to understand the role of specific implementer characteristics on the perceived fairness of policies.

A second consideration from the communication theory standpoint is the way in which a message is presented. In the area of persuasion, it seems clear that the plausibility of the message is critical when listeners are interested in the issue (Petty & Cacioppo, 1981). In the context of affirmative action, it may be the case that the justification for the policy is important. In fact, some studies have examined the effect of the way affirmative action is framed or presented on acceptance of the policies and have found that this has a significant impact on the reactions of individuals to the policies (Kinder & Sanders, 1990; Taylor-Carter, Doverspike, & Alexander, 1995). The specific findings and implications for organizational settings are discussed in the implementation chapter (see Chapter 11).

CHAPTER SUMMARY

Justice theories can provide a solid conceptual foundation for understanding reactions to affirmative action policies. While admittedly a somewhat redundant conclusion, justice theories appear to be most applicable when the criterion of interest is fairness or various types of judgments regarding justice. Furthermore, justice theories would also appear to assume that the decision makers are at least attempting to operate in a rational, fair manner and, conversely, assume that the respondents have some trust in the system and the decision makers. A weakness of all the various justice theories is that they provide little specific guidance as to what actions an individual will take in order to remedy a perceived inequity or unfairness.

The various versions of justice theory can be categorized into those involving outcome, procedural, and interactional justice. Outcome models include equity and referent cognition theories. Procedural justice theories include those offered by Leventhal (1980), Thibaut and Walker (1975) and Nacoste (1996). The concept of interactional justice offers an opportunity to integrate a variety of communication and persuasion theories into a justice perspective.

Outcome theories emphasize the fairness of perceived reward distributions or outcomes. As such, outcomes theories help to explain why self-interest and the weight placed on merit are such critical variables in explaining reactions to affirmative action. At least in American culture, individuals are unlikely to view a policy which results in their being under compensated for merit or where the procedure clearly violates basic rules of merit-based distribution as being a fair policy.

Perhaps the other major contribution of outcome-oriented theories is in predicting when policies will be most closely scrutinized for procedural justice. Researchers have noted that the perception of the violation of rules, or unfair procedures, may motivate one to closely examine a policy. In contrast, fair procedures or those which yield positive outcomes may be given very little scrutiny (Gilliland, 1993; Rutte & Messick, 1995). In other words, violations of policies or inequitable rewards are always going to be more salient than equitable rewards or satisfying policies (Gilliland, 1993).

In organizational settings, people may be less aware of the details of policies than of their outcomes. Basically, we are proposing a two-step model in which unfair outcomes trigger an analysis of procedural justice. It may be the case that the first step in analyzing a procedure in many applied settings is becoming aware that the outcome is unfair. The second step, once the procedure becomes salient, involves a process of judging the fairness of the procedure. Thus, outcomes of procedures should not be ignored when examining the fairness of policies such as affirmative action (Arvey & Sackett, 1993). Decisions regarding the fairness of outcomes may be predicted by equity and referent cognitions theories. But outcome-oriented approaches may be considered deficient in that they fail to reveal how and why people decide a particular procedure is unfair.

Outcome theories of justice can help one predict when policies will be closely evaluated. However, they are not as useful in understanding resistance to affirmative action as are the theories of procedural justice. The specific aspects of policies which evoke feelings of unfairness can be predicted using procedural justice approaches. Although both outcome and procedural justice perspectives are useful in understanding reactions to stronger forms of affirmative action, past research suggests that procedural justice plays a central role in affective reactions to policies and may end up carrying greater weight in these evaluations (Rutte & Messick, 1995). As compared to outcome theories, procedural justice theories attempt to deal with the question of how people decide a policy is unfair in a more direct fashion.

The early work on procedural justice by Leventhal (1980) and Thibaut and Walker (1975) would lead us to expect that stronger forms of affirmative action are likely to be viewed as unfair. Recent contributions by other researchers (Nacoste, 1996; Tyler & Bies, 1990) echoes the suggestions of earlier researchers (Thibaut & Walker, 1975) and extends their work by suggesting that perceptions of unfairness may be strongest in situations where individuals are not given a chance to voice their opinions, and where administrators provide little in the way of explanation for the policies. Again, while the research in this area may allow us to formulate suggestions for implementing affirmative action, current research has not directly examined the impact of voice and policy justification on reactions to affirmative action.

The procedural justice theory which may hold the most promise as a guide to affirmative action research is that offered by Nacoste (1996). One major advantage of Nacoste's theory is that is was developed specifically in order to explain reactions to affirmative action. So, instead of trying to force fit a model to the situation, Nacoste looked at what were the critical elements involved in responses to affirmative action and then developed a theory to explain these critical elements. According to Nacoste's theory, contribution-based claims, the interdependence of the actors, and the effects of the policies on the actors are all critical in understanding reactions to affirmative action. Not only would Nacoste's theory appear to hold great promise in terms of directing future research, it also would appear to be compatible with interactional justice perspectives. This represents an important departure from simple empirical, atheoretical approaches to affirmative action. While these purely data-driven findings are informative, Nacoste's work extends beyond simple description of reactions of affirmative action into the realm of explanation.

Interactional justice and communication theory examine affirmative action at a very personal level and include analysis of situation-specific variables. The use of interactional justice theories would appear to offer an explanation as to why very similar affirmative action policies work effectively in some situations and fail in other organizational settings. More importantly, these perspectives may help us design organizational interventions which are most likely to support the success of affirmative action policies and broaden our view of what variables and what theories, including rhetoric and discourse theories, are useful in understanding reactions to affirmative action policies (Kravitz et al., 1997).

REFERENCES

Adams, J. S. (1965). Inequity in social exchange. In L. Berkowitz (Ed.), *Advances in Experimental Social Psychology* (Vol. 2, pp. 267-299). New York, NY: Academic Press.

Arthur, W., Jr., Doverspike, D., & Fuentes, R. (1992). Recipients' affective responses to affirmative action interventions: A cross-cultural perspective. *Behavioral Sciences and the Law, 10,* 229-243.

Arvey, R. D., & Sackett, P. R. (1993). Fairness in selection: Current developments and perspectives. In N. Schmitt & W. Borman (Eds.), *Personnel selection in organizations* (pp. 171-202). San Francisco: Jossey-Bass.

Bies, R. J., & Shapiro, D. L. (1988). Voice and justification: Their influence on procedural fairness judgments. *Academy of Management Journal, 31,* 676-685.

Folger, R. (1977). Distributive and procedural justice: Combined impact of "voice" and improvement on experienced inequity. *Journal of Personality and Social Psychology, 35,* 108-119.

Folger, R. (1986). Rethinking equity theory: A referent cognitions model. In H. W. Bierhoff, R. L. Cohen, & J. Greenberg (Eds.), *Justice in social relations* (pp. 145-162). New York, NY: Plenum.

Folger, R., & Greenberg, J. (1985). Procedural Justice: An interpretive analysis of personnel systems. In K. M. Rowland and G. R. Ferris (Eds.),

Research in personnel and human resource management: A research annual (Vol. 3, pp. 141-183). Greenwich, CN: JAI Press.

Folger, R., & Martin, C. (1986). Relative deprivation and referent cognitions: Distributive and procedural justice effects. *Journal of Experimental Social Psychology, 22,* 531-546.

Gilliland, S. W. (1993). The perceived fairness of selection systems: An organizational justice perspective. *Academy of Management Review, 18,* 694-734.

Greenberg, J. (1990). Organizational justice: Yesterday, today and tomorrow. *Journal of Management, 16,* 399-432.

Greenberg, J., & Folger, R. (1983). Procedural justice, participation and the fair process effect in groups and organizations. In P. B. Paulus (Ed.), *Basic group processes* (pp. 235-256). New York, NY: Springer Verlag.

Greenwald, A. G. (1968). Cognitive learning, cognitive response to persuasion, and attitude change. In A. G. Greenwald, T. C. Broock, & T. M. Ostrom. (Eds.), *Psychological foundations of attitudes* (pp. 147-170). New York, NY: Academic Press.

Hyer, P. B. (1985). Affirmative action for women faculty: Case studies of three successful institutions. *Journal of Higher Education, 56, 3,* 282-299.

Kelley, H. H., & Thibaut, J. W. (1978). *Interpersonal relations: A theory of interdependence.* New York, NY: John Wiley.

Kinder, D. R., & Sanders, L. M. (1990). Mimicking political debate with survey questions: The case of white opinion on affirmative action for Blacks. *Social Cognition, 8,* 73-103.

Kravitz, D. A., Harrison, D. A., Turner, M. A., Levine, E. L. Chaves, W., Brannick, M. T., Denning, D. L., Russell, C. J., & Conrad, M. A. (1997). *Affirmative action: A review of psychological and behavioral research.* Bowling Green, OH: Society for Industrial and Organizational Psychology.

Kravitz, D. A., & Platania, J. (1993). Attitudes and beliefs about affirmative action: Effects of target and respondent sex and ethnicity. *Journal of Applied Psychology, 78,* 928-938.

Kravitz, D. A., Stinson, V., & Mello, E. W. (1994, August). Public reactions to affirmative action. In M. E. Turner (Chair), *Affirmative action at work: Towards reducing barriers to the integrated workplace.*

Symposium conducted at the annual meeting of the Academy of Management, Dallas, TX.

Leventhal, G. S. (1980). What should be done with equity theory? New approaches to the study of fairness in social relationships. In K. J. Gergen, M. S. Greenberg, & R. H. Willis (Eds.), *Social exchange: Advances in theory and research* (pp. 27-55). New York, NY: Plenum.

Morrison, A. (1992). Developing diversity in organizations. *Business Quarterly,* Summer, 42-48.

Murrell, A. J., Dietz-Uhler, B. L., Dovidio, J. F., Gaertner, S. L., & Drout, C. (1994). Aversive racism and resistance to affirmative action: Perceptions of justice are not necessarily color blind. *Basic and Applied Social Psychology, 15,* 71-86.

Nacoste, R. W. (1985). Selection procedure and responses to affirmative action: The case of favorable treatment. *Law and Human Behavior, 9,* 225-242.

Nacoste, R. W. (1987). But do they care about fairness? The dynamics of preferential treatment and minority interest. *Basic and Applied Social Psychology, 8,*177-191.

Nacoste, R. W. (1990). Sources of stigma: Analyzing the psychology of affirmative action. *Law and Policy, 12,* 175-195.

Nacoste, R. W. (1994). Policy schemas for affirmative action. In L. Heath, R. S. Tindale, J. Edwards, E. J. Posavac, F. B. Bryant, E. Hendeson-King, Y. Suarez-Balcazar, & J. Myers (Eds.), *Applications of heuristics and biases to social issues* (pp. 205-221). New York, NY: Plenum Press.

Nacoste, R. W. (1996). Social psychology and the affirmative action debate. *Journal of Social and Clinical Psychology, 15,* 261-282.

Petty, R. E., & Cacioppo, J. T. (1979). Issues involvement can increase or decrease persuasion by enhancing message-relevant cognitive responses. *Journal of Personality and Social Psychology, 37,* 1915-1926.

Petty, R. E., & Cacioppo, J. T. (1981). *Attitudes and persuasion: Classic and contemporary approaches.* Dubuque, IA: Brown.

Petty, R. E., & Cacioppo, J. T. (1985). Elaboration likelihood model of persuasion. *Advances in Experimental and Social Psychology, 19,* 125-205.

Rutte, C. G., & Messick, D. M. (1995). An integrated model of perceived unfairness in organizations. *Social Justice Research, 8,* 239-261.

Taylor-Carter, M.A., Doverspike, D., & Alexander, R. (1995). Message effects on the perceptions of the fairness of gender-based affirmative action: A cognitive response theory-based analysis. *Social Justice Research, 8,* 285-303.

Taylor-Carter, M.A., Doverspike, D., & Cook, K. (1995). Understanding resistance to sex and race-based affirmative action policies: A review of research policies. *Human Resource Management Review, 5,* 129-157.

Thibaut, J., & Walker, L. (1975). *Procedural justice: A psychological analysis.* Hillsdale, NJ: Erlbaum.

Tyler, T.R., & Bies, R. J. (1990). Beyond formal procedures: The interpersonal context of procedural justice. In J. S. Carroll (Ed.), *Applied Social Psychology and Organizational.* (pp. 77-98). Hillsdale, NJ: Lawrence Erlbaum.

Warner, R. L., & Steel, B. S. (1989). Affirmative action in times of fiscal stress and changing value priorities: the case of women in policing. *Public Personnel Management, 18,* 291- 309.

Chapter 3

THEORETICAL PERSPECTIVES - ATTITUDE AND TRAIT THEORIES

In Chapter 2, the importance of theory to psychological research was noted and the application of various theories of justice to affirmative action issues was discussed. In this chapter, three additional theoretical perspectives which can be applied to affirmative action will be examined.

The first is a basic attitude theory, Fishbein and Ajzen's (1975) theory of reasoned action. Fishbein and Ajzen's (1975) theory represents a comprehensive approach to the prediction of human behavior and to the relationship between attitudes, behavior, and the intention to behave. The power of the theory comes from its unique ability to explain how cognitions are linked to attitudes and how attitudes, in turn, influence behavioral choices.

The second, attribution theory, is also a basic attitude theory. Attribution theory is most applicable to the evaluation of the characteristics of those who benefit from affirmative action policies (i.e., the beneficiaries). The receipt of a job or educational opportunity because of affirmative action policies will affect the evaluation of the beneficiary by others and it will also affect beneficiary self-assessments. Thus, attribution theory can be applied to understanding how others view beneficiaries and how the intended beneficiaries own self-evaluations are influenced by affirmative action.

The third perspective encompasses a variety of personal traits. These personal traits are relatively stable attributes on which individual differences are likely to be related to reactions to affirmative action. Some of the theories of individual differences which can be applied to affirmative action include racism, sexism, individualism-collectivism, liberalism-conservatism, and five-factor personality theory.

FISHBEIN AND AJZEN'S REASONED ACTION THEORY

Fishbein and Ajzen (1975; Ajzen & Fishbein, 1980) theorize that people are rational decision makers and carefully consider available information when forming an attitude. In their theoretical framework, individuals are seen as rather cautious, objective decision-makers (Petty & Cacioppo, 1981). The criterion predicted by Fishbein and Ajzen's (1975) model is the actual behavior of an individual, rather than an affective reaction to a policy or person. The best predictor of this behavior, and one which may be more accessible to researchers than behavior, is the expressed intention to behave. Behavioral intentions are seen as reasonable proxies for actual behavior and as the best predictor of behavior.

In the model, behavior is directed toward an attitude object. In the context of affirmative action, we might be interested in predicting how a White male might behave toward a woman who was hired as part of an affirmative action plan. In this scenario, the attitude object would be the female beneficiary. Alternatively, we might focus on how a personnel officer opposed to affirmative action might behave when asked to implement the policies. In this second scenario, the policy is the attitude object. Reactions and behavior toward either target can be examined by using Fishbein and Ajzen's (1975) framework.

There are several components of the full model of reasoned action (Fishbein, 1980). For our purposes, we will focus on the most central facets of the model. The two most basic components used to predict behavioral intentions are: 1) the individual's attitudes or beliefs about performing the behavior; and 2) the individual's subjective norm, or the pressure on the individual to perform or not perform the behavior. Each of these two factors will be discussed in more detail below.

Attitudes toward a behavior (A_b) stem from two different sources, according to Fishbein (1980). The first source is the individual's estimate of the probability that the behavior will have a particular outcome (b_i). Since a single behavior can have many outcomes, the subscript "i" is used to indicate any number of outcomes, from one to infinity. The second component is the evaluation of each single outcome (e_i), or whether the outcome is favorable or unfavorable. Again, the subscript "i" is used to indicate that any given number of outcomes are being evaluated. Mathematically, a person's attitude toward actually engaging in a behavior can be predicted through two steps: 1) multiplying the evaluation of each particular outcome by the probability that this particular outcome will occur; and, then 2) summing the resulting products.

Take the problem of predicting how a personnel officer will behave when required to implement an affirmative action policy which the officer opposes. In terms of this component of the model, the probability that the personnel officer will sabotage the policy implementation would be a function of: 1) beliefs about whether this behavior will allow the personnel officer to avoid bringing minorities into the firm (a single potential outcome, which will be weighted in terms of its attractiveness to the individual); and, 2) the probability that the sabotaging behavior will actually accomplish the intended goal. Note, this is only one of many possible outcome-probability pairs. Perhaps the personnel officer would also be concerned that their performance appraisal would suffer if they did not meet their affirmative action goals, a likely outcome of sabotaging the implementation of the policies. A weight would again be assigned to this outcome to indicate how attractive or unattractive it is to the personnel officer. Again, the subjective probability of this particular outcome would be assessed by the individual. The aggregate of all the outcome-probability pairs would determine whether the sabotaging behavior would occur.

Note, based on the model, each outcome is carefully assigned a quantitative weight in terms of its attractiveness to the individual. For each individual, a probability estimate of the likelihood that each outcome will occur must also be derived.

At this point, we have only considered the individual's attitude as a predictor of whether the behavior will be executed. Another important force which can help us predict behavior is the subjective norm of the individual. While the attitude of the person can be thought of as an internal force which drives behavior, subjective norms originate externally.

Subjective norms (SN) are external forces which may constrain behavior. They consist of two components: 1) normative beliefs (NB); and 2) motivation to comply (MC; Fishbein, 1980).

Normative beliefs are beliefs about how one's important reference groups would view the behavior. Such reference groups include friends, colleagues, and supervisors. If our personnel officer had spoken to colleagues in the organization who also disliked affirmative action, this could encourage destructive behavior. However, if the officer knew their supervisor would not condone such behavior, this belief would likely discourage sabotage. In this case, there are two normative beliefs which are in conflict.

Given that one's normative beliefs may lead to such conflict, how do we predict behavior? Fishbein and Ajzen (1975) argue that each normative belief is coupled with a motivation to comply with each group. If the personnel officer is more motivated to comply with their colleagues than with their supervisor, then the sabotaging behavior is likely to occur.

Again, the model predicts a very rational process takes place as one weighs these opposing forces. First, our personnel officer would assess the reaction of their colleagues to their behavior (NB). Then the officer would derive a weight corresponding to how important their colleagues' reaction is to them (MC). This process would be repeated for the reaction of the supervisor. Again, Fishbein and Ajzen (1975) suggest that this is a very rational process.

Mathematically, subjective norms can be predicted by two steps: 1) multiplying each normative belief by the motivation to comply with each norm group; and 2) summing the products. Positive force increases the likelihood that the behavior will occur, while a negative force constrains behavior and makes it less likely that the behavior will occur.

In terms of our example, if the personnel officer's colleagues reaction to the sabotaging behavior are less important than the supervisor's reaction, the behavior is less likely to occur. In Fishbein and Ajzen's model (1975), these subjective norms are just as important in determining behavior as are one's own attitudes.

Fishbein and Ajzen's (1975) model depicts a very orderly cognitive process. Whether people engage in such cognitive effort when evaluating policies is not clear. However, a contribution of their model is that they force researchers in the area of procedural justice to consider aspects outside the normal realm of procedural and outcome justice. The focus on normative groups is particularly important in understanding whether affirmative action plans will be supported and carried out in organizations. In addition, the focus on this outside force reminds us that the organizational environment can be a critical factor in determining the success of affirmative action policies and reactions to beneficiaries.

ATTRIBUTION THEORY

The theories discussed thus far, in both the current chapter and Chapter 2, have focused on or been most relevant to the individual's evaluation of the affirmative action policy itself. In this segment, we turn our attention to a theory where the primary application is in understanding how affirmative action procedures affect the evaluation of those persons who are the intended beneficiaries of the affirmative action policies. Attribution theory allows us to attempt to answer questions such as how does the use of affirmative action influence perceptions of the beneficiaries' abilities and does benefitting from affirmative action change the way an individual views their own abilities.

Perhaps one of the most useful theories for examining how people evaluate others and how people make inferences about the causes of individual behavior, as well as about the causes of events, is attribution theory (Heider, 1958; Kelley, 1971, 1973). Basically, attribution theory suggests that people are motivated to understand the underlying causes of human behavior. These causes can be classified as either situational or dispositional (Trope, 1986). Situational attributions are those which assign the cause of the behavior to some external or environmental event. For instance, believing that a person failed a test because the test was too difficult would be a situational attribution. Dispositional attributions place the cause of the behavior within an individual. Believing that a person failed a test because they did not study would be a dispositional attribution.

This attributional approach can easily be adapted to examining how people evaluate beneficiaries of affirmative action. By using attribution theory, one can investigate the way in which these policies affect people's views of the potential and abilities of the minorities and women who benefit from such policies.

Under preferential treatment, minorities and women may be hired or promoted partially because of their protected group status. This does not imply that unqualified people are given employment opportunities. However, research suggests that some people believe that all forms of affirmative action overemphasize group status over ability when employment decisions are made (Eberhardt & Fiske, 1994; Kravitz et al., 1997; Kravitz & Platania, 1993). It is this belief system, rather than an objective assessment of reality, that may drive attitudes toward affirmative action beneficiaries.

Attribution theory would lead to the prediction that people will make situational or external attributions for the success of beneficiaries when they believe that the receipt of desired employment or educational outcomes was the result of preferential treatment. While we would normally expect that attributions for success would be dispositional, or due to the ability of the beneficiary, this may not be the case when decisions are made in an affirmative action environment (Eberhardt & Fiske, 1994). The presence of a race- or sex-based policy gives nonbeneficiaries or independent respondents an alternative explanation for any success achieved as a result of an affirmative action effort. Thus, the competence of a beneficiary may be brought into question when stronger forms of affirmative action are used in order to make decisions or allocate valued opportunities (Garcia, Erskine, Hawn, & Casmay, 1981; Heilman, Block, & Lucas, 1992). Success will tend to be attributed to the policy rather than to the personal attributes of the beneficiary.

A second factor which may lead to negative attributions about beneficiaries is that nonbeneficiaries may overestimate their own abilities and merit when comparing themselves to a minority or woman in competition for an opportunity (Larwood, 1982). Thus, even an "average" nonbeneficiary may believe that they have qualifications which are superior to those of a beneficiary. This belief system would lead them to view the female or minority more negatively, and to make the attribution that a beneficiary's occupational achievements were the consequence of affirmative action.

Beyond the question of attributions by others, attribution theory would predict the presence of similar effects in self-assessment. That is, beneficiaries may attribute their success to external factors and question their own competence. Although attribution theory predicts that the use of affirmative action would potentially also damage beneficiary self-perceptions, this need not always be the case. First, we tend to evaluate ourselves in more positive terms than we evaluate others. This self-serving bias could negate some of the potentially negative effects of affirmative action. Other forces which work against a potential self-stigma are feelings of entitlement to affirmative action benefits (Eberhardt & Fiske, 1994) and beneficiary self-confidence (Heilman, Lucas, & Kaplow, 1990; Stewart & Shapiro, 1999). The extent to which affirmative action influences both the beneficiary's self-perceptions and the reactions of others is discussed in Chapter 8.

PERSONAL TRAITS

In this section, we briefly review the literature on theoretical developments related to what we feel are several key individual difference variables. Basic constructs which appear to be related to reactions to affirmative action policies include racism, sexism, individualism-collectivism, and liberalism-conservatism. We conclude our discussion of personal traits by offering our thoughts regarding the possible existence of a cosmopolitan personality. We have chosen to highlight these key variables because, in our view, they reflect critical, stable traits or attributes which are likely to have a significant impact on reactions to affirmative action.

A number of other individual variables serve both to predict attitudes and to moderate or mediate the relationship between aspects of procedures and perceptions of justice or fairness. These variables include individual-level values related to redistribution of societal resources, perceptions of the needs of the intended beneficiaries, and the perceived outcome of policy use for one's own group. Although these variables are also important individual differences, they tend to be less stable and are more likely to be treated as mediators in models rather than as independent variables. Therefore, we have chosen to discuss research related to these individual difference variables in the chapter on mediators (see Chapter 7). The research related to the relationship between personal traits and reactions to affirmative action is reviewed in Chapter 6.

Racism

It would be reasonable to assume that for Whites, racism would be related to opposition toward affirmative action, especially race-based affirmative action. After all, someone who is racist should be opposed to policies which favor those minority groups toward which negative attitudes are held. In some cases, racism may even be measured by determining if respondents are opposed to policies, including affirmative action, which favor minorities. As a result, it would be surprising if racism were not related to opposition to affirmative action and, in fact, research suggests that a relationship does exist (for a discussion of the research literature, see Chapter 6).

Thus, beliefs about the competencies of Black Americans may be one force which drives resistance to affirmative action policies. Individuals who hold racist beliefs are likely to oppose affirmative action efforts aimed at remedying racial imbalance in education or employment. Moreover, they may also oppose affirmative action in general. The existence of racism may also explain why racially-based affirmative action policies are sometimes met with greater resistance than sex-based policies or affirmative action policies aimed at other groups. In some settings, White males show greater support for affirmative action designed to benefit women or the handicapped than for programs designed for minorities (Reid & Clayton, 1992).

As noted above, in some cases racism may even be defined in terms of opposition to policies such as affirmative action. This is especially likely to be true with measures of what are referred to as "modern racism," a term used to describe the current embodiment of racist beliefs (Brief et al., 1997; Gaertner & Dovidio, 1986; Kinder & Sears, 1981; McConahay & Hough, 1976). Modern racism may be more subtle and may not contain the harsh stereotypes of earlier forms of racism (Pettigrew & Martin, 1987). Instead, modern racism may take the form of beliefs that Blacks now have equal opportunity and have no right to special gains offered through affirmative action (Kinder, 1986; McConahay, 1986). Thus, according to modern racism, a White respondent might be willing to say that Blacks and Whites should have equal opportunity and oppose discrimination against Blacks but still oppose most forms of affirmative action. This more subtle form of racism may stem from sensitivity to the inappropriateness of the early, extreme racist stereotypes.

A number of variations of modern racism have been proposed including symbolic racism and aversive racism (Dovidio, Mann, & Gaertner, 1989; Gaertner & Dovidio, 1986; Kinder & Sears, 1981; McConahay, 1982, 1986; McConahay & Hough, 1976). The core concept underlying modern racism is that individuals are still socialized to have racist views but also realize that society discourages the expression of overt bias. Symbolic racism (McConohay, 1982, 1986; McConahay & Hough, 1976) refers to the tendency of individuals to express their racism in a symbolic fashion rather than through more direct, overt behaviors. It can be considered to be a combination of racism and a conservative world view (Kravitz et al., 1997). Aversive racism is very similar to symbolic racism in that it is based on the idea that an individual who holds biased views is unlikely to express those views or act out in obvious ways (Dovidio et al., 1989; Gaertner & Dovidio, 1986). It can be considered to be a combination of racism and an egalitarian world view. Symbolic and aversive racism scales typically contain items which capture the belief that minorities are no longer disadvantaged, and, therefore, have no right to special governmental support.

Critiques of modern racism exist (Bobo & Kluegel, 1993; Kinder, 1986; Sniderman & Tetlock, 1986), but what is particularly troubling from a research perspective is that measures of modern racism may include items asking for opinions regarding affirmative action. Thus, by definition, modern racism will be related to opposition to affirmative action; there will also be a lack of statistical independence and common construct variance.

It is not necessarily the case that those with negative racial stereotypes automatically evaluate race-based policies more negatively. Even those who have over learned stereotypes can control the influence of this prejudice on their actions (Devine, 1989). The concern of some White majority group members regarding race-based policies may be fueled by extreme arguments or reports of the policies in the media. Attacks on affirmative action may exaggerate the impact of the policies by noting that they benefit a few Blacks at the expense of opportunities for Whites (Reid & Clayton, 1992). Perhaps such attacks account for the fact that beliefs about affirmative action are often erroneous and more extreme than one would expect (Kravitz et al., 1997).

This racist-based resistance to affirmative action for Blacks is exaggerated when no justification is provided for policies (Murrell, Dietz-Uhler, Dovidio, Gaertner, & Drout, 1994). Again, this might stem from exaggerated negative expectations regarding the outcomes of the policies. As we note in the implementation chapter (see Chapter 11), providing a justification for implementing policies may decrease resistance in some settings.

Sexism

Research on the relationship between sexist beliefs and reactions to sex-based affirmative action suggests that similar cognitive mechanisms are at work in this arena, with those who hold more traditional views of women expressing higher opposition to the integration of women into the workforce (see Chapter 6, see also Martin, Price, Bies, & Powers, 1987; Northcraft & Martin, 1982). Thus, one would expect that those who hold sexist views concerning women are likely to oppose affirmative action policies and may view beneficiaries as less competent, particularly for male sex-typed occupations. Although past research has demonstrated that affirmative action can damage the perceived competence of women regardless of the sex stereotype of the job (Heilman et al., 1992), the moderating effects of sexism have not yet been explored. However, one should be careful not to overgeneralize results from race-based affirmative action to sex-based policies. While some research has found similar levels of opposition to the two types of policies (Kravitz et al., 1997; Kravitz & Platania, 1993), the stereotypes underlying sexism and racism may operate quite differently. People tend to be more segregated on the basis of race, and it is under these conditions that stereotypes remain unchallenged and may have their maximal effect (Eberhardt & Fiske, 1994).

As with racism, there are modern versions of sexism. This new form of sexism is referred to as "neosexism" (Tougas, Brown, Beaton, & Joly, 1995). The basis of neosexism is the belief that most people are reluctant to openly admit to bias. Despite the apparent changes in publically expressed beliefs, women still seem to suffer from sex discrimination. Thus, prejudice is a factor even if it is no longer vocalized. As with modern racism, neosexism reflects a conflict between egalitarian values and traditional beliefs concerning individualism and the role of merit. This confound of neosexism with traditional attitudes creates interpretation problems and also measurement problems for modern racism.

Individualism-Collectivism

Individualism-collectivism is often treated as a continuous, bipolar variable on which there are reliable individual and cultural differences. Cultures, and individuals from those cultures, differ in the extent to which they emphasize individualism versus collectivism. People who can be classified as individualistic stress individual efforts and competitiveness.

Triandis (1996) suggested that the attributes defining individualism-collectivism were the meaning of the self, the structure of goals, norms and attitudes, and the degree of focus on the needs of the group. Individualists tend to view the self and social space in terms of individuals, while collectivists rely upon groups as the primary unit of analysis. Individualists give priority to personal goals while collectivists emphasize group goals. For individualists, behavior is a function of attitudes and then group norms, while for collectivists behavior is a function of group norms and then attitudes. Finally, individualists tend to look at relationships in terms of exchange while collectivists view relationships in more communal terms and tend to have beliefs which center around concern for solidarity and group well-being (Hui, 1988).

Affirmative action programs can be viewed as interventions which require individuals to operate and process information in a collectivistic fashion. That is, affirmative action programs often require individuals to subjugate their own goals to the good of the group or the greater societal good. Thus, we would expect and hypothesize that individual differences in individualism-collectivism would be related to attitudes toward affirmative action. Individuals with a collectivistic, as opposed to an individualistic orientation, should react more favorably toward affirmative action policies (for a review of the research see Chapter 6, also see Arthur, Doverspike, & Fuentes, 1992).

One problem with attempting to make predictions concerning the effects of individualism-collectivism relates to the problem of measurement (Dansereau, 1989). Collectivistic individuals subordinate their goals to the goals of the in-group. But how does one identify the relevant in-group? An individual with a collectivistic orientation may belong to multiple in-groups, and some of those in-groups may be harmed by affirmative action policies. It cannot be assumed that the in-group will be viewed by the individual as being society as a whole or even their particular racial or ethnic group. Therefore, it is possible that an individual with a collectivistic orientation would find the goals of affirmative action to be at odds with the goals of their in-group. An individual with a collectivistic orientation could even find themselves in a situation where they perceive themselves as belonging to several in-groups, each with a different goal. Unfortunately, it is difficult to specify in-groups a priori.

Liberalism-Conservatism

A number of researchers (Peterson, 1994; Sidanius, Pratto & Bobo, 1996) have examined the relationship between individualism-collectivism and social values, especially liberalism-conservatism. Those who are individualistic tend to have conservative political beliefs and also tend to oppose social policies designed to redistribute wealth or economic opportunities. In contrast, collectivists tend to have more liberal belief systems and, in some circumstances, are more likely to redistribute economic resources to those in need (Skitka & Tetlock, 1992, 1993). This is not to suggest that the two are perfectly correlated, but there does appear to be a relationship between individualism-collectivism and political belief systems.

Although recent research suggests that there is not a strong direct link between values and opposition to affirmative action, values may have some influence on intermediary fairness judgments of the policies (Peterson, 1994). Liberal political orientation is positively related to attitudes toward Blacks and is also associated with viewing African-Americans as relatively disadvantaged (Lambert & Chasteen, 1997). In contrast to conservative beliefs, this liberal orientation is associated with egalitarianism, a commitment to the equality, and a desire to help disadvantaged groups.

The relationship between political values and support for affirmative action may depend on the extent to which potential beneficiaries are viewed as responsible for employment inequities. For conservative individuals who view the targeted group as responsible for their position in society, one would expect opposition to affirmative action. In fact, a consistent research finding has been that those with a conservative orientation will deny aid to those who are perceived as personally responsible for their predicament (Skitka & Tetlock, 1993), while personal responsibility may play a smaller role in the distributive tendencies of liberals. Given this general finding, one would expect that conservatism would be associated with opposition to affirmative action. There is a tendency for conservatives to respond negatively to sex or race conscious policies. This opposition is probably attributable to a number of variables -- some researchers attribute the relationship to the link between conservatism and social dominance while others emphasize the link between conservatism and racism. Under scarcity, many individuals are unlikely to be as willing to distribute resources as they are when resources are plentiful.

A second factor which may moderate the relationship between individualism-collectivism and reactions to affirmative action is the way in which the policy is presented. Presenting the policy as an unearned advantage for minorities rather than fair restitution for past discrimination leads to more resistance even from collectivists, or those classified as egalitarian (Kinder & Sanders, 1990). Thus, the way the researcher chooses to describe affirmative action may be a critical determinant of the relationship between values and resistance to the policy.

The Big Five and the Cosmopolitan Personality

Personality theories underwent a rebirth with the advent of the "Big Five" approach, also referred to as the five-factor personality model (McCrae & Costa, 1985, 1987; Tupes & Christal, 1961). According to the five-factor model, the over 15,000 possible personality related attributes can be reduced to five primary factors; this reduction can be carried out using any of a number of statistical procedures including factor analysis. This Big Five can also account for much of the variance in personality inventory responses (McCrae & Costa, 1987, 1994).

The Big Five, often referred to by the acronym of NEOAC, are:

1. Neuroticism - a construct which is similar to emotional stability.
2. Extroversion - the tendency to be sociable, assertive, and active.
3. Openness - a somewhat ambiguous construct corresponding to a general, openness to new experiences. Also, sometimes seen as reflecting intelligence or creativity. However, this factor can also be seen as representing culture. Probably the most controversial and hotly debated of the big five factors.
4. Agreeableness - reflects a cooperative and easy-to-get along with attitude. Along with extroversion, also an interpersonal factor.
5. Conscientiousness - corresponds to a person who would be seen as a good worker. Reflects a tendency to be dependable, hard-working, and to set and achieve goals.

Although various individual difference factors have been looked at as predictors of attitudes toward affirmative action, it is surprising that more research has not focused on the set of Big Five personality traits (Barrick & Mount, 1991; McCrae & Costa, 1985, 1987; Tupes & Christal, 1961). Not only would one expect the Big Five personality factors in general to be related to attitudes toward affirmative action, but, in particular, one would expect that openness would be related to judgments of racism and sexism and reactions to affirmative action.

Does a personality type exist which is particularly likely to be open to the acceptance of affirmative action programs? If such a personality type exists, what would be its nature? We believe that a personality profile exists, or really a combination knowledge structure-personality profile exists, which has the effect of making a person more open to the acceptance of diversity programs, including affirmative action. This personality-knowledge structure profile is referred to here as the 'cosmopolitan personality.'

We propose that the cosmopolitan personality reflects the effects of a culturally-open personality combined with a multicultural knowledge structure. That is, a person is more likely to be accepting of programs such as affirmative action, which benefit cultural groups other than their own, if the individual has both a culturally-open personality profile and sufficient experience with a variety of cultures so as to have had the opportunity to develop multicultural knowledge. The culturally-open personality is necessary in order to benefit properly from experience, while the experience is necessary in order to develop the multicultural knowledge structure. It is this combination, then, of an open personality, experience, and the development of the proper knowledge structure which creates the type of person who is likely to be accepting of programs such as affirmative action policies.

Work in the area of international assignees, provides some relevant data on the factors critical to cross-cultural adaptability. Thus, from a personality or five-factor approach the important factors would be adaptability, extra-cultural openness (i.e., openness), and interpersonal skills (i.e., agreeableness and extroversion). Arthur and Bennett (1995, 1997) studied 338 international assignees from diverse countries and found that there were five factors which were important for success. The five factors were family situation, adaptability, job knowledge and motivation, relational skill, and extra-cultural openness. A reanalysis of the data (Arthur & Bennett, 1997) within the context of contextual job performance theory, identified eight factors: adaptability, family situation, management/administration, integrity, effort, tolerance, cross-cultural interests, and openness. Thus, this literature on international assignees would appear to support our hypothesis of the existence of a cosmopolitan personality type who is open to learning from and accepting multicultural environments.

CHAPTER SUMMARY

Theory should direct research and serve as a foundation for implementation. In the case of affirmative action, however, theory often seems to be the follower rather than the leader. As a result, theories are selected so as to explain the obtained results rather than in order to guide research. The fit between the theory and the data is then offered as evidence of the validity of the underlying theory, when in truth many theories could fit the available data. This current state of affairs is not due to a lack of applicable theories. A variety of theoretical approaches exist in the social psychological literature which would appear to be applicable to affirmative action and we have attempted to present an overview of some of the most critical theories here in Chapter 3 and also in Chapter 2.

In the previous chapter, we saw that various justice theories can provide a solid conceptual foundation for understanding reactions to affirmative action policies, especially when the criterion of interest is fairness or various types of judgments regarding justice. In particular, a combination of Nacoste's (1990, 1994, 1996) theory of procedural-interdependence and the theory of interactional justice would appear to offer a framework for understanding why very similar affirmative action policies work effectively in some situations and fail in other organizational settings.

One weakness of all the various justice theories was that they were primarily oriented at predicting attitudes toward affirmative action, affect or fairness ratings, and, thus, appeared to provide little guidance as to what actions an individual might take in order to remedy a perceived inequity or unfairness. Fishbein and Ajzen's (1975) reasoned action theory fills in this gap nicely in that their model leads to specific predictions regarding the influence of attitudes on behaviors. In addition, Fishbein and Ajzen's (1975) model recognized the role of communications from others, including others in the organization through the component of subjective norms. The emphasis on normative beliefs, shaped in part by reference groups, can easily be integrated into the communication perspective previously discussed as being an important feature of theories of interactional justice.

One of the more controversial issues surrounding the affirmative action debate involves the effects of affirmative action policies on the intended beneficiaries. Attribution theory is particularly helpful in understanding the potential effects of the presence of affirmative action policies on both the assessment of beneficiaries by others and also on self-assessment by beneficiaries. The problem in applications of attribution theory is with specifying what impact situational variables, including additional information, will have on evaluations. Specifically, in applying attribution theory to affirmative action, there is a need to identify the factors which might moderate the relationship between affirmative action and negative evaluations from others as well as negative self-evaluations.

It seems likely that many of the individual difference variables discussed in the latter part of the chapter would influence the extent to which individuals make negative evaluations of beneficiaries. There is a need for more programmatic research which investigates the role of these variables, since they may prove important in predicting the type of individual who will be most resistant to affirmative action.

In terms of personal traits, it is logical to expect that both racism and sexism would be related to reactions to affirmative action. In response to the tendency of individuals to be reluctant to admit to more traditional forms of racism and sexism, theories regarding the existence of modern forms of racism and sexism have been developed. However, the testing of theories regarding the effects of racism and sexism is confounded by measurement problems. Measures of modern racism and sexism tend to include items related to opinions regarding affirmative action and, thus, the operation of defining modern racism and sexism may create an artificial correlation between the constructs and affirmative action attitudes.

Individualism-collectivism is a critical, cultural variable (Chen, Chen, & Meindl, 1998). On the surface, it would appear that there should be a simple relationship with attitudes toward affirmative action in that individualists should oppose it based on their belief in the role of individual merit while collectivists should favor affirmative action based on a belief in the common good. However, the relationship between individualism-collectivism and justice perceptions is unlikely to be a simple one. Complicating the relationship is the issue of the identification of the in-group or the individual's reference group. Depending upon the in-group in question, the direction of the relationship between individualism-collectivism and affirmative action may in fact be reversed. Individualism-collectivism is also correlated with other variables, including political beliefs, which may have an impact on attitudes toward affirmative action.

Political values are likely to be related to support for affirmative action. Liberals, as opposed to conservatives, should favor policies which appear to emphasize equality and can be interpreted as helping the disadvantaged. Conservatives should be opposed to policies which involve a greater role for government intervention and de-emphasize the role of merit. Liberalism-conservatism may also be related to various mediating variables, including whether protected class members are seen as the innocent victims of discrimination or as responsible for their current standing in society. Individualism-collectivism effects may be highly sensitive to the way an affirmative action procedure is presented or framed. Emphasizing certain aspects of the policies (e.g., merit versus minority status), justifications for the policies, or potential outcomes of the policies may determine the relationship between values and support of affirmative action.

The Big Five -- neuroticism, extroversion, openness, agreeableness, and conscientiousness -- dominate modern personality theory and measurement. It is, therefore, surprising that more attention has not been paid to the possible role of personality, and in particular the Big Five, in predicting reactions to affirmative action policies. We present in this chapter a theory regarding the existence of a cosmopolitan personality type which corresponds to a person who possesses both a culturally-open personality and a multicultural knowledge structure. The cosmopolitan personality would score high on the openness dimension of the Big Five and also have sufficient previous experience with other cultures so as to have developed a multicultural knowledge structure.

Research on the relationship between personal traits and affirmative action is in its infancy and hampered at times by measurement problems. While it is likely that the relationship between any personal trait or attribute and reactions to a social policy is complex, the exploration of the relationship between individual differences and reactions to affirmative action policies is likely to lead to the development of more comprehensive models of the psychological processes involved in developing and changing attitudes.

The meaningful interpretation of the results of affirmative action research depends upon the existence of sound theories and models of the underlying psychological processes. It would be a mistake, however, to believe that only research based on a good theory can produce valid data. Research on affirmative action has often been driven by practical concerns or the need to answer applied questions. As Nacoste (1996) points out, while it is dangerous to ignore theory, it can be equally treacherous to simply attempt to adapt a theory, even a well-respected theory, to a social problem such as affirmative action without giving full consideration to practical aspects of the settings and situations.

REFERENCES

Arthur, W., Jr., & Bennett, W., Jr. (1995). The international assignee: The relative importance of factors perceived to contribute to success. *Personnel Psychology, 48,* 99-114.

Arthur, W., Jr., & Bennett, W., Jr. (1997). A comparative test of alternative models of international assignee job performance. *New Approaches to Employee Management, 4,* 141-172.

Arthur, W., Jr., Doverspike, D., & Fuentes, R. (1992). Recipients' affective responses to affirmative action interventions: A cross-cultural perspective. *Behavioral Sciences and the Law, 10,* 229-243.

Ajzen, I., & Fishbein, M. (1980). *Understanding attitudes and predicting behavior.* Englewood Cliffs, NJ: Prentice-Hall.

Barrick, M. R., & Mount, M. K. (1991). The Big Five personality dimensions and job performance: A meta-analysis. *Personnel Psychology, 44,* 1-26.

Bobo, L., & Kluegel, J. R. (1993). Opposition to race-targeting: Self-interest, stratification ideology, or racial attitudes? *American Sociological Review, 58,* 443-464.

Brief, A. P., Buttram, R. T., Reizenstein, R. M., Pugh, S. D., Callahan, J. D., McCline, R. L., & Vaslow, J. B. (1997). Beyond good intentions: The next steps toward racial equality in the American workplace. *Academy of Management Executive, 11,* 59-72.

Chen, C. C., Chen, X., & Meindl, J. R. (1998). How can cooperation be fostered? The cultural effects of individualism-collectivism. *Academy of Management Review, 23,* 285-304.

Dansereau, F. (1989). A multiple level of analysis perspective on the debate about individualism. *American Psychologist, 44,* 959-960.

Devine, P. G. (1989). Stereotypes and prejudice: Their automatic and controlled processes. *Journal of Personality and Social Psychology, 56,* 1, 5-18.

Dovidio, J. F., Mann, J., & Gaertner, S. L. (1989). Resistance to affirmative action: The implications of aversive racism. In F. A. Blanchard & F. J. Crosby (Eds.), *Affirmative action in perspective* (pp. 83-102). New York: Springer-Verlag.

Eberhardt, J. L., & Fiske, S. (1994). Affirmative action in theory and practice: Issues of power, ambiguity and gender versus race. *Basic and Applied Social Psychology, 15,* 201-220.

Fishbein, M. (1980). A theory of reasoned action: Some applications and implications. In H. Howe & M. Page (Eds.), *Nebraska Symposium on Motivation* (v. 27, pp. 65-116). Lincoln, NE: University of Nebraska Press.

Fishbein, M., & Ajzen, I. (1975). *Belief, attitude, intention and behavior.* Reading, MA: Addison-Wesley.

Gaertner, S. L., & Dovidio, J. F. (1986). The aversive form of racism. In J. F. Dovidio & S. L. Gaertner (Eds.), *Prejudice, discrimination, and racism* (pp. 61-89). Orlando, FL: Academic Press.

Garcia, L. T., Erskine, N., Hawn, K., & Casmay, S. R. (1981). The effect of affirmative action on attributions about minority group members. *Journal of Personality, 49,* 427-437.

Heider, F. (1958). *The psychology of interpersonal relations.* New York, NY: Wiley.

Heilman, M. E., Block, C. J., & Lucas, J. A. (1992). Presumed incompetent? Stigmatization and affirmative action efforts. *Journal of Applied Psychology, 77,* 536-544.

Heilman, M. E., Lucas, J. A., & Kaplow, S. R. (1990). Self-derogating consequences of sex-based preferential selection: The moderating role of initial self-confidence. *Organizational Behavior and Human Decision Processes, 46,* 202-216.

Hui, C. H. (1988). Measurement of Individualism-Collectivism. *Journal of Research in Personality, 22,* 17-36.

Kelley, H. H. (1971). *Attribution in social interaction.* New York: John Wiley & Sons, Inc.

Kelley, H. H. (1973). The processes of causal attribution. *American Psychologist, 28,* 107-128.

Kinder, D. R. (1986). The continuing American dilemma: White resistance to racial change 40 years after Myrdal. *Journal of Social Issues, 42,* 151-171.

Kinder, D. R., & Sanders, L. M. (1990). Mimicking political debate with survey questions: The case of White opinion of affirmative action for Blacks. *Social Cognition, 8,* 73-103.

Kinder, D. R., & Sears, D. O. (1981). Prejudice and politics: Symbolic racism versus racial threats to the good life. *Journal of Personality and Social Psychology, 40,* 414-431.

Kravitz, D. A., Harrison, D. A., Turner, M. A., Levine, E. L. Chaves, W., Brannick, M. T., Denning, D. L., Russell, C. J., & Conrad, M. A. (1997). *Affirmative action: A review of psychological and behavioral research.* Bowling Green, OH: Society for Industrial and Organizational Psychology.

Kravitz, D. A., & Platania, J. (1993). Attitudes and beliefs about affirmative action: Effects of target and respondent sex and ethnicity. *Journal of Applied Psychology, 78,* 928-938.

Lambert, A. J., & Chasteen, A. L. (1997). Perceptions of disadvantage versus conventionality: Political values and attitudes toward the elderly versus Blacks. *Personality and Social Psychology Bulletin, 23,* 469-481.

Larwood, L. (1982). The importance of being right when you think you are: Self-serving bias in equal employment opportunity. In B. A. Gutek (Ed.), *Sex Role Stereotyping and Affirmative Action Policy* (pp. 65-80). Los Angeles, CA: Institute of Industrial Relations.

Martin, J. R., Price, L., Bies, R. J., & Powers, M.E. (1987). Now that I can have it, I'm not so sure I want it: The effects of opportunity on aspirations and discontent. In B. A. Gutek & L. Larwood (Eds.), *Women's Career Development* (pp. 28-41). Newbury Park, CA: Sage.

McConahay, J. B. (1982). Self-interest versus racial attitudes as correlates of anti-busing attitudes in Louisville: Is it the buses or the blacks? *Journal of Politics, 44,* 692-720.

McConahay, J. B. (1986). Modern racism, ambivalence and the Modern Racism Scale. In J. F. Dovidio & S.L. Gaertner (Eds.), *Prejudice, Discrimination and Racism.* Orlando, FL: Academic Press.

McConahay, J. B., & Hough, J. C., Jr. (1976). Symbolic racism. *Journal of Social Issues, 32*, 23-45.

McCrae, R. R., & Costa, , P. T., Jr. (1985). Updating Norman's "adequate taxonomy": Intelligence and personality dimensions in natural language and in questionnaires. *Journal of Personality and Social Psychology, 49*, 710-721.

McCrae, R. R., & Costa, , P. T., Jr. (1987). Validation of the five-factor model of personality across instruments and observers. *Journal of Personality and Social Psychology, 52*, 81-90.

McCrae, R. R., & Costa, P. T., Jr., (1994). The stability of personality: Observations and evaluations. *Current Directions in Psychological Science, 3*, 173-175.

Murrell, A. J., Dietz-Uhler, B. L., Dovidio, J. F., Gaertner, S. L., & Drout, C. (1994). Aversive racism and resistance to affirmative action: Perceptions of justice are not necessarily color blind. *Basic and Applied Social Psychology, 15*, 71-86.

Nacoste, R. W. (1990). Sources of stigma: Analyzing the psychology of affirmative action. *Law and Policy, 12*, 175-195.

Nacoste, R. W. (1994). Policy schemas for affirmative action. In L. Heath, R. S. Tindale, J. Edwards, E. J. Posavac, F. B. Bryant, E. Hendeson-King, Y. Suarez-Balcazar, & J. Myers (Eds.), *Applications of heuristics and biases to social issues* (pp. 205-221). New York, NY: Plenum Press.

Nacoste, R. W. (1996). Social psychology and the affirmative action debate. *Journal of Social and Clinical Psychology, 15*, 261-282.

Northcraft, G. B., & Martin, J. (1982). Double Jeopardy: Resistance to affirmative action from potential beneficiaries. In B. Gutek (Ed.), *Sex Role Stereotyping and Affirmative Action Policy* (pp. 81-130). Los Angeles, CA: Institute of Industrial Relations.

Peterson, R. S. (1994). The role of values in predicting fairness judgments and support of affirmative action. *Journal of Social Issues, 50*, 95-116.

Pettigrew, T.F., & Martin, J. (1987). Shaping the organizational context for Black American inclusion. *Journal of Social Issues, 43*, 41-78.

Petty, R. E., & Cacioppo, John T. (1981). *Attitudes and Persuasions: Classic and Contemporary Approaches.* Dubuque, IA: Wm. C. Brown.

Reid, P.T., & Clayton, S. (1992). Racism and sexism at work. *Social Justice Research, 5*, 249-268.

60　　　　　　D. Doverspike, M. Taylor and W. Arthur, Jr.

Sidanius, J., Pratto, F., & Bobo, L. (1996). Racism, conservatism, affirmative action, and intellectual sophistication: A matter of principled conservatism or group dominance? *Journal of Personality and Social Psychology, 70,* 476-490.

Skitka, L. J., & Tetlock, P. (1992). Allocating scarce resources: A contingency model of distributive justice. *Journal of Experimental Social Psychology, 28,* 491-522.

Skitka, L. J., & Tetlock, P. (1993). Providing public assistance: Cognitive and motivational processes underlying liberal and conservative policy preferences. *Journal of Personality and Social Psychology, 65,* 1205-1223.

Sniderman, P. M., & Tetlock, P. E. (1986). Symbolic racism: Problems of motive attribution in political analysis. *Journal of Social Issues, 42,* 129-150.

Stewart, M. M., & Shapiro, D. L. (1999, April). *Selection based on merit versus demography: Implications across race and gender lines.* Paper presented at the Society for Industrial and Organizational Psychology, Atlanta, GA.

Tougas, F., Brown, R., Beaton, A. M., & Joly, S. (1995). Neosexism: Plus ca change, plus c'est pareil. *Personality and Social Psychology Bulletin, 8,* 842-849.

Triandis, H. C. (1996). The psychological measurement of cultural syndromes. *American Psychologist, 51,* 407-415.

Trope, Y. (1986). Identification and inferential processes in dispositional attribution. *Psychological Review, 93,* 239-257.

Tupes, E. C., & Christal, R. E. (1961). *Recurrent personality factors based on trait ratings* (ASD-TR-61-97). Lackland Air Force Base, TX: Personnel Laboratory.

Chapter 4

BASIC METHODOLOGICAL APPROACHES

Within psychology, the approach taken to the study of affirmative action is one rooted in the traditions of experimental social psychology. Research participants are either surveyed concerning their opinions or various dimensions of affirmative action are manipulated in artificial situations which are described in written form or created in an artificial work environment. Thus there are four basic research approaches:

1. The opinion survey.
2. The correlational study.
3. The paper-person scenario.
4. The assigned leader paradigm.

A key question in evaluating affirmative action studies is whether the conclusions and inferences reached are valid based on the data obtained from the study. The "validity" of a research study can be defined as "the appropriateness of inferences drawn from the data." There are four, generally recognized types of research validity (for a much more complete discussion of this topic, see the work of Cook and Campbell, 1976, 1979):

1. Internal Validity - refers to the extent to which it can be inferred that any obtained relationship or effect, or lack of effect, corresponds to a true relationship or effect. In the special case where a casual relationship is described, a study has internal validity if a cause-effect relationship

actually exists between the independent and dependent variables when the results of the study indicate that a causal relationship does exist.

2. External Validity - refers to the generalizability of the identified relationships between variables to other persons, settings, and times. In general, field research is seen as having higher external validity than laboratory research, because the persons, settings, and times are more likely to correspond to those found in the populations of interest (i.e., those found in other field settings).

3. Statistical Conclusion Validity - refers to the appropriateness of any conclusions arrived at as a result of the statistical analysis, and, as such, deals with the appropriateness of the statistical methods used by the researcher. Consequently, statistical conclusion validity is more a function of the use of statistical methods in a particular study, or possibly the misuse of statistics, than it is a general property of a class of research designs.

4. Construct Validity - refers to the labels that are used to describe the phenomena or events being studied and the extent to which the labels are theoretically relevant. Thus, construct validity is a question of whether the research results support the theory underlying the research study. That is, is there another theory that could adequately explain the same results? If the labels being used are irrelevant to the theory being researched, then the research study can be said to lack construct validity. There is another meaning of construct validity, which corresponds to its use within psychometrics. In test theory, construct validity refers to the appropriateness of the labels attached to the measurement operations, the extent to which those labels correspond to the theory, and the appropriateness of the resulting theoretical statements. For example, if we infer that a question measured a respondent's judgment of the procedural justice of affirmative action, what evidence do we have that our question actually measures procedural justice as compared to distributive justice or fairness.

Each of the above dimensions or facets of research validity has associated with it various threats to the validity of the design. An analysis of the threats to the various types of validity can be found in a number of research methods textbooks (Cook & Campbell, 1976, 1979; Frankfort-Nachmias & Nachmias, 1996; Rosenthal & Rosnow, 1991). It is also common to view research as often involving a tradeoff between external and internal validity.

In this chapter we will briefly discuss and illustrate the basic methodologies, and the strengths and weaknesses of each of the major approaches. For each approach, we will first discuss the characteristics of the method itself, then discuss some of the major limitations and threats to validity.

Any topology, including this one, can only hope to identify the general features of its subjects and present examples corresponding to prototypical members of each category. In practice, researchers adapt designs to their purposes and may use a mixture of designs, as well as, a wide array of statistical techniques. Thus, any comments regarding strengths and weakness of typical members are intended as general comments and may not apply to specific applications of a design or a specific research study. External validity, in particular, will often be more a function of the specific situation in which a study takes place than of the general design type.

THE OPINION SURVEY

The opinion survey approach involves the measurement and assessment of opinions or attitudes toward a target, in this case affirmative action, by means of responses to simple questions or items. Responses to the questions may be collected through written questionnaires, telephone interviews, or in-person interviews. This type of opinion survey is often used in public opinion polling, and we will soon offer an example from such a poll. However, our concern here and in this book is primarily with the validity of such surveys in psychological research rather than in public opinion polling or in sociological research.

An example of a survey study would be the one conducted recently by *PARADE* (Ciabattarit, 1999), a national magazine frequently distributed with Sunday newspapers. In a story, *PARADE* asked readers to respond to one of four questions. One question was:

'Should the government give preferential treatment in the employment of minorities and women?'

Items on the survey were responded to using a *Yes* or *No* option. In terms of the results, for the question above, approximately 85.9% of the responses were *No* and 9% were *Yes*. Similar rates of response were obtained for questions dealing with college admissions and government contracts; the fourth question dealt with economic need.

In a survey study, it is possible to ask a very, general question or a specific question which thereby limits the definition of affirmative action. For example, a general question would be:

"Do you approve of affirmative action?"

This general type of question leaves it to the discretion and the judgment of the respondent to offer their own definition of affirmative action. While this type of approach allows the respondent to apply their personal definition of affirmative action, a weakness of the approach is that the researcher cannot be sure as to how the respondents choose to define affirmative action (Nacoste, 1996), unless there are follow-up questions.

As in the *PARADE* (Ciabattarit, 1999) survey, it is possible to limit the definition of affirmative action in a question. It also becomes possible to then manipulate the definition of affirmative action and compare the rate of responses. For example, in order to compare attitudes toward race- and sex-based affirmative action, the following two questions could be asked:

"Should organizations be allowed to give preferential treatment in employment to minorities?"
"Should organizations be allowed to give preferential treatment in employment to women?"

The previous two questions would allow a researcher to investigate the presence of statistically significant differences in the proportions of respondents agreeing with each type of affirmative action. If the researcher had the foresight to record responses for each individual, then it would also be possible to correlate responses with other variables, for example, the sex or race of the respondent. Thus, a researcher could investigate whether females, as compared to minorities, are more likely to agree with an item which asks for approval for preferential treatment for women. If the researcher could also compare the responses of females and minorities to responses on another item asking for approval for preferential treatment for minorities, it would then be possible to test a personal benefit or personal entitlement hypothesis. It would also be possible, using the above questions, to correlate responses to the two items. By doing this, a researcher could determine if people who endorse race-based affirmative action are also more likely to also endorse sex-based affirmative action (Note: At this point, the opinion survey is being used as a correlational study).

There are a number of response options which can be used with survey questions beyond the simple *Yes* or *No* response option. Reactions or attitudes toward the target may be collected using a variety of common rating scale formats including those of the type often referred to as Likert, which use some type of graphical, numerical, or verbal anchor (Rosenthal & Rosnow, 1991). Perhaps the most common is one which uses the following options:

1. Strongly disagree
2. Disagree
3. Neither disagree nor agree
4. Agree
5. Strongly Agree

By using a 5-step response scale, the researcher can obtain a greater range of responses than those offered by a simple *Yes* or *No* option. The use of a 5-point scale also makes it easier to use parametric statistics.

Limitations and Threats to Validity

A problem with any type of survey is the manner in which people are sampled. Typically, response rates to surveys may be very low, 30% or less, introducing questions regarding the characteristics of respondents. This is especially likely to be true when the topic or issue is a sensitive or controversial one like affirmative action or racist attitudes.

Although various types of sampling strategies exist, in many cases sampling in psychological research may be haphazard. In psychology, survey studies are often performed with convenience samples, specifically college students enrolled in introduction to psychology classes. In opinion polling, sophisticated sampling strategies are usually employed. Another problem with survey studies is the wording of questions. Potentially, the questions and items themselves can have a major influence on how people will respond. This is not as much of a problem when item content is purposely controlled or manipulated, but it is still always an issue.

In responding to surveys, participants may also rely upon certain response sets or response styles (Pedhazur & Schmelkin, 1991). Response styles refer to the tendency of people to respond to questionnaire items in a specific manner regardless of content. For example, some people will not answer items/questions when they are unsure of their response, while others will simply respond with a random response. Some respondents may simply agree with every item, while other participants will tend to disagree with every item.

Response sets refer to the tendency to respond to questionnaire or test content based on a goal other than accurately responding to the content. The primary example of a response set is social desirability, which refers to the tendency to favorably distort responses to self-report measures. In more recent work, researchers (Paulhus, 1986, 1991; Paulhus, Fridhandler, & Hayes, 1997; Paulhus & John, 1998) have demonstrated differences among two major kinds of social desirability, which Paulhus labels "impression management" and "self-deception." In part, the distinction is related to a test-taker or research participant's presumed conscious strategy for dissimulation. In impression management (Snyder, 1974), a participant's self-report may be based on active attempts to create an image as a liberal, tolerant, open-minded, accepting person, knowing full well that she/he is typically none of these things. Here impression management is in the service of pleasing the researcher and conforming to what are perceived to be acceptable or expected views, attitudes, and behaviors. Other terms that may be used to describe impression management-like related behaviors include intentional distortion, faking, dissimulation, and lying (Furnham, 1986).

In contrast, in self-deception, a participant may be less aware of the motivational processes leading to distortions, but distortions may be apparent to experts and peer raters. Thus, self-deception is unconscious distortion that occurs unbeknownst to the participant. This might occur if the participant lacks self-insight or self-knowledge.

In dealing with a sensitive subject like affirmative action or racism, impression management is likely to be the most pertinent source of response bias. Participants in a survey may try to create a favorable impression of themselves in the eyes of the researchers (Paulhus, 1984). In studies of affirmative action, it is possible to attempt to control for social desirability in general, and impression management in particular, by administering a scale designed to measure individual differences in socially desirable response tendencies. However, the inclusion of a social desirability control in affirmative action studies appears to be rather rare, although some racism measures do attempt to control for social desirability by including "faking" or "lie" scales.

Survey studies are usually analyzed by calculating simple proportions, frequency tables, and/or means. Where proportions or frequency tables are calculated, chi-square tests of significance can also be computed. Finally, the use of survey designs, which do not lend themselves to the manipulation of variables or strong experimental control, makes it impossible to make any statements or inferences about the causality of relationships between the variables studied.

In terms of the four types of validity, the survey study as typically used in psychological research on affirmative action, will probably be weak on internal validity, external validity, and construct validity. The external validity will vary depending on the relevance of the setting (i.e., was the survey conducted with organizational members or was it conducted with college sophomores). The threats to construct validity arise due to problems associated with trying to adequately define and measure constructs within the limits of the survey technique. The advantage of the survey study is that a great deal of information can be collected in a short amount of time at a relatively low cost.

THE CORRELATIONAL STUDY
AND INDIVIDUAL DIFFERENCES

Correlational studies or research designs are those where we simply measure two or more variables and attempt to determine the degree of relationship between the variables. There is no manipulation of variables. Correlational designs are not to be confused with correlations, the test statistic; they are two separate concepts and one does not necessarily imply the other. That is, for instance, the mere fact that a study uses correlations to analyze its data does not necessarily make it a correlational design and vice versa.

Although all the research designs discussed here can incorporate or include individual difference variables, such as racism, sexism, or conservatism, the study of individual differences is most closely associated with correlational designs. Thus, one might be interested in the relationship between racism or sexism and attitudes to affirmative action. In such a study, one would simply administer measures of the specified variables and then assess the relationship between them. Individual difference variables can be measured using only a single item, but they are usually operationalized using standardized tests which provide multi-item measures of a variable or construct. One of the main issues when tests are used in this manner is whether they are doing a good job of measuring the constructs in question. The adequacy of the test can be evaluated using two major criteria - reliability and validity.

Reliability refers to the extent to which a test measures a construct in a consistent fashion. Reliability can refer to consistency over time (i.e., test-retest reliability), consistency over forms (i.e., alternate forms reliability), or internal consistency (i.e., coefficient alpha). Typically, if the reliability of a measure is reported in a study it is based upon internal consistency primarily because this type of reliability requires only a single administration of the test and so is readily available in most studies. For research purposes, internal consistency reliabilities above .70 are generally considered to be adequate. The reliability of measures used in affirmative action studies are commonly not reported and, as a result, the adequacy of the measures may be unknown.

Although there are several types of test validity, the most critical, for research purposes, is construct validity. When evaluating the construct validity of a test, the question is one of whether the test provides an adequate measure of the construct corresponding to the test. Unfortunately, in many studies, only limited information is presented on the construct validity of the individual difference measures used in the research.

Limitations and Threats to Validity

Correlational designs, by their very nature, do not involve the manipulation of variables and the level of experimental control, although study-specific, is typically not very high. As a result, it is very difficult to make causal inferences. In recent years, however, a variety of techniques for arriving at casual inferences based on correlational data have been developed. These techniques are often discussed under the rubric of path analysis or structural equation modeling (Pedhazur & Schmelkin, 1991). However, even when these more sophisticated analytical techniques are used, some methodological and statistical purists still question the validity of these causal inferences, since there is usually some ambiguity present regarding the direction of causality.

Given that correlational studies often use a survey methodology, many of the limitations and threats discussed above for the opinion survey study also apply to the correlational study. Thus, response sets and styles will also be a concern with the correlational study. In terms of the four types of validity, the correlational study will probably be weak on internal validity, external validity, and construct validity. The external validity will vary depending on the relevance of the setting. The advantage of the correlational study is that a great deal of information can be collected in a short amount of time at a relatively low cost.

THE PAPER-PERSON SCENARIO

It is quite common in psychology to ask research participants to read a stimulus story and to then have them react to the hypothetical situation presented in the story. This type of study is often referred to as the paper-person scenario. It is not limited to the study of reactions to affirmative action, but is also used in many areas of social psychology, including decision making. This paper-person methodology has been frequently used in psychological studies of affirmative action primarily because it allows the researcher to manipulate and study any number of factors.

As an example, the following is one of several scenarios from a cross-cultural study of reactions to affirmative action. Research participants were presented with this material, asked to read the material, and then asked to assume a specified role in the hypothetical situation. The situation was one of a student applying for an internship. In this version of the scenario, the research participant is playing the role of a Hispanic, female applicant for an internship position who is less qualified than the other candidate, but still receives the position. In addition, the organization had in place a strong affirmative action program. The research participant read the following material which represents the less qualified, strong policy scenario:

This study involves a role play or simulation. The two main characters in this role play are Anna Hernandez and Michelle Sullivan.

Michelle Sullivan is a college student at Middleton University. She is a 21 year old White female. Her major field of study is Business Administration.

Anna Hernandez is a college student at Middleton University. She is a 21 year old Hispanic female. Her major field of study is Business Administration.

We would like you to place yourself in the position of one of the participants, Anna Hernandez. As you read the case study below, please try to place yourself in the role of Anna Hernandez.

You are a college student at Middleton University. You have applied for a prestigious internship with a local Fortune 500 Corporation called Wharton Corporation. The internship is a one-year paid internship that will open doors to future employment possibilities.

The selection committee has narrowed the field down to two applicants. The two applicants are: Michelle Sullivan and yourself, Anna Hernandez.

The selection committee for Wharton Corporation has just called you into their office. They tell you that the committee has agreed that Michelle Sullivan has a better record as a college student and is more qualified. However, Wharton Corporation has installed a strong affirmative action policy to increase jobs and internships to minorities. The current policy of the corporation states that the race of the applicant is to be considered very important. Based on this consideration, Wharton Corporation is happy to award the internship position to you, Anna Hernandez.

Now, think how you as, Anna Hernandez, would feel at this time and then answer the following questions.

After participants read the scenario, they are then asked to respond to a series of questions which constitute the dependent variables for the study. It is also possible that questions may be developed which correspond to mediator variables. A series of typical questions might be:

How do you feel about affirmative action?

1. Very Good
2. Good
3. Neither Good nor Bad
4. Bad
5. Very Bad

How competent do you feel?

1. Very Competent
2. Competent
3. Neither Competent nor Incompetent
4. Incompetent
5. Very Incompetent

How fair was the decision reached by the committee?

1. Very Fair
2. Fair
3. Neither Fair nor Unfair
4. Unfair
5. Very Unfair

For comparative purposes, the following presents an alternative version of the same role play presented above. Here, the research participant is asked to play the role of a Hispanic, female applicant who is equally qualified and receives the position. In this case, a control condition is created where the organization's affirmative action policy is not mentioned. Alternatively, in other versions of the scenario, the organization would have been described as having a weak affirmative action policy. The research participant would read the following:

This study involves a role play or simulation. The two main characters in this role play are Anna Hernandez and Michelle Sullivan.

Michelle Sullivan is a college student at Middleton University. She is a 21 year old White female. Her major field of study is Business Administration.

Anna Hernandez is a college student at Middleton University. She is a 21 year old Hispanic female. Her major field of study is Business Administration.

We would like you to place yourself in the position of one of the participants, Anna Hernandez. As you read the case study below, please try to think of yourself in the role of Anna Hernandez.

You are a college student at Middleton University. You have applied for a prestigious internship with a local Fortune 500 Corporation called Wharton Corporation. The internship is a one-year paid internship that will open doors to future employment possibilities.

The selection committee has narrowed the field down to two applicants. The two applicants are: Michelle Sullivan and yourself, Anna Hernandez.

The selection committee for Wharton Corporation has just called you into their office. They tell you that the committee has agreed that the two applicants are equally qualified. In conclusion, Wharton Corporation is happy to award the internship position to you, Anna Hernandez.

Again, after reading the scenario, participants respond to a series of questions concerning their attitudes toward the material they have just read.

Limitations and Threats to Validity

Paper-person studies on affirmative action usually involve true experimental designs. In true experimental designs, research participants are randomly assigned to the different treatment conditions; in the paper-person scenario, the treatment conditions are created through variations in the description of the various types of affirmative action policies used to make the selection decision.

Although the race or sex of the participant is usually a non-manipulated factor in affirmative action research, in some studies it may be manipulated by asking participants to play the role of a person of a designated race or sex. Thus, participants, regardless of whether they are male or female, may be told to "pretend you are a female." More typically, race or sex is a given and factors such as the type of affirmative action or the qualifications of the persons in the scenario are manipulated.

In paper-person studies, it is possible to achieve rather strong internal validity, although this promise is not always attained. Due to the ease of administration of materials, large numbers of participants can be recruited and tested at low cost and in a short period of time. The researcher also has maximum control over most, if not all, of the important variables.

The major problem with the paper-person study involves the question of realism and external validity. Paper-person scenario studies are classic laboratory studies. The major distinction between laboratory and field studies has to do with the naturalness or artificiality of the setting. While laboratory settings tend to permit higher degrees of control than field settings, they tend to lack realism.

Thus, in terms of the four types of validity of research designs, the paper-person study will probably be judged as being relatively weak in terms of external validity. On the other hand, this is a very flexible design which allows the researcher to manipulate a number of different variables, while minimizing the time and cost associated with implementing the study.

THE ASSIGNED LEADER PARADIGM

The assigned leader paradigm attempts to capture the realism of the field within the confines of the more controlled environment of the researcher's laboratory. In the prototypical assigned leader paradigm, participants are recruited to take part in a group task. When individuals arrive to take part in the study, they are told that the team leaders are usually selected based on performance on a test (i.e., the merit condition is selection based upon performance on the test). A subsample of the participants are told that they have been selected to be leaders based on their race or sex (i.e., the affirmative action condition). The reason they have been selected on the basis of their race or sex is ostensibly the result of a shortage of members of the respective group. This manipulation is supposed to be analogous to the results of affirmative action; that is, due to low representation, the person has been selected as leader despite low (or equal) merit. Of course, it would be possible, as in the paper-person scenario, to create almost any justification corresponding to a variety of different affirmative action definitions.

As an example, a script is presented below which would be read by an experimenter in an assigned leader paradigm study. This script would be read to participants after they had completed a short test on mathematical ability. In this example, the participant is a Hispanic female. The script which represents the less qualified, race-based selection condition, is as follows:

Thank you for participating in our study on mathematical problem solving. We are studying math problem solving by 5-person groups. Every participant is assigned to a five-person group and is then asked to work 50 math problems as a group. Every group is also assigned a leader from among the five participants.

Normally, the leader of the group is selected based upon their math score from the pretest which you just took. The person who achieves the highest score is made the leader of the group. Unfortunately, your score on the test was not very high; you scored lower than all of the other group members. However, we need to balance the group leaders by race. We have not had very many Hispanic group leaders. Therefore, because you are Hispanic, we have selected you to be the group leader.

After listening to the script, the research participant would then actually serve as leader of the group. The performance of the group on the math problems would be measured. In addition, the leader of the group would then be asked to complete a series of questions on their attitudes toward the study similar to those used following the paper-person scenario study.

Other variables could be manipulated to create other conditions. For example, the following script could be use to create an equally qualified, no mention of affirmative action condition:

Thank you for participating in our study on mathematical problem solving. We are studying math problem solving by 5-person groups. Every participant is assigned to a five-person group and is then asked to work 50 math problems as a group. Every group is also assigned a leader from among the five participants.

Normally, the leader of the group is selected based upon their math score from the pretest which you just took. The person who achieves the highest score is made the leader of the group. Your score on the test was very high; you and another member of the group achieved the exact same score. Based on your score, we have decided to make you the leader of the group.

Limitations and Threats to Validity

The assigned leader paradigm is very similar to the paper-person scenario study in terms of the use of true experimental designs, albeit in an artificial setting. As a result, many of the criticisms, limitations, and threats to validity for the assigned leader paradigm are similar to those previously mentioned for the paper-person scenario study. The major advantage of the assigned leader paradigm over the paper-person scenario study is in the degree of realism or external validity. In the assigned leader paradigm, the participant is not asked to imagine that they have been treated differently, they actually experience the differential treatment. It is also possible to measure the effects of any manipulation on performance. The trade-off is that the assigned leader paradigm will usually be more expensive and take longer than the paper-person scenario study to implement.

Nacoste (1996) also criticizes the assigned leader paradigm for its operationalization of affirmative action. He argues that the assigned leader paradigm involves individual rather than organizational discrimination and that the rationale behind the differential treatment is simply participation rates rather than discrimination. As a result, Nacoste (1996) appears to be arguing that the assigned leader paradigm actually ends up having less external validity than the paper-person scenario. Although this may be true of the of the assigned leader paradigm to date, it would not seem to be an essential or necessary property of this unique design. That is, the assigned leader paradigm could always provide a rationale for the decision to appoint a person a leader which is closer to the definition of affirmative action.

CHAPTER SUMMARY

This chapter has discussed the four major methods or designs used in affirmative action research, and also the inclusion of individual difference variables. In practice, researchers use variations on the different designs or even a mixture of designs. As a result, any comments or criticisms of the various designs are intended as general statements directed at exemplars of each category, and may not apply to the designs as actually used in specific studies.

Of the four designs, the opinion survey and correlational study are the most cost effective and easiest to implement. However, the opinion survey and correlational study also tend to result in the most questions concerning internal validity, external validity, and construct validity. Both the paper-person scenario and assigned leader paradigm allow for the use of true experimental designs. Although the paper-person scenario and assigned leader paradigm have advantages over the opinion survey and correlational study in terms of internal validity, external validity and construct validity, they also tend to be more costly and require more time (see also Nacoste, 1996, for a discussion of the effects of different types of research approaches on the acceptance of psychological studies on affirmative action).

Although individual difference variables can be included in any of the designs discussed, they are most closely associated with the use of correlational designs where the major concern is the adequacy of the measurement processes (i.e., does the individual difference measure or test measure the hypothesized construct in a reliable and valid manner?). The effects of individual difference variables are usually assessed using correlational statistical methods which are conceptually distinct and different from correlational research designs. The use of correlational designs give rise to questions concerning the direction of causation and internal validity. Experimental data from both paper-person studies and the assigned leader paradigm always seem to lead to the same troublesome question -- do the data generalize to real-world or real-life situations? Although there are some field studies, usually survey studies, they typically ask slightly different questions or present there own set of problems. Many field studies do not even involve surveys, but often represent nothing more than case studies or the results of casual observation.

We have chosen to approach the issue of psychological process in affirmative action from a traditional, experimental psychology viewpoint. It could be argued that other approaches within psychology are more appropriate for answering the questions presented. This argument has been effectively made by proponents of Feminist Psychology and Critical Psychology.

REFERENCES

Ciabattarit, J. (1999, April 4). Parade's Special Intelligence Report: Affirmative Action Debate Rages on. *PARADE*, p. 14.

Cook, T. D., & Campbell, D. T. (1976). The design and conduct of quasi-experiments and true experiments and field settings. In M. D. Dunnette (Ed.), *Handbook of Industrial and Organizational Psychology* (pp. 223-326). Chicago, IL: Rand McNally.

Cook, T. D., & Campbell, D. T. (1979). *Quasi-experimentation: Design and analysis issues of field settings*. Chicago, IL: Rand McNally.

Frankfort-Nachmias, C., & Nachmias, D. (1996). *Research methods in the social sciences* (5th Ed.). New York, NY: St. Martin's Press.

Furnham, A. (1986). Response bias, social desirability, and dissimulation. *Personality and Individual Differences, 7*, 385-400.

Nacoste, R. W. (1996). Social psychology and the affirmative action debate. *Journal of Social and Clinical Psychology, 15*, 261-282.

Paulhus, D. L. (1984). Two-component models of socially desirable responding. *Journal of Personality and Social Psychology, 46*, 598-609.

Paulhus, D. L. (1986). Self-deception and impression management in test responses. In A. Angleitner & J. S. Wiggins (Eds.), *Personality assessment via questionnaire* (pp. 143-165). New York, NY: Springer-Verlag.

Paulhus, D. L. (1991). Measurement and control of response biases. In J. P. Robinson, P. R. Shaver, & L. Wrightsman (Eds.), *Measures of personality and social psychological attitudes* (Vol. 1, pp. 1-17). San Diego, CA: Academic Press.

Paulhus, D., Fridhandler, B., & Hayes, S. (1997). Psychological defense: Contemporary theory and research. In R. Hogan, J. Johnson, & S. Briggs (Eds.), *Handbook of personality psychology* (pp. 554-580). San Diego, CA: Academic Press.

Paulhus, D. L., & John, O. P. (1998). Egoistic and moralistic biases in self-perception: The interplay of self-deceptive styles with basic traits and motives. *Journal of Personality, 66,* 1025-1060.

Pedhazur, E. J., & Schmelkin, L. P. (1991). *Measurement, design, and analysis: An integrated approach.* Hillsdale, NJ: Lawrence Erlbaum.

Rosenthal, R., & Rosnow, R. L. (1991). *Essentials of behavioral research: Methods and data analysis* (2nd Ed.). New York: NY. McGraw-Hill.

Snyder, M. (1974). The self-monitoring of expressive behavior. *Journal of Personality and Social Psychology, 30,* 526-537.

Chapter 5

THE MESSAGE: EFFECTS OF THE OPERATIONALIZATION OF AFFIRMATIVE ACTION AND ORGANIZATIONAL CONTEXT

This chapter is concerned with the effects of variations in the description of the affirmative action procedure (i.e., the message), on resulting attitudes. Reactions toward affirmative action policies and toward the results of affirmative action policies are likely to vary as a function of the relative severity of the policy, as captured in the definition of affirmative action, and the organizational context in which the policy is embedded. This is especially likely to be true if the premise that people tend to possess relatively little actual knowledge of affirmative action procedures is accurate. Despite the controversial nature of affirmative action, the general populace appears to have relatively little, accurate information on affirmative action (Kravitz et al., 1997; Kravitz & Patina, 1993; Kravitz, Stinson, & Mello, 1994; Taylor-Carter, Doverspike, & Alexander, 1995).

In considering the impact of variations in the message, both the manner in which affirmative action is described and the organizational context are likely to emerge as critical factors. The typical variations in the definition of affirmative action as operationalized in the psychological literature have already been described in the Introduction (see Chapter 1).

Although the organizational context could be manipulated independent of the operational definition of affirmative action, in the psychological research, information on the affirmative action procedures is usually embedded within the description of the organizational context. Conversely, the researcher may also choose to reverse the procedure and embed information on the organizational context within the description of the affirmative action procedure. Organizational context is used here to refer to variables related to why the organization is implementing affirmative action in the first place and how the organization chooses to communicate the informational message to the recipient, and may also include information on other variables relevant to the decision making environment.

In a similar vein, in survey or laboratory research, the sender of the message is usually the experimenter or an unknown source. Thus, while the sender has been identified in the communication literature as an important factor, in the psychological literature information on the sender is usually unknown, ambiguous, or confounded with information on the organizational context.

OPERATIONALIZATION OF AFFIRMATIVE ACTION

In conducting research on affirmative action, the definition of affirmative action or the description of the actual policies used is often manipulated by the experimenter as a means of testing the effect of changes in the characterization of affirmative action on the research participants. A second option, used by some researchers, is to provide an ambiguous definition of affirmative action, and then capture the respondent's personal definition of what affirmative action means. As discussed in Chapter 1, the three basic dimensions which can be manipulated in order to study the effects of affirmative action are:

1. The relative emphasis on merit or the type of affirmative action.
2. The protected group(s) involved.
3. The type of opportunity (e.g., education or employment).

The Relative Emphasis on Merit

One of the most fundamental questions surrounding the use of affirmative action is whether there are differences in fairness perceptions and attitudes as a function of various affirmative action policies. This can also be conceptualized in terms of differences in reaction as a function of the relative emphasis of the affirmative action policy on merit versus protected group status.

As noted in the Introduction (see Chapter 1), while different authors have slightly different lists, there are basically five levels of affirmative action. The five are (Ledvinka & Scarpello, 1991; Seligman, 1975):

1. Recruitment.
2. Removing discriminatory obstacles.
3. Soft Preferential Treatment.
4. Hard Preferential Treatment.
5. Diversity.

In addition to the five listed here, it is possible to compare a decision made under an affirmative action policy to either a situation in which an organization indicated that it specifically did not have an affirmative action policy, but made a decision based upon only merit, or to a control condition in which there is simply no mention made of the presence or absence of an affirmative action policy. It can be argued, however, that the failure to specify whether an organization has an affirmative action policy or not leaves open the possibility that a respondent may assume the organization has an affirmative action policy.

The types of affirmative action have been listed in an order which approximates their relative emphasis on merit versus protected group status, with the possible exception of diversity policies. The weaker forms include recruiting and removing discriminatory attitudes. The stronger forms include soft and hard preferential treatment. Diversity is the newest type and most of the research described in this book was planned or completed before the emergence of diversity as a popular trend in the applied and popular literatures. From a research perspective, exactly what would constitute diversity is also relatively difficult to specify. Perceptions of and attitudes toward the different forms of affirmative action have been examined in a number of studies involving opinion surveys, correlational studies, and laboratory research of both the paper-person scenario and assigned leader paradigm types. The main dependent variables have been some measure of affect or fairness, or some similar concept such as degree of agreement. In some cases, measures have also been taken on possible mediator variables.

Based upon opinion polls conducted since the 1970s, and with only slight changes over time, the general public tends to support equal opportunity and very weak forms of affirmative action while opposing stronger forms of affirmative action such as preferential treatment and quotas (Bruno, 1998; Lipset & Schneider, 1978; Sigelman & Welch, 1991). Thus, forms of affirmative action such as recruitment or special training programs tend to receive support from most Americans, including most Whites. On the other hand, a majority of Americans, probably between 50% and 80%, oppose preferential treatment strategies (Kravitz et al., 1997).

The results of both opinion surveys and correlational studies suggest that weaker forms of affirmative action are viewed more favorably than stronger forms by all respondents in general, and White males in particular. In a summary of a Harris poll, Jacobson (1985) reported that 70% of White respondents agreed it was fair to set up special programs and special training for Blacks and females. White respondents in the Harris poll also favored the use of affirmative action programs for employment purposes as long as there were no quotas. Summarizing Gallup poll research, Warner and Steel (1989) found that while 83% endorsed the use of merit in selection for education and employment opportunities, only 10% favored race- and sex-based preferential treatment. Studies conducted by Kluegel (1985) and Kravitz and Platania (1993) found similar results. For Whites, resistance or negative reactions to affirmative action increases as the emphasis on sex or race increases and the emphasis on merit decreases.

Similar results were also found using the paper-person scenario study paradigm. Nacoste (1985, 1987) found that as the emphasis on sex increased, ratings of fairness decreased. In a study on reactions to race-based affirmative action, Arthur, Doverspike, and Fuentes (1992; Doverspike & Arthur, 1995) found that participants in a soft preferential treatment condition had more favorable responses than those in the hard preferential treatment condition.

Research which has allowed respondents to supply their own definition of affirmative action also suggests that not all affirmative action programs are seen as equally unfair, with perceived fairness being correlated with the emphasis on merit. Perhaps the best series of studies on the question of personal definitions of affirmative action has been the program of research on affirmative action components which has been conducted by Kravitz and associates (Kravitz & Platania, 1993; Kravitz et al., 1997). The results of the componential research and related studies (Kluegel & Smith, 1983) revealed that respondents tended to approve of affirmative action efforts which involved equal opportunity, training, and recruitment (Arthur et al., 1992;

Kravitz & Platania, 1993; Kravitz et al., 1997), eliminating discrimination (Kravitz & Platania, 1993; Kravitz et al., 1997), and ignoring race (Kravitz & Platania, 1993; Kravitz et al., 1997), while opposing policies which involve quotas and preferential treatment (Johnson, 1980; Kluegel, 1985; Kluegel & Smith, 1983; Kravitz & Platania, 1993; Kravitz, Stinson, & Mello, 1994; Veilleux & Tougas, 1989). In terms of personal definitions, respondents tended to believe that affirmative action involved the use of quotas, the hiring and promoting of certain numbers of Blacks, consideration of minority group status, and additional recruiting (Kravitz & Platania, 1993; Kravitz et al., 1997). The most negative ratings were attached to procedures which involved the hiring of unqualified Blacks (Kravitz & Platania, 1993; Kravitz et al., 1997). For unfavorable components, the greater the rated likelihood that a component would be included in an affirmative action plan, the more unfavorable the respondent's attitude toward affirmative action (Kravitz & Platania, 1993; Kravitz et al., 1997). For favorable components, the greater the rated likelihood that a component would be included in an affirmative action plan, the more favorable the respondent's attitude toward affirmative action (Kravitz & Platania, 1993; Kravitz et al., 1997). An interesting finding emerging from the component research was that quotas were differentiated from preferential treatment, with respondents interpreting quotas in terms of a certain number of a protected group being hired while the definition of preferential treatment was seen as being more ambiguous (Kravitz et al., 1997; Kravitz et al., 1994). Thus, while researchers may see the terms "quota" and "preferential treatment" as relatively interchangeable, the general public does not.

Females tend to view affirmative action, including both race-based and sex-based, more favorably than do males (Dovidio, Gaertner, & Murrell, 1994; Kravitz & Platania, 1993; Kravitz et al., 1997; Singer, 1992, 1993,1996). Females also tend to view quota systems and stronger forms of affirmative action more negatively than they do softer forms of affirmative action. The greater the emphasis on sex rather than merit in allowing one to gain employment opportunities, the more unfair the affirmative action policies are perceived to be (Kravitz & Platania, 1993). The finding that policies which emphasize both applicant sex and merit in decision making are viewed negatively has also emerged in studies of leader selection (Jacobson & Koch, 1977), selection into managerial tasks (Heilman, Rivero, & Brett, 1991), and leadership roles (Heilman, Lucas, & Kaplow, 1990), and in studies where participants are explicitly asked to rate the fairness of stronger and weaker forms of sex-based affirmative action in selection decisions (Taylor & Doverspike, 1990).

Results of opinions polls and other available research (Kravitz & Platania, 1993; Kravitz et al., 1997) suggest that reactions to strong race-based affirmative action parallel reactions to sex-based affirmative action. Strong forms of affirmative action such as preferential treatment are often viewed as unfair by Whites. Softer forms of affirmative action such as training and recruiting evoke more positive responses from nonbeneficiaries. Blacks showed only slightly less negative affect toward strong race-based preferential treatment than did Whites (Arthur & Doverspike, 1990; Arthur et al., 1992), while attitudes toward race-based affirmative action techniques designed to recruit and retain Blacks were viewed more positively (Ponterotto, Martinez, & Hayden, 1986). However, it should be noted that females and Blacks tend to evaluate all forms of affirmative action more positively than do White males (Kravitz & Platania, 1993; Kravitz et al., 1997).

PROTECTED GROUP

Although affirmative action could be granted to a variety of groups based on their protected status, most of the psychological research has been directed at either race- or sex-based affirmative action. The potentially negative impact of sex-based affirmative action on beneficiaries has long been an area of concern for organizational and psychological researchers and, perhaps surprisingly to some, sex-based affirmative action has attracted as much and sometimes more research attention than has race-based affirmative action. This emphasis on sex-based affirmative action in the psychological research literature would appear to be primarily a matter of convenience. Research on sex-based affirmative action is often easier to conduct than research on race-based affirmative action, as female research participants are much more prevalent in the typical research pools, especially introduction to psychology students, than are minority subjects. Minority students may also resist participating in psychological studies.

Survey research would appear to indicate that sex-based affirmative action is more acceptable than is race-based affirmative action (Clayton, 1992; Kravitz et al., 1997; Kravitz & Platania, 1993; Sniderman, Piazza,

Tetlock, & Kendrick, 1991). This finding might seem to be a bit unexpected, in that one might think that the general public would see Blacks as having been more likely to be the victims of past discrimination. However, it may be that the general public views sex discrimination as more pervasive than race discrimination (Smith & Kluegel, 1984).

Research has not been limited to sex- and race-based affirmative action. Kravitz and Platania (1993) investigated attitudes toward affirmative action for the disabled, in addition to sex- and race-based policies. Overall, attitudes did not differ as a function of the targeted group. Similar results were found in a scenario study with undergraduate students conducted by Gilliland and Haptonstahl (1995). In a comparison of race-based affirmative action with affirmative action for the elderly and the disabled, Murrell, Dietz-Uhler, Dovidio, Gaertner, and Drout (1994) found that attitudes were more positive for policies directed at the elderly and the disabled.

Older workers clearly face potential discrimination in the workforce. This discriminatory behavior can affect hiring, promotion, and pay, but is most likely to be a factor in layoffs and forced retirement. In the United States, older adults, defined usually as those over 40, are protected by provisions of the Age Discrimination in Employment Act of 1967, as amended in 1974, 1978, and 1986. The issue of whether there should be affirmative action based on age led to an interesting exchange between Sterns and Sterns (1997a, 1997b) and Longman (1997a, 1997b). In their published debate, Sterns and Sterns (1997a, 1997b) took the position that the answer should be yes, based on the argument that older workers are discriminated against, are a minority, need to work longer, and should have legislative protections. On the other hand, Longman (1997a, 1997b) argued that older workers do not fit the traditional definition of discrimination, having suffered no real history of discrimination, and, therefore, affirmative action was not a proper remedy as the aged already receive substantial entitlements not available to younger workers, including protections under both the ADEA and ADA (Doverspike & Hollis, 1995; Hollis-Sawyer & Doverspike, in press).

Type of Opportunity

In the research literature, it is often difficult to differentiate research on affirmative action in education from affirmative action in employment. Should a study on internships be considered education or employment? Should a laboratory study where research credit is given to students be considered education or employment? What if the laboratory study involves pay instead of class credit? Although relatively few experimental studies would appear to assess a purely educational situation (e.g., high school students being selected into a prestigious college), a number of survey studies have collected comparative data on affirmative action in education versus employment. Based on opinion surveys, it would appear that there is greater public support for affirmative action plans in education than in employment (Bobo & Smith, 1994; Fine, 1992; Kinder & Sanders, 1990; Kluegel & Smith, 1983; Kravitz et al., 1997).

Although the type of organization, public or private, could be manipulated, this does not appear to have been a major area of concern in the psychological literature. As mentioned previously, this is surprising given that the difference between the public and private sectors is often a major issue in political arguments over affirmative action.

ORGANIZATIONAL CONTEXT

In addition to describing or defining the nature of the affirmative action procedures used, researchers will often provide the participant with an organizational context. This is especially likely to be true in studies which use the paper-person scenario approach. Perhaps situational context would be a better term to use here, except that the term "situational" could be seen as carrying with it surplus meaning corresponding to the setting of the research or the type of opportunity. Therefore, we have chosen to use the term "organizational context." Based on the literature, organizational context can be divided into four main dimensions:

1. Relative Qualifications of Candidates.
2. Previous History of Discrimination.
3. Managerial Support.
4. Framing of the Message.

Relative Qualifications of Candidates

As has already been discussed, the relative emphasis that affirmative action policies place on merit as opposed to protected class status affects their acceptance. Given the widespread belief in merit as a distribution rule, and the role of merit in a number of applicable psychological theories, this consideration of the tradeoff between merit and protected class status is consistent with theoretical and practical expectations. Thus, it would be reasonable to expect that the relative qualifications, or the relative merit, of the candidates involved in the decision making situation would affect ratings of fairness or attitudes toward the procedures.

Consider three possible scenarios involving sex-based affirmative action, which could be easily manipulated in the paper-person scenario or in the assigned leader paradigm. In scenario one, a male and female apply for the same job in an organization which has a policy of showing preferential treatment on the basis of sex. The female is selected but also has higher qualifications than the male. In this first scenario, despite the presence of the affirmative action policy, the principle of distribution of jobs based on merit has not been violated; the female candidate had higher merit and was selected. In this situation, even though an affirmative action policy was in place, the final decision was still consistent with basic fairness principles (i.e., the individual with higher merit received the job).

In scenario two, a male and female apply for the same job in an organization which has a policy of showing preferential treatment on the basis of sex. The female is selected and has qualifications equal to that of the male. In this second scenario, it is unclear as to whether this is a chance occurrence or whether the principle of distribution of jobs based on merit has been violated.

In scenario three, a male and female apply for the same job in an organization which has a policy of showing preferential treatment on the basis of sex. The female is selected but also has lower qualifications than the male. In this third scenario, despite lower merit, the female candidate is selected which would appear to clearly violate the principle of distribution of jobs based on merit and thus basic equity and fairness principles.

A number of paper-person scenario studies have investigated the effects of the varying qualifications of the candidates on attitude or fairness ratings. Arthur et al. (1992; Doverspike & Arthur, 1985) found that fairness ratings were more positive when the qualifications of the selected Black candidate were described as equal to rather than lower than the qualifications of the rejected White candidate for an internship (Doverspike & Arthur, 1995). Nacoste (1985, 1987; Nacoste & Lehman, 1987) and Gilliland and Haptonstahl (1995) also found that fairness ratings were related to the differences in qualifications, with fairness ratings being higher when the more qualified candidate was selected. Similar results for the effect of qualifications have been found in other studies (Heilman, McCullough, & Gilbert, 1996; Kravitz et al., 1997), including research by Singer (1990, 1992, 1993), where by manipulating test scores, a monotonic relationship between fairness ratings and difference scores was identified.

Research on qualifications clearly reveals that attitudes and fairness ratings are affected by the relative merit of the respective candidates. Thus, the weight given to merit is important in the comparison of candidates and in the definition of the affirmative action policy. This finding is consistent with the finding that the relative emphasis on merit in the operationalization of affirmative action policies has a major impact on fairness ratings and on attitudes.

Previous History of Discrimination

One of the most basic arguments offered in favor of affirmative action is that it serves as a form of remediation or compensation for past discrimination. It is common in the United States to grant special preference to certain groups based on past sacrifices or past discrimination. For example, seniority, which compensates for employee loyalty, is often viewed as a principle which can trump even merit considerations. Veterans of foreign wars and military service have often been the recipients of special protection or special benefits including those offered by the Vietnam Era Veterans Readjustment Act of 1974. Thus, there is a tradition in the United States of granting persons or groups special rights based on past sacrifices or past losses. As a result, it could be hypothesized that attitudes toward affirmative action would be more favorable when the affirmative action policy was adopted on the basis of remedying past discrimination. On the other hand, it could be argued that granting privileges on the basis of historical events is different from awarding special privileges based upon personal experiences such as seniority or having served as a veteran; again, we are not considering here cases in which the adoption of affirmative action is non-voluntary or is court-ordered based on a legal finding of discrimination.

In laboratory research using the paper-person scenario, the past history of discrimination can be easily manipulated by including statements to the effect that the organization had implemented affirmative action as a way of compensating for past discrimination. Nacoste (1985; Nacoste & Lehman, 1987) conducted a series of studies using the paper-person scenario paradigm in which the history of discrimination was manipulated along with other variables. Overall, history of discrimination had very little effect (see also Matheson, Echenberg, Taylor, Rivers, & Chow, 1994; and the discussion in Kravitz et al., 1997).

In the Kravitz (Kravitz & Platania, 1993; Kravitz et al., 1994) studies, using the component methodology, one of the evaluated components was whether the affirmative action program compensated for past discrimination. In Kravitz's survey studies, history of past discrimination was a factor which was seen as creating more favorable attitudes toward the use of affirmative action, especially among Black and Hispanic respondents.

As Kravitz et al. (1997) note, an alternative way to operationalize past history of discrimination would be by offering data on economic indicators and utilization ratios. To the best of our knowledge, research has not been conducted which has used this approach, although it would be an interesting variation to traditional research.

Thus, while it seems reasonable to hypothesize that attitudes toward affirmative action would be more favorable when information was presented justifying the action based upon previous discrimination by the organization, the research evidence has been unclear and far less than convincing on this point. This may be because simply presenting information on past discrimination by the firm is not enough to change attitudes. Societal discrimination may be a more important factor than organizational discrimination in shaping attitudes (Kravitz et al., 1997), and societal discrimination is not a factor which is easily manipulated in laboratory research.

Managerial Support

For any type of organizational intervention, managerial support stands out as one of the most critical factors related to success. If upper management does not support an organizational intervention, the new policy is likely to meet with resistance and end in failure (Hitt & Keats, 1984; Marino, 1980; Rodgers, Hunter, & Rogers, 1993). If supervisors do not support the intervention and communicate their support to subordinates, then the policy is likely to meet with resistence and end in failure.

The effectiveness of affirmative action programs has been found to be linked to managerial and supervisory support (Hitt & Keats, 1984; Marino, 1980). Rynes and Rosen (1995) surveyed seven hundred and eighty-five human resource professionals. The results of their analyses of the survey data indicated that both the adoption of diversity programs and the success of diversity programs were strongly associated with the presence of top management support.

Gard (1996) conducted a field study with a large manufacturing company in which she investigated predictors of employee satisfaction with diversity efforts. Little support was found in her study for conceptualizing valuing diversity as a prosocial organizational behavior. No evidence was found that individuals who felt a sense of fit with the organization were more or less positive toward diversity. However, individuals who felt that their supervisor supported diversity were also themselves more positive toward diversity.

Framing

Social psychological research suggests that the way messages are presented, sometimes referred to as "framing," influences the persuasive value of the communication, especially where the message deals with sensitive or controversial topics (Petty & Cacioppo, 1981). One of the basic findings regarding persuasive messages is that factual communications which present both negative and positive aspects of the policy may actually enhance acceptance among those who resist the policies. On the other hand, presenting just one side of a message may lead to a polarization or boomerang effect among those holding viewpoints in a direction opposed to the message (Petty & Cacioppo, 1981).

As part of an opinion survey on race-based affirmative action in both employment and education, Kinder and Sanders (1990) manipulated the type of information presented to the respondents. Affirmative action was described as being needed for remedial action, as being an unfair advantage, or reverse discrimination. Although Whites tended to oppose affirmative action in all three cases, their attitude toward affirmative action varied as a function of the frame. Kinder and Sanders (1990) found that the way the policy was framed determined the amount of policy support from respondents with egalitarian value systems. This suggests that framing effects may be as important as some values in determining responses to affirmative action.

A study specifically designed to test for framing effects was conducted by Taylor-Carter et al. (1995). Their study was based on a theory known as cognitive response theory (Petty & Cacioppo, 1981, 1985). Research participants attended a training session in which sex-based soft preferential treatment was defined and followed by a brief discussion of affirmative action. During the training, affirmative action arguments were presented based on either a reverse discrimination or equity-restoring explanation. The initial attitude of the respondent toward affirmative action was used to predict reactions to either the negative or positive presentation. The research participants were not persuaded by the one-sided messages when the message was inconsistent with their initial attitude. Rather, the one-sided messages had the effect of moving respondents' attitudes to a more polarized or extreme position, a finding consistent with a boomerang effect.

As part of the Taylor-Carter et al. (1995) study, the researchers collected information on the thoughts generated by the research participants as they read the message containing the information on affirmative action (i.e., the framing manipulation). Based on the analysis of the thoughts, Taylor-Carter et al. (1995) concluded that the arguments a person makes while receiving a message, either pro or con, were related to final attitude. Thus, when presented with a message, the intended receiver is an active processor of the content of the signal, and it is the person's own internal arguments which lead to attitude change. In general, providing a justification for the implementation of an affirmative action effort has the effect of producing more positive reactions toward the polices as long as the argument is logical and believable, and is presented by a trustworthy source (Bobocel & Farrell, 1996; Heilman et al., 1996; Murrell et al., 1994). However, in some cases, a message can have unexpected and unintended effects on attitudes.

A study by Singer (1996) was unique in that it examined the gender of the sender of the message, referred to as the informant, as well as the frame supplied for the affirmative action message. The interpretation of the results was complicated by the presence of interactions plus the manner in which the dependent variables were calculated. Overall, both the frame and the gender of the sender did affect attitudes toward sex-based affirmative action, with the most support being observed in a condition where a male informant presented a message emphasizing the advantages of diversity-based selection.

CHAPTER SUMMARY

The relative emphasis of an affirmative action policy on merit as opposed to protected class status is a major factor in determining reactions toward the policy. Given the widespread nature of the belief in merit as a distribution rule, and the role of merit in a number of applicable psychological theories, this consideration of the tradeoff between merit and protected class status is consistent with theoretical and practical expectations. White males tend to view stronger forms of affirmative action as unfair and unacceptable. A negative correlation exists between positive attitude ratings and the degree of emphasis on race or sex in decision making. Blacks tend to view all forms of affirmative action more favorably than do Whites, but also view stronger forms as being more unfair than weaker forms. Similar results are obtained for females. There also seems to be an interaction between sex and race of the respondent and affirmative action policy such that smaller sex and race differences are found in attitudes toward policies which strongly emphasize protected group status relative to merit.

Basically, then, harder forms of preferential treatment are unlikely to be seen as fair in most circumstances. Studies reveal that the stronger forms are the most controversial and are most likely to evoke resistance from organizational members. Support for more general policies such as equal opportunity, or support for policies such as training, are much more prevalent. On the other hand, softer forms of preferential treatment, where the exact weighting of merit and protected group status may be ambiguous, are likely to result in the greatest variance in attitudinal reactions.

The group targeted by the affirmative action effort does appear to affect fairness and attitude ratings. Somewhat surprisingly, race-based affirmative action appears to be viewed less favorably than interventions directed at other groups. On the surface, this would appear to be inconsistent with the argument (discussed below) that the previous history of discrimination affects attitudes, unless one accepts the argument that women and other possible groups (e.g., the elderly and the disabled) have suffered more as a result of discrimination than have Blacks and other racial minorities/Another possibility, although it would seem remote, is that males may not see sex-based affirmative action as necessarily inconsistent with their own self-interest (i.e., if they share income with females).

The type of opportunity (i.e., employment or education) appears to have a relatively small effect on acceptance of affirmative action, with more favorable attitudes being expressed toward affirmative action in education than in employment/This may be because education is viewed as a type of training in preparation for employment. It may also reflect a philosophical orientation in which education is seen as a way of equalizing opportunities and, therefore, the consideration of factors other than merit in awarding educational opportunities is seen as acceptable. Another related possibility is that education in the United States is viewed as a right, whereas employment opportunities are to be earned through the accumulation of sufficient merit.

Research on qualifications clearly reveals that attitudes and fairness ratings are affected by the relative merit of the respective candidates. Thus, the weight given to merit is important in the comparison of candidates and in the definition of the affirmative action policy. This finding is consistent with the finding that the relative emphasis on merit in the operationalization of the affirmative action policy has a major impact on fairness ratings and on attitudes.

The history of previous discrimination by the organization does not appear to have a major effect on attitudes. This may be because societal discrimination is a more important factor than organizational discrimination or it may be because it is the individual's perception of the previous history of discrimination which is the critical variable. Societal discrimination may be a more important factor than organizational discrimination in shaping attitudes, and societal discrimination is not a factor which is easily manipulated in laboratory research. Individuals may also have previous opinions regarding past discrimination which may influence their ratings. It may also be that past history of discrimination is better treated as a mediating variable; that is, it is the perception of past discrimination which is critical and not the simple manipulation of information on past discrimination by the firm (see Chapter 7). Individuals may also vary in their attitudes toward the target group, and in Chapter 6 we consider the effects of individual difference variables such as racism and sexism on attitudes toward affirmative action.

Both managerial and supervisory support are critical in determining the effectiveness of affirmative action interventions. Managerial and supervisory support is communicated through both verbal pronouncements and subsequent behavior. Such support should extend beyond simple verbal promises and monitoring to incorporating progress toward affirmative action goals in performance assessments, in the allocation of resources, and in reward systems.

How information on the affirmative action policy is presented or "framed" affects the interpretation and acceptance of the information in the message. That is, the way a message or argument is organized and the type of information presented, positive or negative, affects the attitudes of the recipient of the message, although sometimes in unexpected directions. The person receiving the message is an active processor of the message. As part of the processing of the message, the target may engage in internal arguments regarding the content of the message, and it is these internal cognitive arguments which influence attitude change.

Of course, almost all of the research previously discussed in this chapter on the operationalization of affirmative action and on the organizational context could be considered as offering evidence for the importance of the framing of the message. That is, when the organization defines what it means by affirmative action or when it offers a compensatory explanation, the organization is framing its message. This framing of the message is critical in the attitude change process and in the acceptance of or resistance to affirmative action policies.

REFERENCES

Arthur, W., Jr., & Doverspike, D. (1990, August). *Affective responses to affirmative action interventions: A cross-cultural perspective.* Presented at the 98th annual convention of the American Psychological Association, Boston, MA.

Arthur, W., Jr., Doverspike, D., & Fuentes, R. (1992). Recipients' affective responses to affirmative action interventions: A cross-cultural perspective. *Behavioral Sciences and the Law, 10,* 229-243.

Bobo, L., & Smith, R. A. (1994). Antipoverty policies, affirmative action, and racial attitudes. In S. H. Danziger, G. D. Sandefur, & D. H. Weinberg (Eds.), *Confronting poverty: Prescriptions for change* (pp. 365-395). Cambridge, MA: Harvard.

Bobocel, D. R., & Farrell, A. (1996). Sex-based promotion decisions and interactional fairness: Investigating the influence of managerial accounts. *Journal of Applied Psychology, 81,* 22-35.

Bruno, A. (1998). California Civil Rights Initiative. In S. N. Colamery (Ed.), *Affirmative action: Catalyst or albatross* (pp. 53-57). Commack, NY: Nova.

Clayton, S. D. (1992). Remedies for discrimination: Race, sex and affirmative action. *Behavioral Sciences and the Law, 10,* 245-257.

Doverspike, D., & Arthur, W., Jr. (1995). Race and sex differences in reactions to a simulated selection decision involving race-based affirmative action. *Journal of Black Psychology, 21,* 181-200.

Doverspike, D., & Hollis, L. (1995, May). Diversity issues in testing: Assessing older adults. *IPMA Assessment Council News, 5,* 10-12.

Dovidio, J. F., Gaertner, S. L., & Murrell, A. J. (1994, August). Why people resist affirmative action. In S. M. Burn (Chair), *Psychological perspectives on affirmative action.* Symposium presented at the meeting of the American Psychological Association, Los Angeles, CA.

Fine, T. S. (1992). The impact of issue framing on public opinion: Toward affirmative action programs. *The Social Science Journal, 29,* 323-334.

Gard, J. (1996). *Valuing diversity as a prosocial organizational behavior.* Unpublished doctoral dissertation, University of Akron, Akron, Ohio.

Gilliland, S. W., & Haptonstahl, D. E. (1995, May). *Distributive justice of preferential hiring decisions.* Poster presented at the annual meeting of the Society for Industrial and Organizational Psychology, Orlando, FL.

Heilman, M. E., Lucas, J. A., & Kaplow, S. R. (1990). Self-derogating consequences of sex-based preferential selection: The moderating role of initial self-confidence. *Organizational Behavior and Human Decision Processes, 46,* 202-216.

Heilman, M. E., McCullough, W. F., & Gilbert, D. (1996). The other side of affirmative action: Reactions of nonbeneficiaries to sex-based preferential selection. *Journal of Applied Psychology, 81,* 346-357.

Heilman, M. E., Rivero, J. C., & Brett, J. F. (1991). Skirting the competence issue: Effects of sex-based preferential selection on task choices of women and men. *Journal of Applied Psychology, 76,* 99-105.

Hollis-Sawyer, L. & Doverspike D. (in press). Reasonable accommodation in the workplace: Implications of the ADEA and ADA for older workers. *Journal of Ethics, Law and Aging.*

Hitt, M. A., & Keats, B. W. (1984). Empirical identification of the criteria for effective affirmative action programs. *Journal of Applied Behavioral Science, 20,* 203-222.

Jacobson, C. K. (1985). Resistance to affirmative action: Self-interest or racism? *Journal of Conflict Resolution, 29,* 306-329.

Jacobson, M. B., & Koch, W. (1977). Women as leaders: Performance evaluation as a function of method of leader selection. *Organizational Behavior and Human Performance, 20,* 149-157.

Johnson, S. D. (1980). Reverse discrimination and aggressive behavior. *Journal of Psychology, 104,* 11-19.

Kinder, D. R., & Sanders, L. M. (1990). Mimicking political debate with survey questions: The case of white opinion on affirmative action for Blacks. *Social Cognition, 8,* 73-103.

Kluegel, J. R. (1985). "If there isn't a problem, you don't need a solution": The bases of contemporary affirmative action attitudes. *American Behavioral Scientist, 28,* 761-784.

Kluegel, J. R., & Smith, E. R. (1983). Affirmative action attitudes: Effects of self-interest, racial affect, and stratification beliefs on Whites' views. *Social Forces, 61,* 797-824.

Kravitz, D. A., Harrison, D. A., Turner, M. A., Levine, E. L. Chaves, W., Brannick, M. T., Denning, D. L., Russell, C. J., & Conrad, M. A. (1997). *Affirmative action: A review of psychological and behavioral research.* Bowling Green, OH: Society for Industrial and Organizational Psychology.

Kravitz, D. A., & Platania, J. (1993). Attitudes and beliefs about affirmative action: Effects of target and respondent sex and ethnicity. *Journal of Applied Psychology, 78,* 928-938.

Kravitz, D. A., Stinson, V., & Mello, E. W. (1994, August). Public reactions to affirmative action. In M. E. Turner (Chair), *Affirmative action at work: Towards reducing barriers to the integrated workplace.* Symposium conducted at the annual meeting of the Academy of Management, Dallas, TX.

Ledvinka, J., & Scarpello, V. G. (1991). *Federal regulation of personnel and human resource management.* Boston, MA: PWS-Kent.

Lipset, S. M., & Schneider, W. (1978). The Bakke case: How would it be decided at the bar of public opinion? *Public Opinion, 1,* 38-44.

Longman, P. (1997a). Should there be an affirmative action policy for hiring older persons? No. In A. E. Scharlach & L. W. Kaye (Eds.), *Controversial issues in aging* (pp. 40-43). Boston, MA: Allyn and Bacon.

Longman, P. (1997b). Should there be an affirmative action policy for hiring older persons? Rejoinder to Professor Sterns and Mr. Sterns. In A. E. Scharlach & L. W. Kaye (Eds.), *Controversial issues in aging* (p. 39). Boston, MA: Allyn and Bacon.

Marino, K. E. (1980). A preliminary investigation into the behavioral dimensions of affirmative action compliance. *Journal of Applied Psychology, 65,* 346-350.

Matheson, K., Echenberg, A., Taylor, D. M., Rivers, D., & Chow, I. (1994). Women's attitudes toward affirmative action: Putting actions in context. *Journal of Applied Social Psychology, 24,* 2075-2096.

Murrell, A. J., Dietz-Uhler, B. L., Dovidio, J. F., Gaertner, S. L., & Drout, C. (1994). Aversive racism and resistance to affirmative action: Perceptions of justice are not necessarily color blind. *Basic and Applied Social Psychology, 15,* 71-86.

Nacoste, R. W. (1985). Selection procedure and responses to affirmative action: The case of favorable treatment. *Law and Human Behavior, 9,* 225-242.

Nacoste, R. W. (1987). But do they care about fairness? The dynamics of preferential treatment and minority interest. *Basic and Applied Social Psychology, 8,* 177-191.

Nacoste, R. W., & Lehman, D. (1987). Procedural stigma. *Representative Research in Social Psychology, 17,* 25-38.

Petty, R. E., & Cacioppo, J. T. (1981). *Attitudes and persuasion: Classic and contemporary approaches.* Dubuque, IA: Brown.

Petty, R. E., & Cacioppo, J. T. (1985). Elaboration likelihood model of persuasion. *Advances in Experimental and Social Psychology, 19,* 125-205.

Ponterotto, J. G., Martinez, F. M., & Hayden, D. C. (1986, July). Student affirmative action programs: A help or hindrance to development of minority graduate students? *Journal of College Student Personnel,* pp. 318-325.

Rodgers, R., Hunter, J. E., & Rogers, D. L. (1993). Influence of top management commitment on management program success. *Journal of Applied Psychology, 78,* 151-155.

Rynes, S.L., & Rosen, B. (1995). A field survey of factors affecting the adoption and perceived success of diversity training. *Personnel Psychology, 48,* 247-270.

Seligman, D. (1975). How "equal opportunity" turned into employment quotas. In K. N. Wexley & G. A. Yukl (Eds.), (pp. 470-479). *Organizational behavior and industrial psychology.* New York, NY: Oxford Press.

Sigelman, L., & Welch, F. (1991). *Black American's views of racial inequality.* Cambridge, MA: Cambridge University Press.

Singer, M. (1996). 'Merit', 'preferential' or 'diversity-based selection': Effect of information frame and informant gender on the public's views on preferential treatment in selection. *International Journal of Selection and Assessment, 4,* 1-11.

Singer, M. S. (1990). Individual differences in category width and fairness perception of selection decisions. *Social Behavior and Personality, 18,* 87-94.

Singer, M. S. (1992). The application of relative deprivation theory to justice perception of preferential selection. *Current Psychology: Research & Reviews, 11,* 128-144.

Singer, M. S. (1993). Gender-based preferential selection: Perceptions of injustice and empathy of deprivation. *International Journal of Selection and Assessment, 1,* 184-202.

Smith, E. R., & Kluegel, J. R. (1984). Beliefs and attitudes about women's opportunity: Comparisons with beliefs about blacks and a general perspective. *Social Psychology Quarterly, 47,* 81-95.

Sniderman, P. M., Piazza, T., Tetlock, P. E., & Kendrick, A. (1991). The new racism. *American Journal of Political Science, 35,* 423-447.

Sterns, A. A., & Sterns, H. L. (1997a). Should there be an affirmative action policy for hiring older persons? Rejoinder to Mr. Longman. In A. E. Scharlach & L. W. Kaye (Eds.), *Controversial issues in aging* (pp. 43-44). Boston, MA: Allyn and Bacon.

Sterns, A. A., & Sterns, H. L. (1997b). Should there be an affirmative action policy for hiring older persons? Yes. In A. E. Scharlach & L. W. Kaye (Eds.), *Controversial issues in aging* (pp. 35-39). Boston, MA: Allyn and Bacon.

Taylor, M. A., & Doverspike, D. (1990, August). *Reactions to soft and hard preferential treatment.* Paper presented at the 98th annual convention of the American Psychological Association, Boston, MA.

Taylor-Carter, M.A., Doverspike, D., & Alexander, R. (1995). Message effects on the perceptions of the fairness of gender-based affirmative action: A cognitive response theory-based analysis. *Social Justice Research, 8,* 285-303.

Veilleux, F., & Tougas, F. (1989). Male acceptance of affirmative action programs for women: The results of altruistic or egotistical motives. *International Journal of Psychology, 24,* 485-496.

Warner, R. L., & Steel, B. S. (1989). Affirmative action in times of fiscal stress and changing value priorities: the case of women in policing. *Public Personnel Management, 18,* 291- 309.

Chapter 6

RESPONDENT CHARACTERISTICS: DEMOGRAPHICS AND PERSONAL TRAITS

In this chapter, we review the psychological research relevant to characteristics of the respondent. The term "respondent" is used here to refer to the subject or participant in the study or the target of the affirmative action message. There are two main classes of respondent characteristics that appear to affect reactions to affirmative action. These are:

1. Demographic Variables - the two major demographic variables are respondent race and sex. In most cases, demographic variables are confounded with beneficiary status. That is, women and minorities are likely to see themselves as benefitting from affirmative action policies, especially those aimed at their group, whereas, White males are likely to see themselves as gaining little or losing as a result of affirmative action policies.

2. Personal Traits - this includes measurable characteristics of the individual for which reliable, individual differences have been shown to exist. In terms of the affirmative action research, the major attributes with which we will concern ourselves are racism, sexism, individualism-collectivism, liberalism-conservatism, and personality.

DEMOGRAPHIC VARIABLES AND BENEFICIARY STATUS

A factor which would be expected to influence reactions to affirmative action is self-interest or the likelihood of personal gain. Affirmative action can be seen as resulting in individual losses and individual gains, and in group losses and group gains. There will be those individuals who stand to gain from affirmative action because of their protected group status (i.e., the beneficiaries). Conversely, there will be those individuals who will lose desired spots in educational programs or desired jobs because they are not members of the protected group (i.e., the nonbeneficiaries). In the case of sex-based affirmative action, the beneficiaries are females and the nonbeneficiaries are males. In the case of race-based affirmative action, the beneficiaries are ethnic or racial minorities, usually Black or sometimes Hispanic, while the nonbeneficiaries are White. The design of the typical study results in Whites or males being treated as the comparison group (i.e., the nonbeneficiary group). It is also true that not all members of a targeted group will necessarily benefit from affirmative action. Nevertheless, the whole group can be seen as potential beneficiaries.

Beneficiary status, then, will often be confounded with sex or race differences, although it is possible to create designs where the two are at least experimentally, albeit artificially, independent. The lack of independence between beneficiary status and race, or sex, is unfortunate in that it is likely that race and sex are important factors in determining reactions to affirmative action, yet the effects are difficult to separate out. As a result, we consider here race and sex together with the related topic of beneficiary status. It should also be noted that we have already discussed the role of both race and sex in terms of their interaction with message factors (see Chapter 5).

There is also a shortage of research on demographic variables other than race and sex. Research on age and education has not led to consistent findings across studies (Fine, 1992b; Jacobson, 1985; Kluegel, 1990; Kluegel & Smith 1983; Sidanius, Pratto, & Bobbo, 1996; Stoker 1998).

Race

The results of opinion polls and experimental research generally find that support for affirmative action, hiring preferences, preferential treatment, and quotas is higher, in many cases substantially higher, for Blacks than for Whites (Bobo & Smith, 1994; Bruno, 1998; Lipset & Schneider, 1978; Sigelman & Welch, 1991). For race-based affirmative action, Blacks' ratings of affect or fairness are more positive than the ratings of Whites, with the ratings of Hispanics falling somewhere in between those of Whites and Blacks (Bell, Harrison, & McLaughlin, 1997; Bobo & Smith, 1994; Citrin, 1996; Dovidio, Gaertner & Murrell, 1994; Fine, 1992a; Kinder and Sanders, 1990, 1996; Kravitz et al., 1997; Kravitz & Platania, 1993; Kravitz, Stinson, & Mello, 1994; Lipset & Schneider, 1978; Stoker, 1998).

Of course, Black support for affirmative action may reflect self-interest in that Blacks are likely to be the beneficiaries of affirmative action efforts. Racial differences in attitudes may also reflect differences in the definition of affirmative action. Kravitz et al. (1997) suggested that race differences were largely due to differences in beliefs about affirmative action and evaluations of those beliefs (Bobo & Smith, 1994; Citrin, 1996; Fine, 1992a; Kinder & Sanders, 1990, 1996; Lipset & Schneider, 1978; Sigelman & Welch, 1991). Research has also found greater support for affirmative action among political liberals or moderates than conservatives (Sidanius et al., 1996; Sniderman, Piazza, Tetlock, & Kendrick, 1991).

As mentioned previously, it is possible to construct designs in the laboratory where race and sex are independent of beneficiary status. Doverspike and Arthur (1995) created such a situation using a paper-person scenario by having all research participants play the role of a Black who had received a prestigious graduate fellowship. In the study, there was a significant main effect for race for ratings of fairness but not for negative affect. Blacks saw the decision as fairer than did Whites. This finding was complicated by the presence of a three-way interaction between sex, race, and qualifications. In Arthur, Doverspike, and Fuentes (1992), which used some of the same data, the ratings of affect by minority students were lower than the ratings of international students and of White students.

Sex

A large body of research encompassing a variety of research designs supports the general finding that females react more favorably to all types of affirmative action than do males (Goldsmith, Cordova, Dwyer, Langlois, & Crosby, 1989; Konrad & Linnehan, 1995; Kravitz & Platania, 1993; Matheson, Echenberg, Taylor, Rivers, & Chow, 1994; Ozawa, Crosby, & Crosby, 1996; Summers, 1995; Tickamyer, Scollay, Bokemeier, & Wood, 1989; Tougas, Brown, Beaton, & Joly, 1995). This could again reflect a self-interest factor as women are more likely to benefit from affirmative action efforts.

However, in a recent, paper-person scenario study conducted by Struchul (1999), male respondents were more likely to express positive fairness reactions toward affirmative action than were female participants. This seems contrary to previous research that suggests females will generally respond more favorably to affirmative action than males, even when their own group is not the specific target of affirmative action (Kravitz et al., 1997; although also see Kravitz, Stinson, & Mello, 1994).

Clearly, self-interest or beneficiary status plays a role in the higher fairness and affect rating attributed to affirmative action policies by females as compared to males. However, self-interest does not seem to explain all of the results. As was the case with Blacks, females may differ in their definition of affirmative action and in their evaluation of the individual components of affirmative action. There may also be differences in the belief in various distribution rules. Women may prefer the use of an equality rule to an equity rule. As a result, they may feel a result is unfair when it subverts instead of enhances equality (Gilliland & Haptonstahl, 1995).

Beneficiary Status

As might be expected, beneficiaries tend to hold more positive attitudes toward affirmative action than do nonbeneficiaries. Even individuals, who might otherwise be opposed to affirmative action, may favor affirmative action when they stand to benefit from its policies. The effect of beneficiary status can and has been studied primarily by comparing the responses of Blacks to Whites or by comparing the responses of females to males (see above). However, this has the disadvantage of confounding beneficiary status with race or sex. It would be natural to expect that the effects of beneficiary status would be moderated by the likelihood of personal benefit, personal gain or self-interest. The mediating role of self-interest is considered in greater detail in Chapter 6.

One method of trying to separate beneficiary status from race or sex would be to look at or manipulate the role of the respondent. For example, in a paper-person scenario study by Struchul (1999), she asked research participants to play either the role of a White student who had lost an internship position due to an affirmative action policy or a faculty member who was responsible for supervising the program. Thus, she created a nonbeneficiary versus an involved observer. The nonbeneficiaries, as compared to the faculty observers, reported greater negative affect toward affirmative action and provided lower fairness ratings. As expected then, after controlling for race, nonbeneficiaries reported more negative attitudes than did observers.

Survey studies have also looked at the role of the respondent. Studies in an academic environment by both Noble and Winett (1978) and Goldsmith et al. (1989) found no evidence of differences in attitudes toward affirmative action or toward decisions based upon affirmative action policies as a function of the role of the respondent (i.e., student, faculty members, administrator). The Noble and Winett (1978) study compared department chairs and faculty while the Goldsmith et al. (1989) study compared students, faculty, staff, and administrators.

A second method of investigating the independent contribution of role is to compare responses based upon sex and race in the same study. To do this, sufficient numbers of minorities must be included in the study in order to have an adequate sample of both males and females. The Doverspike and Arthur (1995) study included large numbers of both Black males and females. In this study, respondents were asked to play the role of a beneficiary. Black females reported more negative affect than did Black males, but the fairness ratings for Black females were higher than the fairness ratings for Black males. However, this difference may reflect affect toward the beneficiary status rather than toward the affirmative action policy.

PERSONAL TRAITS

The term "personal trait" is used here in a broad sense to refer to attributes or characteristics of the individual for which important, stable individual differences have been shown to exist. Personal traits include social traits, motives, values, interests, and various personality dimensions. Tests or standardized measures are often used to measure personal traits. Tests of personal traits should possess the properties of both reliability and validity. Unfortunately, one of the major problems facing modern psychology is the adequacy of the psychometric properties of our measurement instruments. In terms of the affirmative action research, the major attributes with which we will concern ourselves are racism, sexism, individualism-collectivism, liberalism-conservatism, and personality.

Racism

As was discussed in Chapter 3, it would be reasonable to assume that for Whites racism would be related to opposition toward affirmative action, especially race-based affirmative action. Unfortunately, in some cases, racism may be defined in terms of the opposition to policies such as affirmative action. This is especially likely to be true with measures of what are referred to as modern racism.

Based on data from national surveys there appears to be a relationship between agreement with racism items and opposition to affirmative action. In an analysis of the responses of White individuals, as part of a national survey, Kluegel and Smith (1983) found that responses to items reflecting symbolic racism were correlated with attitudes toward affirmative action in employment and education. Jacobson (1985), based on a national Harris survey conducted in the fall of 1978 for the National Conference of Christians and Jews, found that reactions to affirmative action were a function of symbolic and traditional racism.

Surveys of undergraduate students have resulted in similar findings. For example, Kravitz (1995) found that racism was correlated with opposition to affirmative action in general, as well as toward specific race-based, affirmative action plans. Kravitz's study was somewhat unique in that it was based on a survey of both White and Hispanic undergraduates. In a survey study conducted with 148 White undergraduates, Sidanius et al. (1996) investigated the relationship between classic racism, a construct similar to overt racism, and affirmative action. In their study, classic racism was correlated with opposition to affirmative action (similar results were obtained in Sidanius, Devereux, & Pratto, 1992).

The studies discussed above used a survey approach to collecting data. A recent, unpublished study conducted by Struchul (1999), used a paper-person scenario approach. Participants in her study included 107 male and female participants recruited from a University and the surrounding community. An affirmative action scenario based on Arthur et al. (1992) was utilized which described a White and an African-American college student who were the two final candidates for a prestigious internship program. Both candidates were equally qualified for an internship program that would facilitate future opportunities. Based on the strong affirmative action policy of the college, the African-American applicant was awarded the internship. Thus, the scenario involved an education-employment type situation and race-based affirmative action. Racism was measured using McConahay's (1982) modern racism scale and an inequity measure based upon Kluegel and Bobo (1993). Although no significant relationship was found between racism and affective reactions to affirmative action, a significant relationship was found between racism and fairness reactions to affirmative action.

Thus, psychological research supports the common sense hypothesis that racism would be related to opposition to affirmative action. Based upon the data reported in the literature, the correlation appears to be somewhere in the range of .20 to .40 (uncorrected for any artifacts or unreliability of measures). There are two confounds which affect the interpretation of the relationship between racism and resistance to affirmative action policies. First, some racism measures may include items which involve assessing attitudes toward affirmative action. Second, racism may be related to self-interest. That is, Whites who see themselves as most likely to suffer employment, educational, or financial losses as a result of affirmative action may also be those Whites who are most likely to express racist attitudes (Kravitz et al., 1997). Thus, it would appear that the effect of racism on attitudes may be mediated by judgments of justice and self-interest.

Sexism

As with racism, it would be expected that sexism will be associated with opposition to affirmative action, especially sex-based affirmative action. In survey studies of male Canadians, Tougas and associates (Tougas, Brown et al., 1995; Tougas Crosby, Joly, & Pelchat, 1995), found that sexism and neosexism, predicted resistance toward affirmative action, although the effect of sexism was through its effect on neosexism. A study by Joly, Pelchat, and Tougas (1993) also found that neosexism was related to attitudes toward affirmative action in general and sex-based affirmative action.

Thus, sexism would appear to be related to resistence to affirmative action. Based on the available date, the correlation appears to be in the range of .35 to .60 (uncorrected for artifacts or unreliability in the measures). It seems likely that the effects of sexism would be mediated by judgments of justice and self-interest.

Individualism-Collectivism

Affirmative action plans may be viewed as interventions to correct past inequities which on occasion require individuals to be cooperative and noncompetitive, and to some extent, subjugate their personal goals for the greater good of society. Using this theoretical framework, Arthur et al., (1992) investigated whether individualism-collectivism differences would account for the observed relationship between ethnic group status and affective responses to race-based affirmative action. They found that although ethnicity was related to individualism-collectivism (i.e., international and minority participants were more collectivist than majority participants), individualism-collectivism was not related to attitudes to affirmative action plans. However, international and minority participants reported similar and more positive attitudes to affirmative action plans than did majority participants.

In a similar study of United States' Asian Americans' beliefs and attitudes toward a race-based affirmative action plan, Bell et al. (1997) found greater attitudinal similarity among Asians, Blacks, and Hispanics than between Asians and Whites. Bell et al. (1977) also argued that Asian Americans may have a more collectivist orientation.

Like Arthur et al. (1992), Ozawa et al., (1996) investigated the role of individualism-collectivism in attitudes toward affirmative action. They posited that part of the resistance to affirmative action in the United States derived from the individualistic and competitive nature of the culture with its strong emphasis on individualistic meritocracy. Using a sample of Japanese and United States citizens, Ozawa et al. (1996) found the Japanese sample to be more collectivist than the United States sample. Furthermore, they displayed significantly more favorable attitudes toward a sex-based affirmative action plan than did the United States sample.

Individualism-collectivism is correlated with a number of other variables, including political beliefs (Arthur et al., 1992; Peterson, 1994; Sidanius et al., 1996). This relationship with other critical variables complicates any interpretation of a relationship between individualism-collectivism and attitudes toward affirmative action. In addition, the construct of individualism-collectivism is closely tied to the concept of an in-group (see Chapter 3). In order to predict how a person with a collective orientation will respond to an affirmative action intervention, we must be able to specify the relevant in-group. Unfortunately, it is difficult to predict a priori what group will be a person's in-group.

Liberalism-Conservatism

As discussed in Chapter 3, a liberal political orientation is positively related to attitudes toward Blacks and is also associated with viewing African-Americans as relatively disadvantaged (Lambert & Chasteen, 1997). Conservatives tend to be opposed to most government interventions including affirmative action (Jacobson, 1985; Kluegel, 1990; Kluegel & Smith, 1983; Sidanius et al, 1996; Sniderman et al., 1991; Stoker, 1998; Stout & Buffum, 1993). A problem with many of the studies is that liberalism-conservatism has been operationalized using a small number of unstandardized questions rather than based upon some standardized scale or measure of liberalism-conservatism.

The relationship between political values, including liberalism-conservatism, and attitudes toward affirmative action is complex, and cannot be reduced to a single underlying variable (Peterson, 1994; Sidanius et al., 1996; Taylor-Carter, Doverspike, & Cook, 1995). Although attitudes toward affirmative action do appear to be associated with political perspective, the strength of the relationship doubtless varies with the way in which political ideology is assessed. There is a need for more research in this area using valid measures of political ideology.

Personality

Although various individual difference factors have been investigate as predictors of attitudes toward affirmative action, it is surprising that research has not focused on personality traits, especially those personality traits included in the five-factor model of personality. Based on the relationship between racism and reactions to affirmative action, we would expect the openness to experience personality factor to be related to support for affirmative action.

As part of Struchul's (1999) thesis, she looked at the relationship between personality, racism, and reactions to affirmative action. Small negative correlations were found between openness to experience and racism, and a small positive relationship was found between conscientiousness and racism. Racism and reactions to affirmative action were correlated, and self-interest and gender influenced reactions to affirmative action. Given the central role of the Big Five in modern personality theory, it is surprising that more research has not been conducted exploring the relationship between personality and reactions to affirmative action.

CHAPTER SUMMARY

The research indicates that both race and sex are related to fairness ratings of affirmative action and attitude ratings toward affirmative action. Blacks have more favorable attitudes toward affirmative action than do Whites. Females have more favorable attitudes toward affirmative action than do males. Beneficiary status is also related to fairness ratings of affirmative action and attitude ratings toward affirmative action. Potential beneficiaries have more favorable attitudes than those who are likely to experience no benefit or a loss of potential employment or educational opportunities.

Unfortunately, at least from a research perspective, it is very difficult to separate the role of beneficiary status, and thus self-interest, from race and sex effects. Beneficiary status and race and sex do appear to have independent effects, but statistically estimating the size of the effects would be next to impossible, and would not generalize to the real world where beneficiary status and race, or sex, are closely yoked. It is possible, albeit difficult, to design studies which separate beneficiary status from demographic characteristics. The question is whether it is worth the investment of time and effort required in order to separate the various effects. Beneficiary status is also highly related to self-interest (see Chapter 7), and may be related to differences in the perception of the definition of affirmative action and evaluations of the individual components. The general lack of empirical research on groups such as Native Americans and Asians is an area of concern. Membership in particular ethnic groups may be accompanied by group-specific stereotypes and other unique barriers. Again, the problem is that it is much more difficult to conduct research involving adequate sampling of various minority groups, including Blacks (Taylor-Carter, Doverspike, & Cook, 1996).

Both racism and sexism, and their modern variants, are related to resistence to affirmative action policies. This is not meant to imply that everyone who opposes affirmative action is a racist or a sexist, but there is substantial evidence of at least a moderate correlation between bias and opposition to affirmative action. From a research perspective, there is a significant methodological problem in that measures of racism and sexism may include items inquiring as to attitudes with respect to affirmative action. However, this problem is relatively easily overcome through the development of measures of racism and sexism which avoid this confound. There is clearly a need for additional research on the relationship between racism and sexism and affirmative action, and also for research on changing racist and sexist attitudes.

Individualism-collectivism and liberalism-conservatism both appear to be related to reactions to affirmative action. Although high levels of individualism should lead to negative attitudes toward affirmative action, the relationship between collectivism and affirmative action would appear to be dependent upon the definition of the in-group. A collectivist should be motivated by group goals, but there may be many potential groups with which an individual could identify, and those groups may have very different objectives with respect to affirmative action.

One corollary of belief in the American economic system, is a belief in limited government intervention. Conservatives and other individuals who are opposed to government intervention are likely to be opposed to government-sponsored affirmative action. Thus, affirmative action may be opposed by conservatives because it violates strongly held beliefs regarding the role of government. Similarly, individuals who believe in the role of merit and are opposed to government intervention, may also be opposed to government assistance and hold a negative view of those who receive government assistance. More research is needed in order to explore the role of these beliefs in predicting resistance to different forms of affirmative action.

Finally, it is quite surprising that psychologists have ignored personality as a predictor of reactions to affirmative action policies. We have developed a theory of the cosmopolitan personality which predicts that attitudes toward affirmative action would be related to openness. The study conducted by Struchul's (1999) confirmed that there was a negative relationship between openness and racism. A small positive relationship was also found between conscientiousness and racism. Of course, if personality does predict reactions to affirmative action, then the question would remain as to whether it is possible or feasible to change personality. The question of malleability would apply to all of the individual difference variables discussed in this chapter.

REFERENCES

Arthur, W., Jr., Doverspike, D., & Fuentes, R. (1992). Recipients' affective responses to affirmative action interventions: A cross-cultural perspective. *Behavioral Sciences and the Law, 10,* 229-243.

Bell, M. P., Harrison, D. A., & McLaughlin, M. E. (1997). Asian American attitudes toward affirmative action in employment. *Journal of Applied Behavioral Science, 33,* 356-377.

Bobo, L., & Smith, R. A. (1994). Antipoverty policies, affirmative action, and racial attitudes. In S. H. Danziger, G. D. Sandefur, & D. H. Weinberg (Eds.), *Confronting poverty: Prescriptions for change* (pp. 365-395). Cambridge, MA: Harvard.

Bruno, A. (1998). Affirmative action in employment. In S. N. Colamery (Ed.), *Affirmative action: Catalyst or albatross* (pp. 59-109). Commack, NY: Nova.

Citrin, J. (1996, Winter). Affirmative action in the people's court. *The Public Interest,* 39-48.

Doverspike, D., & Arthur, W., Jr. (1995). Race and sex differences in reactions to a simulated selection decision involving race-based affirmative action. *Journal of Black Psychology, 21,* 181-200.

Dovidio, J. F., Gaertner, S. L., & Murrell, A. J. (1994, August). Why people resist affirmative action. In S. M. Burn (Chair), *Psychological perspectives on affirmative action.* Symposium presented at the meeting of the American Psychological Association, Los Angeles, CA.

Fine, T. S. (1992a). The impact of issue framing on public opinion: Toward affirmative action programs. *The Social Science Journal, 29,* 323-334.

Fine, T. F. (1992b). Public opinion toward equal opportunity issues: The role of attitudinal and demographic forces among African Americans. *Sociological Perspectives, 35,* 705-720.

Gilliland, S. W., & Haptonstahl, D. E. (1995, May). *Distributive justice of preferential hiring decisions.* Poster presented at the annual meeting of the Society for Industrial and Organizational Psychology, Orlando, FL.

Goldsmith, N., Cordova, D., Dwyer, K., Langlois, B., & Crosby, F. J. (1989). Reactions to affirmative action: A case study. In F. A. Blanchard & F. J. Crosby (Eds.), *Affirmative action in perspective,* (pp. 139-146). New York: Springer-Verlag.

Jacobson, C. K. (1985). Resistance to affirmative action: Self-interest or racism? *Journal of Conflict Resolution, 29,* 306-329.

Joly, S., Pelchat, D., & Tougas, F. (1993, May). *Men and affirmative action: Opposition or misconception?* Poster session presented at the annual meeting of the Canadian Psychological Association, Montreal, Canada.

Kinder, D. R., & Sanders, L. M. (1990). Mimicking political debate with survey questions: The case of white opinion on affirmative action for blacks. *Social Cognition, 8,* 73-103.

Kinder, D. R., & Sanders, L. M. (1996). *Divided by color: Racial politics and democratic ideals.* Chicago, IL: University of Chicago Press.

Kluegel, J. R. (1990). Trends in Whites' explanations of the Black-White gap in socioeconomic status, 1977-1989. *American Sociological Review, 55,* 512-525.

Kluegel, J.R., & Bobo, L. (1993). Dimensions of whites' beliefs about the black-white socioeconomic gap. In P.M. Sniderman, P.E. Tetlock, & E.G. Carmines (Eds.), *Prejudice, politics, and the American dilemma* (pp. 127 - 147). Stanford, CA.: Stanford University Press.

Kluegel, J. R., & Smith, E. R. (1983). Affirmative action attitudes: Effects of self-interest, racial affect, and stratification beliefs on Whites' views. *Social Forces, 61,* 797-824.

Konrad, A. M., & Linnehan, F. (1995). Race and sex differences in line managers' reactions to equal employment opportunity and affirmative action interventions. *Group and Organization Management, 20,* 409-439.

Kravitz, D. A. (1995). Attitudes toward affirmative action plans directed at Blacks: Effects of plan and individual differences. *Journal of Applied Social Psychology, 25,* 2192-2220.

Kravitz, D. A., Harrison, D. A., Turner, M. A., Levine, E. L. Chaves, W., Brannick, M. T., Denning, D. L., Russell, C. J., & Conrad, M. A. (1997). *Affirmative action: A review of psychological and behavioral research.* Bowling Green, OH: Society for Industrial and Organizational Psychology.

Kravitz, D. A., & Platania, J. (1993). Attitudes and beliefs about affirmative action: Effects of target and of respondent sex and ethnicity. *Journal of Applied Psychology, 78,* 928-938.

Kravitz, D. A., Stinson, V., & Mello, E. W. (1994, August). Public reactions to affirmative action. In M. E. Turner (Chair), *Affirmative action at work: Towards reducing barriers to the integrated workplace.* Symposium conducted at the annual meeting of the Academy of Management, Dallas, TX.

Lambert, A. J., & Chasteen, A. L. (1997). Perceptions of disadvantage versus conventionality: Political values and attitudes toward the elderly versus Blacks. *Personality and Social Psychology Bulletin, 23,* 469-481.

Lipset, S. M., & Schneider, W. (1978). The Bakke case: How would it be decided at the bar of public opinion? *Public Opinion, 1,* 38-44.

Matheson, K., Echenberg, A., Taylor, D. M., Rivers, D., & Chow, I. (1994). Women's attitudes toward affirmative action: Putting actions in context. *Journal of Applied Social Psychology, 24,* 2075-2096.

McConahay, J.B. (1982). Self-interest versus racial attitudes as correlates of anti-busing attitudes in Louisville: Is it the buses or the blacks? *The Journal of Politics, 44,* 692-720.

Noble, A., & Winett, R. A. (1978). Chairpersons' and hirees' opinions, knowledge, and experiences with affirmative action guidelines. *Journal of Community Psychology, 6,* 194-199.

Ozawa, K., Crosby, M., & Crosby, F. (1996). Individualism and resistance to affirmative action: A comparison of Japanese and American samples. *Journal of Applied Social Psychology, 26,* 1138-1152.

Peterson, R. S. (1994). The role of values in predicting fairness judgments and support of affirmative action. *Journal of Social Issues, 50,* 95-116.

Sidanius, J., Devereux, E., & Pratto, F. (1992). A comparison of symbolic racism theory and social dominance theory as explanations for racial policy attitudes. *Journal of Social Psychology, 132,* 377-395.

Sidanius, J., Pratto, F., & Bobo, L. (1996). Racism, conservatism, affirmative action, and intellectual sophistication: A matter of principled conservatism or group dominance? *Journal of Personality and Social Psychology, 70,* 476-490.

Sigelman, L., & Welch, F. (1991). *Black American's views of racial inequality.* Cambridge, MA: Cambridge University Press.

Sniderman, P. M., Piazza, T., Tetlock, P. E., & Kendrick, A. (1991). The new racism. *American Journal of Political Science, 35,* 423-447.

Stoker, L. (1998). Understanding Whites' resistance to affirmative action: The role of principled commitments and racial prejudice. In J. Hurwitz & M. Peffley (Eds.), *Perception and prejudice: Race and politics in the United States* (pp. 135-170). New Haven, CT: Yale University Press.

Stout, K. D., & Buffum, W. E. (1993). The commitment of social workers to affirmative action. *Journal of Sociology and Social Welfare, 20,* 123-135.

Struchul, A. L. (1999). *Personality predictors of racist attitudes and attitudes toward affirmative action.* Unpublished Masters Thesis, University of Akron.

Summers, R. J. (1995). Attitudes toward different methods of affirmative action. *Journal of Applied Social Psychology, 25,* 1090-1104.

Taylor-Carter, M., Doverspike, D., & Cook, K. (1995). Understanding resistance to sex and race-based affirmative action: A review of research findings. *Human Resource Management Review, 5,* 129-157.

Taylor-Carter, M. A., Doverspike, D., & Cook, K. D. (1996). The effects of affirmative action on the female beneficiary. *Human Resource Development Quarterly, 7,* 31-54.

Tickamyer, A., Scollay, S., Bokemeier, J., & Wood, T. (1989). Administrators' perceptions of affirmative action in higher education. In F. A. Blanchard & F. J. Crosby (Eds.), *Affirmative action in perspective* (pp. 125-138). New York: Springer-Verlag.

Tougas, F., Brown, R., Beaton, A.M., & Joly, S. (1995). Neosexism: Plus ca change, plus c'est pareil. *Personality and Social Psychology Bulletin, 21,* 842-849.

Tougas, F., Crosby, F., Joly, S., & Pelchat, D. (1995). Men's attitudes toward affirmative action: Justice and intergroup relations at the crossroads. *Social Justice Research, 8,* 57-71.

Chapter 7

MEDIATING MECHANISMS

Independent variables do not always have a direct effect on dependent variables. Sometimes, the effect of an independent variables is transmitted through its effect on another variable. That is, the independent variable has its effect on an intervening variable which then effects the dependent variable. The intervening variables are referred to as "mediators" or "mediating variables."

In this chapter, we have chosen to feature three possible mediator variables. The mediators are perceptions of justice and fairness, self-interest, and beliefs concerning the relative distribution of educational and employment opportunities.

PERCEPTIONS OF JUSTICE AND FAIRNESS

One researcher's mediator can be another researcher's independent or dependent variable. Nowhere would this seem to be truer than in the case of fairness. In most research or theoretical models, fairness is treated as one of the main dependent variables. However, fairness can also be conceptualized as a mediator of the effect of other variables onto attitudes. That is, independent variables such as the type of affirmative action can be viewed as affecting fairness which then causes changes in attitudes.

The problem is that depending upon how fairness is measured, it can be virtually impossible to differentiate fairness from general attitudes toward affirmative action. Measures of fairness are typically very highly correlated with measures of attitudes toward affirmative action. There are problems not just of common method variance but also of common content variance. Trying to separate out fairness and attitudes leads to a maze of definitional and measurement problems.

In our research, we have differentiated between affect, measured using bipolar mood adjective items, and fairness, measured using perceptions of fairness and agreement with the decision. Another method of distinguishing between the two concepts would be to define fairness in terms of procedural and distributive justice, both of which, it could be argued, include more of a cognitive component, and then to define attitude in terms of general agreement or satisfaction with affirmative action policies.

A field survey study of federal employees, conducted by Parker, Baltes and Christiansen (1997) specifically tested perceptions of justice as a mediator of the effects of affirmative action, actually organizational support for affirmative action, on satisfaction. For White males, perceptions of organizational support for affirmative action were not related to justice perception nor negative work attitudes. For females and minorities, perceptions of organizational support for affirmative action were associated with ratings of organizational justice and attitudes. Limited support was found for the overall model involving justice perceptions as a mediator.

Kravitz (1995) also directly tested the role of fairness in a study of reactions to race-based affirmative action. Based on a hierarchical regression analysis, fairness did serve as a mediator of the effects of type of affirmative action on attitudes.

Our opinion would be that it is very hard to differentiate between fairness and attitudes toward affirmative action. To attempt to do so also leads to a number of troubling questions including if fairness is not an attitude what is it. Nevertheless, it appears that the trend in recent research is to treat fairness as a separate concept from attitude and as a mediator variable. The solution, we would argue, is to treat perceptions of justice as a variable separate from fairness. Ratings could be made of distributive justice, procedural justice, and interactional justice. Then fairness can remain a dependent variable in psychological models.

SELF-INTEREST

Self-interest would appear to be one of the major predictors of reactions to affirmative action policies and a major mediator of the effects of other variables on attitudes. The previously documented difference in reactions of beneficiaries and nonbeneficiaries is completely consistent with a self-interest explanation. Research in the area of race-based interventions has documented the important role self-interest plays in reactions to a variety of social policies (Jacobson, 1985; McConahay, 1982), including affirmative action (Jacobson, 1985; Kravitz et al., 1997; Tougas & Beaton, 1993). Individuals who see race- or sex-based policies as being beneficial for their group are likely to support the policies. Individuals who see the same policies as leading to the loss of opportunities for their own group are likely to oppose the same policies (Kluegel, 1985; Veilleux and Tougas, 1989).

In a study involving respondents to a national survey poll, Jacobson (1985) investigated the role of modern racism, traditional racism, and self-interest as mediators of attitudes toward affirmative action. Based on the results of a regression analysis, all three variables were predictive of attitudes toward affirmative action programs, with modern racism having the strongest relationship.

A direct test of self-interest as a possible mediator was conducted by Kravitz (1995). The perceived costs and benefits of affirmative action partially mediated the effects of type of affirmative action on fairness perceptions. Thus, self-interest was a mediator of the effects of variations in affirmative action procedures on reactions (Kravitz, 1995).

Arguments concerning affirmative action often turn into morality plays with those who support or oppose the policies accusing the opposing side of self-serving interests. This often shifts analyses of the policies away from legitimate topics. Concerns of majority group members about the potential outcome of affirmative action should be addressed in theoretical analyses of the policies and in "real world" settings where their opposition is driven by economic concerns. Across a wide range of research settings, self-interest predicts reactions to affirmative action, particularly when strong policies are used.

BELIEFS CONCERNING OPPORTUNITIES
AND THE ROLE OF DISCRIMINATION

A possible mediator of attitudes toward affirmative action is beliefs concerning the relative availability of opportunities in education and employment for minorities and women and the causes of any differences in opportunities (Taylor-Carter, Doverspike, & Cook, 1995). The hypothesis that the perceptions of inequities in equal opportunity would result in more support for affirmative action would appear to be a relatively straightforward one (Taylor-Carter et al., 1995). However, the relationship is not so simple.

The relative availability of educational or employment opportunities is a difficult variable to categorize since it could be considered to be an organizational variable, a respondent variable, or a mediator variable. Availability of opportunities could be considered to be an organizational variable when information is provided or manipulated concerning past employment opportunities. It could be considered to be a respondent variable when we are looking at preexisting beliefs or attitudes regarding opportunities. Finally, it could be a mediator variable when the concern is with measuring the effect of manipulating information on past opportunities on attitudes regarding opportunities, especially when the variable being measured is the attributions made regarding the differences in opportunities across protected classes.

We have chosen to treat the availability of opportunities as a mediating variable which is closely related to perceptions of past discrimination. In practice, it would appear very difficult to separate out perceptions regarding past discrimination from perception regarding the availability of opportunities, although in research settings the two could be manipulated separately.

In investigating White males' beliefs about the need for race-based affirmative action, Whites who believed that Blacks were already favored in employment opportunities were less likely to support affirmative action (Jacobson,1985). Among males, the belief that females had fewer employment opportunities was correlated with favorable attitudes toward affirmative action Veilleux and Tougas (1989). Thus, the existence of a perception that women or minorities have been deprived of previous opportunities appears to lead to greater support for affirmative action, while the perception that women and minorities have had equal or better past opportunities leads to negative attitudes and resistance toward affirmative action.

Beliefs concerning the distribution of employment and educational opportunities for minorities and women would appear to be a major factor in shaping attitudes toward affirmative action efforts. If a person believes that differences do not exist in the availability of educational and employment opportunities, then there would appear to be no reason to have affirmative action efforts in place; of course, this assumes that the causation is not reversed (i.e., that opposition to affirmative action efforts is not leading to the perception that there are no race or sex differences in opportunities). On the other hand, when a difference is perceived in educational and employment opportunities, then the individual respondent may look for additional information, such as the history of past discrimination, in order to make an attribution to the cause of the differences in opportunities. When the differences in opportunities can not be explained or are seen as the result of discrimination, then this should lead to greater support for affirmative action policies.

Simply presenting information on previous discrimination by an organization does not in and of itself appear to lead consistently to more favorable attitudes toward affirmative action. As we argued in Chapter 5, this may be because individuals have previous opinions regarding past discrimination and, perhaps, the past history of discrimination is better treated as a mediating variable. Thus, it is individual differences in the perception of past discrimination which are critical, but these perceptions are influenced by a variety of respondent and message characteristics.

Perceptions of discrimination do appear to be correlated with attitudes toward affirmative action (Belliveau, 1996; Jacobson, 1985; Tougas & Beaton, 1993; Tougas, Joly, Beaton, & St.-Pierre, 1996; Tougas & Veilleux, 1988). However, data from both national opinion surveys and other research suggests that Whites often attribute differences in representation and opportunities to factors other than discrimination (Bobo & Kluegel, 1993; Kluegel & Smith 1982, 1983; Kravitz, Stinson, & Mello, 1994; Tougas & Veilleux, 1988, 1989).

Thus, even when confronted with incontrovertible evidence of differences in representation among groups, the differences need not be attributed to discrimination. Instead, differences in opportunities may be attributed to a lack of skills or abilities (Kluegel, 1985) or stereotypes regarding the fit between characteristics of groups of people and occupations (Heilman, 1983; Kleugel, 1985; Larwood, 1982). White Americans appear to want to believe in the fairness of the economic system and in its basis in merit (Kluegel, 1985) and thus there is a tendency among both the general public and among White males to attribute inequities in opportunities to the members of the protected class, especially minorities, rather than to discrimination (Kluegel, 1985; Lovrich, 1987).

Framing affirmative action as a type of help for those in need leads to more favorable attitudes (Pratkanis & Turner, 1996; Turner & Pratkanis, 1993, 1994; Turner, Pratkanis, & Hardaway, 1991). However, the strength of the policy may determine reactions to procedures, regardless of need, with stronger forms of affirmative action often being viewed as unnecessary (Veilleux & Tougas, 1989).

For the intended beneficiaries (i.e., women and Blacks), the process of assessing opportunities may operate somewhat differently than for White males. Stating that one's own sexual or racial group is underrepresented may lead to self-blame and feelings of stigmatization. If remedies are not available, then women and minorities may ignore the presence of discrimination in order to avoid feelings of discomfort. Since labeling oneself as a victim may be unacceptable, people exposed to discrimination may acknowledge problems at a group level and still deny personally experiencing discrimination (Crosby, 1982, 1984). Minorities and women may also fear stigmatization by others (Nacoste, 1990; Nacoste & Lehman, 1987), as there is a tendency for others to view the beneficiaries of affirmative action as less competent (see Chapter 8). Beneficiaries may also fear retaliation on the part of others (Martin, Price, Bies, & Powers, 1987).

This fear of stigmatization may lead to resistance toward preferential treatment and to even stronger opposition when the policy has personal consequences for the respondent. Thus, women and Blacks may oppose affirmative action because they fear that the policies will damage perceptions of their own competence or the competence of those in their racial or gender group. In addition, they may fear that affirmative action efforts will result in negative reactions from majority group members (Kravitz et al., 1997).

An important concept in understanding perceptions of past discrimination is "collective relative deprivation," which is the feeling that one's group has fewer or less attractive opportunities relative to the majority group (Taylor-Carter et al., 1995). Based on social identity theory (Tajfel,

1978), if an individual identifies with a group, then a collective action which is target toward that group may be seen as more favorable if the individual believes that the group has been collectively deprived. Affirmative action can be seen as a collective action and past discrimination as a form of collective relative deprivation. Many women and minorities in organizations may experience feelings of collective relative deprivation related to their belief that fewer employment opportunities exist for females and minority groups members than for White males (Clayton & Crosby, 1985; Tougas & Veilleux, 1988), although affirmative action could also result in White males experiencing feelings of collective relative deprivation. The belief that fewer opportunities exist for females than for males has been found to be related to support for affirmative action efforts in general, although less strongly to support for forms of sex-based preferential treatment policies (Tougas & Veilleux, 1988).

CHAPTER SUMMARY

Mediator variables fill in the black boxes in our theories by explaining why it is that independent variables have the effects they do on dependent variables. In this chapter, we discussed three possible mediator variables: justice and fairness, self-interest, and beliefs concerning the relative distribution of educational and employment opportunities.

Although fairness has been treated as a mediator of the effects of independent variables on attitudes, in our opinion it is very difficult to separate the concepts of fairness and attitudes, as this leads to a variety of definitional and methodological problems. We propose treating perceptions of justice as a mediator and retaining fairness as a dependent variable.

Self-interest predicts reactions to affirmative action. Beneficiaries have more favorable attitudes toward affirmative action and this can be explained by the effect of beneficiary status on self-interest. Individuals who see themselves as gaining from affirmative action are likely to support specific affirmative action efforts even if they are opposed to affirmative action as a general social policy.

Beliefs concerning equal employment opportunities and the distribution of employment and educational opportunities for minorities and women is a major factor in shaping attitudes toward affirmative action efforts. When differences in opportunities are seen as the result of discrimination, this leads to greater support for affirmative action policies. However, White males may attribute differences in opportunities to factors other than discrimination. Women and minorities may resist attributing differences in opportunities to discrimination if it leads to self-blame or stigmatization. On the other hand, the feeling that one's group has fewer or less attractive opportunities relative to the majority group (i.e., collective relative deprivation) has been found to be related to support for affirmative action policies.

REFERENCES

Belliveau, M. A. (1996). The paradoxical influence of policy exposure on affirmative action attitudes. *Journal of Social Issues, 52,* 99-104.

Bobo, L., & Kluegel, J. R. (1993). Opposition to race-targeting: Self-interest, stratification ideology, or racial attitudes? *American Sociological Review, 58,* 443-464.

Clayton, S.D., & Crosby, F. J. (1985). *Justice, Gender and Affirmative Action.* Ann Arbor, MI: University of Michigan Press.

Crosby, F. J. (1982). *Relative deprivation and Working Women.* New York: Oxford University Press.

Crosby, F. J. (1984). Relative deprivation in organizational settings. In B. M. Staw & L. L. Cummings (Eds.), *Research in organizational behavior* (Vol. 6, pp. 51-93). Greenwich, CT: JAI Press.

Heilman, M. E. (1983). Sex bias in work settings: The lack of fit model. *Research in Organizational Behavior, 5,* 269-298.

Jacobson, C. K. (1985). Resistance to affirmative action: Self-interest or racism? *Journal of Conflict Resolution, 29,* 306-329.

Kluegel, J. R. (1985). "If there isn't a problem, you don't need a solution": The bases of contemporary affirmative action attitudes. *American Behavioral Scientist, 28,* 761-784.

Kluegel, J. R., & Smith, E. R. (1982). Whites' beliefs about blacks' opportunity. *American Sociological Review, 47,* 518-532.

Kluegel, J. R., & Smith, E. R. (1983). Affirmative action attitudes: Effects of self-interest, racial affect, and stratification beliefs on Whites' views. *Social Forces, 61,* 797-824.

Kravitz, D. A., Stinson, V., & Mello, E. W. (1994, August). Public reactions to affirmative action. In M. E. Turner (Chair), *Affirmative action at work: Towards reducing barriers to the integrated workplace.*

Symposium conducted at the annual meeting of the Academy of Management, Dallas, TX.

Kravitz, D.A. (1995). Attitudes toward affirmative action plans directed at Blacks: Effects of plan and individual differences. *Journal of Applied Social Psychology, 25,* 2192-2220.

Kravitz, D. A., Harrison, D. A., Turner, M. A., Levine, E. L. Chaves, W., Brannick, M. T., Denning, D. L., Russell, C. J., & Conrad, M. A. (1997). *Affirmative action: A review of psychological and behavioral research.* Bowling Green, OH: Society for Industrial and Organizational Psychology.

Larwood, L. (1982). The importance of being right when you think you are: Self-serving bias in equal employment opportunity. In B. Gutek (Ed.), *Sex Role Stereotyping and Affirmative Action Policy* (pp. 65-80). Los Angeles, CA: Institute of Industrial Relations.

Lovrich, N. P. (1987). Equality and efficiency tradeoffs in affirmative action: Real or imagined? The case of women in policing. *The Social Science Journal, 24,* 53-70.

Martin, J.R., Price, L., Bies, R. J., & Powers, M.E. (1987). Now that I can have it, I'm not so sure I want it: The effects of opportunity on aspirations and discontent. In B. A. Gutek & L. Larwood (Eds.), *Women's Career Development* (pp. 28-41). Newbury Park, CA: Sage.

McConahay, J.B. (1982). Self-interest versus racial attitudes as correlates of anti-busing attitudes in Louisville: Is it the buses or the blacks? *The Journal of Politics, 44,* 692-720.

Nacoste, R. B. (1990). Sources of stigma: Analyzing the psychology of affirmative action. Law and Policy, 12, 175-195.

Nacoste, R. W., & Lehman, D. (1987). Procedural stigma. *Representative Research in Social Psychology,17,* 25-38.

Parker, C. P., Baltes, B.B., & Christiansen, N.D. (1997). Support for affirmative action, justice perceptions, and work attitudes: A study of gender and racial-ethnic group differences. *Journal of Applied Psychology, 82,* 376-389.

Pratkanis, A. R., & Turner, M. E. (1996). The proactive removal of discriminatory barriers: Affirmative action as effective help. *Journal of Social Issues, 52,* 111-132.

Tajfel, H. (1978). *Differentiation between social groups: Studies in the social psychology of intergroup relations.* London, England: Academic Press.

Taylor-Carter, M. A., Doverspike, D., & Cook, K. (1995). Understanding resistance to sex and race-based affirmative action: A review of research findings. *Human Resource Management Review, 5,* 129-157.

Tougas, F., & Beaton, A. M. (1993). Affirmative action in the work place: For better or for worse. *Applied Psychology: An International Review, 42,* 253-264.

Tougas, F., Joly, S., Beaton, A. M., & St.-Pierre, L. (1996). Reactions of beneficiaries to preferential treatment: A reality check. *Human Relations, 49,* 453-464.

Tougas, F., & Veilleux, F. (1988). The influence of identification, collective relative deprivation, and procedure of implementation of women's response to affirmative action: A causal modeling approach. *Canadian Journal of Behavioral Science, 20,* 15-28.

Tougas, F., & Veilleux, F. (1989). Who likes affirmative action: Attitudinal processes among men and women. In F. A. Blanchard & F. J. Crosby (Eds.), *Affirmative action in perspective* (pp. 111-124). New York: Springer-Verlag.

Turner, M. E., & Pratkanis, A. R. (1993). Effects of preferential and meritorious selection on performance: An examination of intuitive and self-handicapping perspectives. *Personality and Social Psychology Bulletin, 19,* 47-58.

Turner, M. E., & Pratkanis, A. R. (1994). Affirmative action as help: A review of recipient reactions to preferential selection and affirmative action. *Basic and Applied Social Psychology, 15,* 43-69.

Turner, M. E., Pratkanis, A. R., & Hardaway, T. (1991). Sex differences in reactions to preferential selection: Towards a model of preferential selection as help. *Journal of Social Behavior and Personality, 6,* 797-814.

Veilleux, F., & Tougas, F. (1989). Male acceptance of affirmative action programs for women: The results of altruistic or egotistical motives. *International Journal of Psychology, 24,* 485-496.

Chapter 8

POTENTIAL COSTS TO BENEFICIARIES

One of the main goals of affirmative action procedures is to increase the proportion of members of protected groups in educational programs, jobs, occupations and industries where they have been traditionally underrepresented. Thus, affirmative action efforts should lead to substantial benefits, both economic and social, for members of the targeted groups. Consequently, because it would appear to be in their best interest to support affirmative action policies, minorities and females are generally more supportive of affirmative action efforts than are White males, and self-benefit appears to be a key variable in predicting reactions to affirmative action. At first, then, it seems odd to even ask the question as to whether affirmative action can harm its intended beneficiaries. Although some social commentators have dismissed the possibility (Glasser, 1988; Shaw, 1988), affirmative action policies appear to have the potential to result in social psychological costs for the intended beneficiaries. There are two types of costs to beneficiaries which could result from the implementation of affirmative action procedures. First, the negative reactions of nonbeneficiaries toward affirmative action could also be directed at the beneficiaries themselves. If a White male knows that he was passed over for a promotion because a woman received the position through affirmative action, then he may feel resentment and hostility toward the woman as well as toward the organization and the policy. Second, affirmative action policies could result in the intended beneficiaries experiencing negative self-evaluations and self-perceptions. If a Black female knows that she was admitted into medical school as a result of a special minority recruitment program, then she may feel less competent than a classmate receiving a regular admission.

Thus, the potential paradox -- is it possible that a procedure which is designed to benefit minorities and females may actually have significant costs, at least psychological costs, for the intended beneficiaries? This question would seem to be one for which the psychological literature should offer a unique perspective, and indeed this issue has attracted a good deal of research attention. The question of the effect of the presence of affirmative action programs on the evaluation of beneficiaries has been a dominant theme in the psychological research on affirmative action. In this chapter, we review the research evidence related to the potential costs of affirmative action in terms of both the reactions of others toward beneficiaries and the effects on beneficiaries' self-assessments.

REACTIONS OF OTHERS TOWARD BENEFICIARIES

In order to achieve a truly diverse workforce, organizations must decrease the negative reactions of majority group members toward affirmative action policies and also toward the intended beneficiaries of these policies. There is a real need to understand the reasons why nonbeneficiaries respond to and react to affirmative action as they do and how these reactions affect their perceptions of minorities and women in the organization. Based on attribution and stigma theories (Austin, Friedman, Martz, Hooe, & Pregerson Ball, 1977; Chacko, 1982; Kelley, 1973; Nacoste, 1989), as well as a number of other theories discussed in Chapters 2 and 3, we would expect that when presented with an alternative explanation for minority or female success, in this case affirmative action policies, nonbeneficiaries would discount minority or female ability and merit as a causative factor.

Attribution theory (Kelley, 1973) proposes that people take a rational approach to understanding the causes of behavior (see Chapter 3). Behavior and its outcomes can be explained as either being the result of personal characteristics, such as ability and personality variables, or situational characteristics. The attributional process is not totally rational, but also reflects inferences about the roles of others and situational variables in the production of behavior. The role of situational variables is often overestimated in attributions for success. There is a corresponding tendency to overestimate the role of personal factors in attributions concerning failure (Huber, Podsakoff, & Todor, 1985).

Based on attribution theory, it would be expected that when women or minorities succeed in the presence of an affirmative action policy, they will receive less credit for their performance, since their accomplishments can be attributed to the presence of the affirmative action policy. Thus, an affirmative action hire will be seen by their coworkers as less competent than if they were hired under normal hiring procedures; the hiring of the person in question will be seen as a result of the organizational policy of affirmative action rather than as a result of merit.

An example of a typical study involving the evaluation of the competence of the beneficiaries of affirmative action was conducted by Jacobson and Koch (1977). In this early study, the leader of a group was described as having been selected based upon her sex, chance factors, or her ability. Thus, this study was of the assigned leader paradigm type. After completion of a group task, false feedback, either positive or negative, was given on the group's performance. The group members were then asked to evaluate the leader's effectiveness and to explain or provide reasons for the group's success or failure. A female leader selected on the basis of her sex was perceived to be the cause of poor performance by the group. Conversely, a female leader selected on the basis of her sex did not receive credit for successful performance by the group.

Research by Summers (1991) provides an example of the use of the paper-person scenario study approach to study the effect of affirmative action on assessments of beneficiary competence. Participants were asked to rate a female manager who was employed by an organization which was described as either having a pro-affirmative action policy or being an anti-affirmative action company. Male and female participants rated the manager as actually being less competent when the company had a pro-affirmative action policy. Thus, the presence of an affirmative action policy led to a degrading of the female beneficiary's ability. For the anti-affirmative action description, there was a sex difference such that female participants viewed the manager as more competent than did male participants.

Perhaps the most complete set of studies on the effects of affirmative action policies on attitudes toward beneficiaries can be found in the research conducted by Heilman and her associates. For example, in a laboratory study completed by Heilman, Block, and Lucas (1992), they asked undergraduates to evaluate a new hire for either a male sex-typed or a more neutral sex-typed job. In the condition in which there was no affirmative action policy, the female was seen as being less competent than the male for the male sex-typed job but not for the more neutral job. However, in the presence of an affirmative action policy, the female applicant was rated as less competent for both jobs.

The previous laboratory study by Heilman et al. (1992) was followed up using a field study in which respondents were asked to rate a coworker's competence and the degree to which affirmative action had been a factor in the coworker's hiring. Competence ratings were highly negatively correlated with the respondents' belief that affirmative action had played a role in the hiring of the coworker. Black and White females hired under affirmative action policies were viewed as less competent, less qualified, and having less desirable interpersonal characteristics than other coworkers. This negative effect was more pronounced in evaluations of Black women. The combined effects of racial and sexual stereotypes may have been responsible for the particularly negative reactions to Black, female beneficiaries. A problem with the sex-based research on affirmative action is that there is an extremely limited number of studies on the interaction effects of race or ethnicity. A few studies have investigated reactions of Black females; however, research on other minorities is virtually nonexistent and many researchers do not even report data on the race of participants in studies dealing primarily with sex-based affirmative action.

In a laboratory study involving race-based affirmative action, Garcia, Erskine, Hawn, and Casmay (1981) had White undergraduates rate minority applicants to a graduate program. The described presence of an affirmative action program affected the respondents' ratings of the minority applicants' qualifications. When the minority applicant was viewed as having been accepted into the program based upon affirmative action, the respondents tended to discount the role of personal ability in achieving success.

Although most of the research on reactions to beneficiaries has dealt with questions of ratings of competence, the results of a laboratory study by Rosen and Mericle (1979) provide some data on salary recommendations. Females, who were described as having been hired into the organization under an affirmative action policy, were awarded significantly lower starting salaries than those in a no-strong policy condition. One possible explanation for this results is that the research participants discounted the ability of the females hired as a result of affirmative action. As a result, when it came to making a salary offer, the participants in the study offered salaries consistent with depressed evaluations of ability.

Providing information on qualifications or merit was previously found to have an effect on reactions toward affirmative action policies (see Chapter 5). A similar effect for information on qualifications has been found for attitudes toward the beneficiary (Heilman, McCullough & Gilbert, 1996; Nacoste, 1987a; Nacoste, 1987b; Nacoste & Lehman, 1987). In a situation involving an affirmative action hire, providing qualification information has the effect of increasing competence ratings. As part of a series of three studies using a variety of methods, Heilman, Battle, Keller, and Lee (1998) found that some of the negative effects of sex-based selection were eliminated by including information regarding the use of merit in decision making. However, information on merit had less of a positive effect on participants in the role of onlooker and on nonbeneficiaries' intent to engage in citizenship behavior.

In a recent study, Traver and Alliger (1999) found that male raters viewed female police officers hired through affirmative action as relatively inferior to officers who were not hired through affirmative action. However, this effect did not emerge when information on the female beneficiary's competence was presented. This provides further information which suggests that stigmatization may only occur under conditions of extremely limited information.

In summary, not only does affirmative action result in general feelings of negative affect, some of that negative affect also appears to be directed at the intended beneficiaries. Specifically, and consistent with attribution theory, the possibility that an educational or employment opportunity could have resulted from affirmative action leads to a discounting of the role of beneficiary motivation, ability, and merit. The tendency is to attribute the successful acquisition of the desired outcome to the existence of the affirmative action policy, rather than to the competencies of the recipient. Affirmative action hires are seen as less competent by others, because their performance or outcomes can be attributed to situational or external factors.

BENEFICIARY SELF-ASSESSMENTS

Given the effects of affirmative action programs on other's evaluations of beneficiaries, do similar or parallel effects occur when beneficiaries assess their own merit and ability? In the presence of an affirmative action program, will a beneficiary question their own competence? Based on attribution theory, similar effects would be expected for self-assessments, although we might expect beneficiaries to engage in some self-serving bias and to also have greater access to information on their own competence.

Using the paper-person scenario, Nacoste (1985) had research participants role play a female professor who had been awarded a grant based either on merit or her sex. In the sex-based condition, the beneficiaries experienced more negative affect and reported feeling less deserving of the award. Similar results were obtained by Nacoste and Lehman (1987) where beneficiaries reported being less confident in their ability and in their future performance. Thus, female participants who were told they were hired on the basis of their sex felt less competent, but providing information that the hiring reflected qualifications resulted in more positive affect. In a follow up study, Nacoste (1989) found that affirmative action resulted in feelings of reduced competence and lower self-efficacy for those participants who thought that affirmative action was unfair.

Using the assigned leader paradigm, Heilman, Simon, and Repper (1987) found that selection based upon sex had a negative effect on self-assessments. Females selected on the basis of their sex lowered their rating of ability, took less credit for group performance, and had less desire to remain in the leader role. This effect was not found for male participants who were told that they were appointed to the leadership position because of their sex.

Similar results were found in a study by Major, Feinstein, and Crocker (1994), which also used the assigned leader paradigm. For women, the perception that they had been selected based upon sex rather than merit led to feelings of reduced competence. This effect did not occur in a condition where selection was based upon sex plus merit (i.e., a condition similar to soft preferential treatment). In addition, selection based upon sex did not have a negative effect on males' ratings of competence. In fact, the males evaluated their competence more highly when told they had been selected based upon sex.

One possible explanation for the above sex-based results is that males are simply more confident in their abilities than females and that their self-assessment are less affected by external information (Doverspike & Arthur, 1995). A related, but slightly different interpretation of the results, is that leadership is a male sex-typed position requiring stereotypical male abilities (Lord, Foti, & DeVader, 1984). Therefore, the male participants expected to succeed in this situation and, therefore, saw their performance as consistent with their expectations. Female participants, on the other hand, could have seen themselves in a token role and expected to have trouble fitting in to the role required by the task. This leads to the potentially unpleasant conclusion that selection based upon group status may have the greatest negative effect on a woman's self assessment in the types of occupations and situations where affirmative action is most needed (i.e., male sex-typed tasks or jobs).

The findings of Arthur, Doverspike and Fuentes (1992) also lend support to these results and reveal the presence of similar effects for race. In a role playing scenario similar to that used by Nacoste (1985), participants who were told that they had received a fellowship based on a race-based preferential treatment program reported less positive affect than those who received the fellowship as a result of merit. Again, being told that sex or race was a deciding factor in the selection decision or award decision was related to negative emotional reactions from the beneficiary.

In an extension of this study, Doverspike and Arthur (1995) explored the impact of soft and hard preferential treatment on self-rated competency using the paper-person scenario method. The study was designed to include a large number of White males, White females, Black males and Black females, in order to allow for a test of a race by sex effect. Participants in the study read a scenario in which they were informed that they had received a graduate fellowship. The fellowship award had been given because of a hard or soft preferential treatment policy. The information provided to each participant also indicated that they had been less qualified than the other potential recipient of the fellowship or equally qualified. Although the results were confounded by the presence of a number of interactions, one unexpected finding was that soft preferential treatment resulted in lower reported competence than did hard preferential treatment (i.e., being told that the qualifications were equal as opposed to lower, resulted in higher competence ratings). Overall, Black males and White males reported fairly high levels of competence across all conditions. When told that they were less qualified,

White females reported relatively low levels of competence. The negative effect of hard preferential treatment was more severe on the ratings of competence made by White participants than on the ratings provided by Black participants.

In a rare study which jointly examined sex and race effects of affirmative action, Stewart and Shapiro (1999) found that preferential treatment did not have negative effects on Black male beneficiaries. Black male participants actually rated their leadership ability highest when chosen preferentially and when given negative information about their ability. The findings did not generalize to Black or White women. While preferential selection did not affect women's confidence when they were given no information on their performance, their self-evaluations did drop when they were preferentially selected and given negative performance feedback. Stewart and Shapiro (1999) note that this effect may have emerged because leadership is a typically masculine job, making women relatively less confident in their performance than men.

Although there are studies which examine dependent variables other than evaluations of competence or merit, the research results have been inconsistent and somewhat difficult to reconcile into simple conclusions or summary statements. Affirmative action does appear to have effects on commitment and job satisfaction. Chacko (1982), in a survey study, found that both commitment and satisfaction were lower for females who saw themselves as having been hired as a result of sex as opposed to merit. However, studies conducted by a number of other researchers (Graves & Powell, 1994; Heilman et al. 1987; Taylor, 1994; Turner & Pratkanis, 1993, 1994; Turner, Pratkanis, & Hardaway, 1991) suggest that any effects of affirmative action on motivation or on job satisfaction are less than clear (Kravitz et al., 1997). Based on data from a 1990 General Social Survey, Taylor (1994) concluded that there was no evidence that beneficiaries suffered any negative effects and that for Blacks affirmative action resulted in greater occupational ambition.

The presence of affirmative action procedures does affect occupational choice and the desire to engage in sex-typed tasks, although interpreting the results of the studies is another matter. There does appear to be some research evidence which indicates that the presence of strong preferential treatment may lead to less of a desire among potential beneficiaries to enter an occupation or an organization (Heilman & Herlihy, 1984; Heilman,

Lucas, & Kaplow, 1990; Heilman, Rivero, & Brett, 1991; Heilman et al., 1987; Nacoste, 1987a; Nacoste, 1987b; Stanush, Arthur, & Doverspike, 1988).

For example, Heilman et al. (1990) manipulated information on ability in a laboratory study using the assigned leader paradigm. When selected based upon their sex and given no information on ability, females were far more negative in their self-evaluations than when selected based upon merit. When females were provided with positive information on their ability, the effect for selection method was nonsignificant. Heilman et al. (1991) conducted two laboratory studies in which participants were told that they had been selected based upon either sex or merit. For females, but not for males, selection based upon sex affected their choice of tasks. The effect of selection on task choice was mediated by perceptions of competence.

On the other hand, other research suggests that affirmative action may have either a positive or neutral effect on organizational or occupational attraction (Graves & Powell, 1994). In that this research can be considered as involving attitudes directed toward the organization, rather than self-assessments, we will discuss the topic of the effects of affirmative action on organizational attraction more thoroughly in Chapter 11.

There have been a few studies which have investigated the effects of affirmative action policies on performance. As part of Nacoste's (1989) research, he did not find an effect on performance for the type of affirmative action procedure nor for judgments of fairness. Turner and Pratkanis (1993) found that the effect of type of affirmative action procedure on performance depended upon a number of other factors including the description of the competencies required by the task. It is difficult to reach conclusions regarding performance as a dependent variable given the limited number of studies which have been conducted and the likelihood that substantial amounts of variance in performance may be explained by task-related abilities.

In many areas of social psychology, providing information on the qualifications or actual merit of the target person reduces the strength of any other effects including those occurring as a result of the use of stereotypes. As a result, one could reasonably ask whether providing information on the actual merit or qualifications of the beneficiaries will attenuate the effects of the presence of affirmative action procedures. Further, as previously discussed, reactions to affirmative action procedures seem to depend on the relative emphasis placed upon protected groups status versus merit. Therefore, providing information on the relative merit of the beneficiary should reduce the tendency of individuals to attribute success to the policy rather than to individual factors.

A number of studies have included some type of condition where information was provided on qualifications. Based on laboratory studies, the presence of information on qualifications results in more positive affect and higher competence ratings (Arthur et al., 1992; Heilman et al., 1990; Nacoste, 1985), although in the Arthur et al. (1992) study, Black males reported relatively high levels of perceived competence independent of information on qualifications. Using an assigned leader paradigm, Heilman et al. (1998) found that the presence of information on the inclusion of merit as a factor in decision making reduced the negative effects of selection based upon sex on beneficiaries' self-assessments.

The presence of an information effect may also partially explain why the fit in terms of the sex appropriateness of the task is important. Basically, it might be hypothesized that when potential beneficiaries see a mismatch between their group status and the sex- or race-type of the task, job, or occupation, they will perceive a lower likelihood of success or adequate performance. These lowered expectations of success will in turn lead to lowered overall feelings of competence and general negative affect. Thus, there may be an interaction between sex-type of task or job and the use of affirmative action, such that the more extreme the sex typing of the task, the greater the potential negative impact of the presence of affirmative action policies on beneficiary competence.

CHAPTER SUMMARY

The theme which emerges from studies of the effect of affirmative action on assessments of beneficiaries is that those women or minorities who are brought into an organization as part of an affirmative action effort may be viewed as less competent. Nonbeneficiaries will view beneficiaries as less competent and affirmative action will have a negative impact on the beneficiary's own self-assessments. However, the simple act of providing information on beneficiary qualifications does attenuate the effect of affirmative action on assessments of competence. The observed effects of affirmative action on assessments of beneficiaries are consistent with the predictions of attribution theory.

The use of affirmative action is most likely to produce negative attributions in situations where the policy is stronger and when respondents have very little information concerning beneficiary ability. It is important to note that understanding these inferences is not a simple process, and conflicting findings exist in this body of research. Males may still stigmatize females even when their performance is acceptable.

Although initial research on the effects of affirmative action on nonbeneficiaries' attributions about beneficiaries was quite discouraging, more recent research suggests that these negative attributions may not occur as strongly in applied settings as the experimental research would suggest. In general, negative inferences about beneficiaries are less likely to occur when positive information about beneficiary ability is emphasized, when their performance is strong, and when weaker forms of affirmative action are used.

Early research led to the conclusion that sex-based affirmative action can have negative effects on self-rated competence of female beneficiaries and may lead women to "self-select" out of challenging tasks. However, the negative impact of benefitting from affirmative action is lessened in situations where beneficiaries have confidence in their abilities and where specific feedback is provided to beneficiaries regarding their abilities. It is also worth noting that affirmative action may not have negative effects on the self-perceptions of Blacks, especially Black males. Thus, it may be the case that beneficiary attributions about their own performance are not as negative as once believed. A number of factors may also moderate the relationship between affirmative action and self-perceptions.

Limited research exists on variables other than competence. There is the possibility that negative beliefs about beneficiaries may become translated into less attractive rewards for female job applicants. The effects of the presence of affirmative action policies on job satisfaction, organizational satisfaction, and motivation is unclear. A topic which will be covered in more detail in Chapter 11 is the effect of affirmative action on the attractiveness of organizations.

A problem with the research on beneficiary's self-assessments is that much of it has been based on sex-based affirmative action, although in our research we have tried to investigate more thoroughly the question of race-based affirmative action. Much of the sex-based literature seems to be based on White females, although this is only an educated guess since data on ethnicity is typically not reported. Not only is there a need for more research on race-based affirmative action, there is also a real need for more research on the interaction between race or ethnicity and sex-based affirmative action. That is, how do minority women, including American Indians, Hispanics, and Asians, respond to sex-based affirmative action.

An important issue which has attracted very little research attention is whether negative self-assessments also generalize to one's group (Kravitz et al., 1997). For example, if a female manager experiences feelings of lowered competence and self-efficacy due to her selection based upon sex-based affirmative action, will those negative feelings generalize to other female managers? Will those negative feelings generalize to other females in the organizational? Will they generalize to female employees in general? An intriguing possibility to consider is that the likelihood of negative evaluations generalizing is a function of group identity, group consciousness or stigma consciousness (Pinel, 1999). Although the constructs differ in their technical definitions, they all basically involve the degree to which people perceive themselves as similar to other members of the designated group (Pinel, 1999). Thus, we might hypothesize that the greater one's sense of group identity, the more likely it is that negative self-evaluations will also be attributed to the group at large.

At the beginning of this chapter, we posed the question of whether affirmative action can have costs for its potential beneficiaries. The answer would appear to be a qualified "yes." That is, when a woman or a minority is selected on the basis of affirmative action, nonbeneficiaries will question the ability and competence of the recipient. It does appear, especially for women, that the beneficiary will question their own competence. However, these effects have been demonstrated primarily in the laboratory and may be of relatively short duration. Furthermore, providing information on the qualifications of the beneficiary reduces these negative effects.

In conclusion, there is evidence that there may be costs, both self- and other-imposed, on the intended beneficiary. However, the costs are primarily psychological and may be relatively short in duration. In addition, it could be argued that the long-term benefits, acquiring employment and educational opportunities, of affirmative action will far outweigh the short-term costs (Plous, 1996).

REFERENCES

Arthur, W., Jr., Doverspike, D., & Fuentes, R. (1992). Recipients' affective responses to affirmative action interventions: A cross-cultural perspective. *Behavioral Sciences and the Law, 10,* 229-243.

Austin, W., Jr., Friedman, J. S., Martz, R. A., Hooe, G. S., & Pregerson Ball, K. (1977). Responses to favorable sex discrimination. *Law and Human Behavior, 1,* 283-298.

Chacko, T. I. (1982). Women and equal employment opportunity: Some unintended effects. *Journal of Applied Psychology, 67,* 119-123.

Doverspike, D., & Arthur, W. (1995). Race and sex differences in reactions to a simulated selection decision involving race-based affirmative action. *Journal of Black Psychology, 21,* 181-200.

Garcia, L. T., Erskine, N., Hawn, K., & Casmay, S. R. (1981). The effect of affirmative action on attributions about minority group members. *Journal of Personality, 49,* 427-437.

Glasser, I. (1998). Affirmative action and the legacy of racial injustice. In P. A. Katz & D. A. Taylor (Eds.), *Eliminating racism: Profiles in controversy* (pp. 341-357). New York, NY: Plenum.

Graves, L. M., & Powell, G. N. (1994). Effects of sex-based preferential selection and discrimination on job attitudes. *Human Relations, 47,* 133-157.

Heilman, M. E., Battle, W. S., Keller, C. E., & Lee, R. A., (1998). Type of affirmative action policy: A determinant of reactions to sex-based preferential selection. *Journal of Applied Psychology, 83,* 190-205.

Heilman, M. E., Block, C. J., & Lucas, J. A. (1992) Presumed incompetent? Stigmatization and affirmative action efforts. *Journal of Applied Psychology, 77,* 536-544.

Heilman, M. E., & Herlihy, J. M. (1984). Affirmative action, negative reaction? Some moderating conditions. *Organizational Behavior and Human Performance, 33,* 204-213.

Heilman, M. E., Lucas, J. A., & Kaplow, S. R. (1990). Self-derogating consequences of sex-based preferential selection: The moderating role of initial self-confidence. *Organizational Behavior and Human Decision Processes, 46,* 202-216.

Heilman, M. E., McCullough, W. F., & Gilbert, D. (1996). The other side of affirmative action: Reactions of nonbeneficiaries to sex-based preferential selection. *Journal of Applied Psychology, 81,* 346-357.

Heilman, M. E., Rivero, J. C., & Brett, J. F. (1991). Skirting the competence issue: Effects of sex-based preferential selection on task choices of women and men. *Journal of Applied Psychology, 76,* 99-105.

Heilman, M. E., Simon, M. C., & Repper, D. P. (1987). Intentionally favored, unintentionally harmed? Impact of sex-based preferential selection on self-perceptions and self-evaluations. *Journal of Applied Psychology, 72,* 62-68.

Huber, V. L., Podsakoff, P. M., & Todor, W. D. (1985). A dimensional analysis of supervisor and subordinate attributions of success and failure. *Journal of Occupational Behavior, 6,* 131-142.

Jacobson, M. B., & Koch, W. (1977). Women as leaders: Performance evaluation as a function of method of leader selection. *Organizational Behavior and Human Performance, 20,* 149-157.

Kelley, H. H. (1973). The processes of causal attribution. *American Psychologist, 28,* 107-128.

Kravitz, D. A., Harrison, D. A., Turner, M. A., Levine, E. L. Chaves, W., Brannick, M. T., Denning, D. L., Russell, C. J., & Conrad, M. A. (1997). *Affirmative action: A review of psychological and behavioral research.* Bowling Green, OH: Society for Industrial and Organizational Psychology.

Lord, R. G., Foti, R. J., & DeVader, C. L. (1984) A test of leadership categorization theory: Internal structure, information processing, and leadership perceptions. *Organizational Behavior and Human Performance, 34,* 343-378.

Major, B., Feinstein, J., & Crocker, J. (1994). Attributional ambiguity of affirmative action. *Basic and Applied Social Psychology, 15,* 113-141.

Nacoste, R. W. (1985). Selection procedure and responses to affirmative action: The case of favorable treatment. *Law and Human Behavior, 9,* 225-242.

Nacoste, R. W. (1987a). But do they care about fairness? The dynamics of preferential treatment and minority interest. *Basic and Applied Social Psychology, 8,*177-191.

Nacoste, R. W. (1987b). Social psychology and affirmative action: The importance of policy analysis. *Journal of Social Issues 43,* 127-132.

Nacoste, R. W. (1989). Affirmative action and self-evaluation. In F. A. Blanchard & F. J. Crosby (Eds.), *Affirmative action in perspective* (pp. 103-109). New York, NY: Springer-Verlag.

Nacoste, R. W., & Lehman, D. (1987). Procedural stigma. *Representative Research in Social Psychology, 17,* 25-38.

Pinel, E. C. (1999). Stigma consciousness: The psychological legacy of social stereotypes. *Journal of Personality and Social Psychology, 76,* 114-128.

Plous, S. (1996). Ten myths about affirmative action. *Journal of Social Issues, 52,* 111-132.

Rosen, B., & Mericle, M. F. (1979). Influence of strong versus weak fair employment policies and applicant's sex on selection decisions and salary recommendations in a management simulation. *Journal of Applied Psychology, 64,* 435-439.

Shaw, B. (1988). Affirmative action: An ethical evaluation. *Journal of Business Ethics, 7,* 763-770.

Stewart, M. M., & Shapiro, D. L. (1999, April). *Selection based on merit versus demography: Implications across race and gender lines.* Presented at the Society for Industrial and Organizational Psychologists Conference, Atlanta, GA.

Stanush, P., Arthue, W.A., Jr., & Doverspike, D. (1998). Hispanic and African-American reactions to a simulated race-based affirmative action scenario. *Hispanic Journal of Behavioral Sciences, 20* (1), 3-16.

Summers, R. J. (1991). The influence of affirmative action on perceptions of a beneficiary's qualifications. *Journal of Applied Social Psychology, 21,* 1265-1276.

Taylor, M. C. (1994). Impact of affirmative action on beneficiary groups: Evidence from the 1990 General Social Survey. *Basic and Applied Social Psychology, 15,* 143-178.

Traver, H. A., & Alliger, G. M. (1999). *Evaluations and attributions of beneficiaries and nonbeneficiaries of affirmative action in mental and physical tasks.* Presented at the Society for Industrial and Organizational Psychologists Conference, Atlanta, GA.

Turner, M. E., & Pratkanis, A. R. (1993). Effects of preferential and meritorious selection on performance: An examination of intuitive and self-handicapping perspectives. *Personality and Social Psychology Bulletin, 19,* 47-58.

Turner, M. E., & Pratkanis, A. R. (1994). Affirmative action as help: A review of recipient reactions to preferential selection and affirmative action. *Basic and Applied Social Psychology, 15,* 43-69.

Turner, M. E., Pratkanis, A. R., & Hardaway, T. (1991). Sex differences in reactions to preferential selection: Towards a model of preferential selection as help. *Journal of Social Behavior and Personality, 6,* 797-814.

Chapter 9

ALTERNATIVE METHODS FOR INCREASING MINORITY REPRESENTATION

As the title suggests, in this chapter alternative methods for increasing minority representation are reviewed. The methods discussed here have been singled out from among many other possible alternatives, because they have attracted a great deal of research attention and, in some cases, resulted in quite a bit of controversy among research professionals. The three alternatives which will be discussed here are within-group norming, banding, and attempts to reduce test score differences. All three approaches are applicable primarily in situations where testing is used for selection for employment or educational opportunities.

WITHIN-GROUP NORMING

The principle of within-group norming is a simple one and has a long tradition in psychological testing. The development of norms is a standard psychometric practice and raw scores on tests are frequently translated into standardized test scores using tables of norms which are broken down by race, sex, and age. Norms have long been used in scoring intelligence and ability tests and are an integral part of the interpretation of personality tests. The use of separate sex and age norms is also important in analyzing physical agility and capacity. In the case of some personality test scales, for example masculinity-femininity scales, it would seem to be invalid, and in less professional terminology, quite silly, to even try to interpret a score in the absence of the use of separate norms for males and females.

Of course, if standard scores are taken from separate norming tables which use a common mean and standard deviation, then the means and standard deviations for males and females and for different racial or ethnic groups will be the same. As a result, members of a group, or a protected group, end up being compared only to other members of the group and the group data is equated. Thus, the net effect of the use of within-group norming is much the same as that of using a quota, except that the use of separate lists is concealed by the mysterious process of score conversion. Further, political arguments concerning affirmative action can be avoided and replaced by arguments over the appropriateness of the underlying psychometric theories.

The practice of within-group norming attracted a great deal of professional attention due to the United States Department of Labor's use of race norming in making score adjustments on the General Aptitude Test Battery. The arguments for and against race norming were the subject of a special report issued by the National Academy of Science (Hartigan & Wigdor, 1989), a report which was not without its critics (Gottfredson, 1988, 1994).

On the surface, within-group norming would appear to be a reasonable compromise which still involves rewarding merit, thus conforming to various merit-based distribution rules, while increasing the inclusion of underrepresented groups. Unfortunately, stripped of its scientific coating, within-group norming is difficult to differentiate from race- or sex-based score adjustments or from preferential treatment approaches. Following the passage of The Civil Rights Act of 1991, the debate over within-group norming subsided as a result of the prohibition on score adjustments contained in Section 106. The scientific debate has shifted from within-group norming to a procedure known as banding.

However, regardless of our judgments of the scientific and social utility of within-group norming, any type of score adjustment based upon race or sex is likely to lead to strong attitudinal reactions from beneficiaries and nonbeneficiaries. Therefore, while we know of no research on reactions to within-group norming, the psychological processes are likely to be similar to those described for strong preferential treatment.

BANDING

Banding shares much in common with within-group norming in that it attempts to achieve a social goal, increasing the inclusion of underrepresented groups, through psychometric arguments and, thereby, avoid the stigma associated with political polemics over affirmative action issues (Barrett, Doverspike, & Arthur, 1995; Cascio, Outtz, Zedeck, & Goldstein, 1991; Murphy, 1994; Schmidt, 1991; Zedeck, Cascio, Goldstein, & Outtz, 1994). The principle behind banding is very simple. It is argued that test scores which are very close together are not really all that different, after all if we gave the same test over and over again individual scores on the test would vary (Note: The variation in test scores over repeated administrations corresponds to the reliability of the test). In practice, scores that are close together can then be considered to represent the same true score. As a result, similar scores can be treated as equivalent or grouped together. Then, in theory, once people are banded together based upon their scores, they can then be selected based upon other factors including race and sex. Thus, banding comes very close to the definition of soft preferential treatment.

Banding, it is argued by its proponents, occurs in academic settings all of the time without generating any controversy. Students who score between 90 and 100 are grouped together in an A band. Students who score between 80 and 89 are grouped into a B band. This grouping of students' scores would be an example of a fixed band. A number of other methods exist for creating bands. Another procedure uses sliding bands in which the bands are continually recalculated based upon the highest remaining, unselected score.

The method used for selecting from within the band may also vary. Decisions within the band may be made at random, based on protected group status, or based upon other criteria (Sackett & Roth, 1991). If selection is made based upon other criteria, then the effect of banding will depend upon the correlation between scores on the other criteria and protected group status.

For example, consider a university which wants to increase its selection of Black students into its graduate programs. The university uses the average Graduate Record Examination (GRE) score for making admission decisions. As a means of increasing Black representation, scores are banded together so that band one equals 650 - 800, band two equals 500 - 650, band three equals 350 - 500, and band four equals 200 - 350. All individuals within a band are treated as if they had the same score. Within a band, the university then selects one White applicant for every Black applicant (Note: The university could use some other criterion. If Blacks and Whites have the same average college grade point average, then selection on the basis of college grade point average would also have the effect of increasing Black representation). As a result of the use of the bands, more Blacks should be selected than would be selected without using the banding, since within a band equal numbers of Blacks and Whites should be identified as eligible for admission into graduate school.

The City of San Francisco used banding in making its decisions for promotion from the rank of police officers to police sergeant (Cascio et al., 1991; Murphy, 1994; *Officers for Justice v. Civil Service Commission of the City & County of San Francisco*, 1991, 1992, 1993; Report of the Scientific Affairs Committee, 1994; Sackett & Roth, 1991; Zedeck et al., 1994). Following an initial selection process based upon rank ordering, the remaining police sergeants were selected based upon recommendations made by a panel of three persons, and two alternates. The panel based its recommendations upon the selection of candidates from sliding bands based upon a number of factors including the department's affirmative action goals.

Whether explicitly or implicitly, the goal of banding is a societal one rather than a psychometric objective. Regardless of the deemed worthiness of banding's ultimate outcomes, any type of score adjustment based upon race or sex is likely to lead to strong attitudinal reactions, as well as potential legal challenges. Furthermore, reactions to banding are likely to be very similar to reactions to within-group norming and strong preferential action.

A field study of reactions to test score banding was conducted with applicants for police officer positions (Truxillo & Bauer, 1999). Across three separate samples, race interacted with the applicant's belief that banding was associated with affirmative action in explaining reactions to the banding procedure. Black reactions to banding were more favorable when it was seen as linked to affirmative action and when it increased their likelihood of a favorable outcome. White reactions to banding were less favorable when it was seen as linked to affirmative action and when it decreased their likelihood of a favorable outcome. Thus, the results of this study were very consistent with a self-interest explanation and also with the argument that the psychological processes involved in reactions to banding would be very similar to those hypothesized to exist for affirmative action.

REDUCING TEST SCORE DIFFERENCES

One of the reasons for underrepresentation is that minorities, and, to a lesser extent females, often have less merit, where merit is defined in terms of scores on employment tests, than do White males. Thus, even if minorities and Whites are recruited in equal numbers, minorities will still tend to have lower selection rates (e.g., the difference between Black and White scores on intelligence or general ability tests is usually found to be one standard deviation or approximately 15 intelligence score points). Thus, one method of increasing minority representation would be to increase minority test scores or to reduce the difference between White and Black test scores.

Methods of reducing adverse impact through reductions in test score differences have received a great deal of research attention over the last 30 years, and with good reason. A consulting firm or individual who could develop a means of reducing the mean difference in Black-White test scores would find the proverbial world beating a path to their front door. Thus, it is not for lack of trying that methods for reducing adverse impact have not been developed; it has just proved to be very difficult to find the right techniques. However, research efforts continue, and some encouraging results have been obtained with test-wiseness training, research on motivational differences, and alternative testing formats.

Test-Wiseness Training

A possible explanation for the differences found in test scores between Black and Whites is that Whites are simply more adept at the task of taking tests. Specifically, Whites could be more test-wise (Miguel-Feruito, 1997). If that is true, then by increasing Black test-wiseness through training, it should be possible to reduce adverse impact.

One of the most common definitions of test-wiseness is that it reflects a person's ability to use the characteristics of the test, such as clues hidden in the questions, to achieve a higher score than should be received based upon ability alone (Millman, Bishop, & Ebel, 1965). This definition can be expanded to include the participant's motivation or confidence levels, factors which should also affect test performance. Test-wiseness has been found to affect test performance (Dolly & Vick, 1986; Fagley, 1987), but test-wiseness can be learned (Dolly & Vick, 1986; Dolly & Williams, 1985).

While there is a paucity of test-wiseness research that deals specifically with minority groups (Benson, Urman, & Hocevar, 1986), a few studies have empirically addressed the issue of test-wiseness and race. For example, test-wiseness training has been found to increase reading achievement among Black children (Dillard, Warrior-Benjamin, & Perrin, 1977), although the study conducted by Benson et al. (1986) found no evidence of an interaction between race and test-wiseness training.

Miguel-Feruito (1997) conducted a study on the effects of a test-wiseness training program on test performance. The participants, 64 Black and 70 White university students, were randomly assigned to either a test-wiseness training group or a control group. In addition to receiving test-wiseness training, participants completed a number of measures including various versions of reading tests, a test taking self-efficacy measure, a measure of test-wiseness, and general ability tests. Test-wiseness and prior knowledge of the content of the reading tests were both fairly consistently found to be significant predictors for reading comprehension tests with and without the passages. In addition, test-wiseness was found to be an important variable in explaining race differences, although the test-wiseness training program was not found to significantly effect test performance. Training did interact with prior knowledge such that individuals with higher prior knowledge of the content benefitted more from the training. Thus, it would appear that the topic of test-wiseness is one deserving of greater research attention.

Motivational Differences

Even if Blacks and Whites are equated in terms of test-wiseness, Blacks may be less motivated to perform well on selection tests. This difference in motivation may reflect differences in attitudes toward tests, long-standing beliefs regarding the fairness of the selection systems, or a general mistrust of the whole testing enterprise (Gould, 1996; Grubb, 1987; Grubb & Ollendick, 1986; Nobles, 1987). Recently, research efforts have been directed at examining the question of whether Whites and Blacks differ in their attitudes toward testing and what effects difference in attitudes might have on adverse impact (McKay & Doverspike, 1999; McKay, Doverspike, Bowen-Hilton, & Martin, 1999).

Perhaps the best known studies, primarily due to the extensive publicity and media attention they received, in this line of research have been the studies on stereotype threat completed by Steele and Aronson (1995). Stereotype threat is a form of anxiety that results when a person is concerned that their performance on a test may substantiate a negative stereotype that exists about their group. According to stereotype threat theory, if a person fears that performing poorly on a test will lead to a negative impression of their group, they suffer a decrease in concentration and attention which leads to a lowering of their test score. The results of a series of studies completed by Steele and Aronson (1995) partially confirmed the above hypothesis.

The findings of Steele and Aronson (1995) have since been supported by other researchers (Aronson, Quinn, & Spencer, 1998; Shih, Pittinsky, & Ambady, 1999). In a study with a large sample of Black and White undergraduates, McKay et al. (1999) replicated the race by test description interaction as predicted by stereotype threat theory (Steele & Aronson, 1995). After controlling for age and socioeconomic status, the Black-White intelligence test score difference was largest among participants assigned to a condition where they believed the test was diagnostic of their intelligence. Thus, the framing of a test as indicative or nonindicative of one's intellectual ability can alter the performance of Black test takers on cognitive measures.

In a series of studies completed with public sector employees and job applicants, Arvey, Strickland, Drauden, and Martin (1990) found that there were differences between Black and White job applicants in terms of their test-taking motivation. Race was significantly correlated with test-taking motivation and motivation explained part of the race difference in scores on employment tests. Test score differences between Black and White applicants were significantly reduced when test-taking attitudes were held constant.

The effect of test-taking motivation was further explored in a study by Chan, Schmitt, DeShon, Clause, and Delbridge (1997). In this study with undergraduate students, the Black-White difference in test performance on a cognitive ability battery was partially mediated by race differences in test-taking motivation. The test-taking motivation of Blacks was significantly lower than that of Whites and, when test-taking motivation was held constant, the race difference on the cognitive ability test battery was significantly reduced.

Alternative Testing Formats

Adverse impact can be reduced by using noncognitive measures. However, the solution of simply using noncognitive measures is less than satisfactory in that cognitive ability tests, intelligence and similar general ability tests, are consistently found to be the most valid predictors of both school and on-the-job performance (Ree, Earles, & Teachout, 1994; Schmidt, 1988; Schmidt & Hunter, 1998; Thorndike, 1986). The elimination of cognitive ability tests for selection purposes would be inefficient and costly. An alternative option is to try to find ways to change the format of cognitive ability tests so as to reduce the amount of adverse impact. The size of the Black-White test score difference on cognitive ability tests does appear to be partially a function of the format used for testing (Goldstein, Yusko, Braverman, Smith, & Chung, 1998).

Alternatives to typical paper-and-pencil tests, such as computer, video or oral presentation can increase perceptions of the validity of the tests and reduce adverse impact (Chan & Schmitt, 1997). In a study with undergraduates, Chan and Schmitt (1997) demonstrated that the race difference on a situational judgment test performance could be reduced through the use of a video format as opposed to a written format and that the video format was perceived by Black test takers as being more valid. One possibility is that race differences on paper-and-pencil tests may partially reflect an artifact, due to the effect of race differences in reading ability (Barrett, Miguel, & Doverspike, 1997).

Another alternative to the use of paper-and-pencil cognitive ability tests is the use of computerized tests of information processing skills. Information processing tests are based on computer models of the mind and measure cognitive skills at a more basic level than standard intelligence tests. A series of studies completed over the past 30 years by Barrett and associates has supported the use of information processing tests as a substitute for traditional cognitive tests in predicting job and skilled performance (Arthur, Barrett, & Doverspike, 1990; Axton, Doverspike, Park, & Barrett, 1997; Barrett, Alexander, Cellar, Doverspike, & Thomas, 1983; Barrett, Alexander, Doverspike, Cellar, & Thomas, 1982; Barrett, Carobine, & Doverspike, in press; Cellar et al., 1982; Doverspike, 1990; Doverspike, 1996; Doverspike, Cellar, & Barrett, 1986; Doverspike, Cellar, Barrett, & Alexander, 1984; Kandra, Barrett, & Doverspike, 1993). The question then is whether information processing tests can reduce adverse impact. In a laboratory study conducted by McKay, Barrett, Doverspike, and Randle (1998), a task-specific information processing test and a computer simulation criterion task did not result in any adverse impact against Black test takers, and the information processing test was a valid predictor of simulator performance. Thus, information processing tests may result in less adverse impact, although clearly additional studies are required. There are also practical problems to overcome regarding the time and costs involved in the use of information processing tests in large-scale testing programs.

CHAPTER SUMMARY

Both within-group norming and banding are methods of increasing minority or female representation which rest on psychometric theory rather than political arguments, although the parallels between within-group norming and strong preferential action and banding and weak preferential action would seem to be rather obvious. The reactions of both beneficiaries and nonbeneficiaries to within-group norming and banding would appear to depend upon the extent to which the methods are perceived as linked to affirmative action and the favorability of the perceived outcomes.

In situations in which differences in representation among groups exist due to Black-White differences in test scores, procedures aimed at reducing the adverse impact inherent in tests offer an alternative to affirmative action as a means of increasing representation. Until recently, efforts to reduce adverse impact on cognitive ability tests have not met with much success. However, recent research has proved promising in the areas of test-wiseness training, motivational differences, and alternative testing formats. Additional research is needed in each area as the strength of the effects appears to be rather small when compared to the large differences in Black and White scores on cognitive ability tests.

Based on current research, it does appear that there are identifiable and measurable racial differences in attitudes toward testing. The studies completed to date are fairly consistent in finding that Black test-taking attitudes have the effect of reducing performance on tests labeled or seen as measures of cognitive ability, although the size of the effect appears to be relatively small. The next step is the development of methods for changing these test-taking attitudes or creating situations in which the test-taking attitudes have less of an effect on test scores.

One obvious approach would be to change the attitudes toward testing held by Black test takers. This could be attempted through various types of training programs including those currently described as test-wiseness training. Test-wiseness training programs should emphasize the development of positive attitudes toward the test and the testing enterprise and the importance of working hard and doing well. A problem with many current test-wiseness training programs, especially those marketed to the general public, is that the programs appear to encourage a negative attitude toward testing where tests are a type of magic trick where through training the test taker can learn to beat the test. Test-wiseness training programs should encourage a positive attitude and attempt to increase test taking motivation.

Test-wiseness training programs should also deal with methods for reducing test-related anxiety. This is especially critical given the recent finding that Black test takers may experience stereotype threat which can lead to even higher levels of test anxiety than might be expected given the testing situation. As a result, Black test takers may benefit from the inclusion of training modules aimed at teaching participants how to identify and handle test anxiety.

REFERENCES

Aronson, J., Quinn, D. M., & Spencer, S. J. (1998). Stereotype threat and the academic underperformance of minorities and women. In J. Swim & C. Stangor (Eds.), *Prejudice: The target's perspective* (pp. 83-103). San Diego, CA: Academic Press.

Arthur, W., Jr., Barrett, G. V., & Doverspike, D. (1990). Validation of an information processing based test battery for the prediction of handling accidents among petroleum product transport drivers. *Journal of Applied Psychology, 75*, 621-628.

Arvey, R. D., Strickland, W., Drauden, G., & Martin, C. (1990). Motivational components of test taking. *Personnel Psychology, 43*, 695-716.

Axton, T. R., Doverspike, D., Park, S. R., & Barrett, G. V. (1997). A model of the information-processing and cognitive abilities requirements for mechanical troubleshooting. *International Journal of Cognitive Ergonomics, 1*, 245-266.

Barrett, G. V., Alexander, R. A., Cellar, D. C., Doverspike, D., & Thomas, J. C. (1983). Use of an information processing based test battery in an applied setting: Prediction of monitoring performance. *Perceptual and Motor Skills, 56,* 939-945.

Barrett, G. V., Alexander, R. A., Doverspike, D., Cellar, D., & Thomas, J. C. (1982). The development and application of a computerized information processing test battery. *Applied Psychological Measurement, 6,* 13-29.

Barrett, G. V., Carobine, R. G., & Doverspike, D. (in press). The reduction of adverse impact in an employment setting using a short-term memory test. *Journal of Business and Psychology.*

Barrett, G. V., Doverspike, D., & Arthur, W., Jr. (1995). The current status of the judicial review of banding: A clarification. *The Industrial-Organizational Psychologist, 33(1),* 39-41.

Barrett, G. V., Miguel, R. F., & Doverspike, D. (1997). Race differences on a reading comprehension test with and without passages. *Journal of Business and Psychology, 12,* 19-24.

Benson, J., Urman, H., & Hocevar, D. (1986). Effects of test-wiseness training and ethnicity on achievement of third- and fifth- grade students. *Measurement and Evaluation in Counseling and Development, 22,* 154-162.

Cascio, W. F., Outtz, J., Zedeck, S., & Goldstein, I. L. (1991). Statistical implications of six methods of test score us in personnel selection. *Human Performance, 4,* 233-264.

Cellar, D., Barrett, G. V., Alexander, R. A., Doverspike, D., Thomas, J. C., Binning, J. A., & Kroeck, G. (1982). Cognitive information processing measures as predictors of monitoring performance. *Perceptual and Motor Skills, 54,* 1299-1302.

Chan, D., & Schmitt, N. (1997). Video-based versus paper-and-pencil method of assessment in situational judgment tests: Subgroup differences in test performance and face validity perceptions. *Journal of Applied Psychology, 82,* 143-159.

Chan, D., Schmitt, N., DeShon, R. P., Clause, C. S., & Delbridge, K. (1997). Reactions to cognitive ability tests: The relationships between race, test performance, face validity, and test-taking motivation. *Journal of Applied Psychology, 82,* 300-310.

Dillard, J. M., Warrior-Benjamin, J., & Perrin, D. W. (1977). Efficacy of test-wiseness on test anxiety and reading achievement among black youth. *Psychological Reports, 41*, 1135-1140.

Dolly, J. P., & Vick, D. S. (1986). An attempt to identify predictors of test-wiseness. *Psychological Reports, 58*, 663-672.

Dolly, J. P., & Williams, K. S. (1985). *Maximizing multiple-choice test scores: Generalizability of test-wiseness training.* Paper presented at the annual meeting of the American Educational Research Association, Chicago, IL.

Doverspike, D. (1990). Information processing approaches to test development and instruction as evidence for test validity. *Proceedings of the 1990 IPMAAC Conference on Personnel Assessment.*

Doverspike, D. (1996, December). Information processing approaches to test development and construction as evidence for test validity. *IPMA Assessment Council News*, pp. 15-16.

Doverspike, D., Cellar, D., & Barrett, G. V. (1986). The auditory selective attention test: A review of field and laboratory studies. *Educational and Psychological Measurement, 46*, 1095-1104.

Doverspike, D., Cellar, D., Barrett, G. V., & Alexander, R. A. (1984). Sex differences in short-term memory processing. *Perceptual and Motor Skills, 58*, 135-139.

Fagley, N. S. (1987). Positional response bias in multiple-choice tests of learning: Its relation to testwiseness and guessing strategy. *Journal of Educational Psychology, 79*, 95-97.

Goldstein, H. W., Yusko, K. P., Braverman, E. P., Smith, D. B., & Chung, B. (1998). The role of cognitive ability in the subgroup differences and incremental validity of assessment center exercises. *Personnel Psychology, 51*, 357-374.

Gottfredson, L. S. (1988). Reconsidering fairness; A matter of social and ethical priorities. *Journal of Vocational Behavior, 33*, 293-319.

Gottfredson, L. S. (1994). The science and politics of race-norming. *American Psychologist, 49*, 955-963.

Gould, S. J. (1996). *The mismeasure of man.* New York: W. W. Norton.

Grubb, H. J. (1987). Intelligence at the low end of the curve: Where are the racial differences? *The Journal of Black Psychology, 14*, 25-34.

Grubb, H. J., & Ollendick, T. H. (1986). Cultural-distance perspective: An exploratory analysis of its effect on learning and intelligence. *International Journal of Intercultural Relations, 10,* 399-414.

Hartigan, J. A., & Wigdor, A. K. (Eds.). (1989). *Fairness in employment testing: Validity generalization, minority issues, and the General Aptitude Test Battery.* Washington, DC: National Academy Press.

Kandra, J., Barrett, G. V., & Doverspike, D. (1993). Validity of a computerized information-processing-based test battery for the prediction of performance in a transport driver simulation. *Educational and Psychological Measurement, 53,* 965-971.

McKay, P. F., Barrett, G. V., Doverspike, D., & Randle, S. (1998). *Prediction of book purchasing task performance using a task-specific information processing test and cognitive ability: Black and White differences.* Unpublished manuscript, The University of Akron.

McKay, P. F., & Doverspike, D. (1999). *African-Americans' test-taking attitudes and their effect on cognitive ability test performance: Implications for public personnel management selection practice.* Unpublished manuscript, University of Akron, Akron, Ohio.

McKay, P. F., Doverspike, D., Bowen-Hilton, D., & Martin, Q. D. (1999). *Stereotype threat effects on the Raven's scores of African-Americans.* Unpublished manuscript, University of Akron, Akron, OH.

Miguel-Feruito, R. F. (1997). *Explaining passage independence: An analysis of the ability to respond to reading comprehension test items when the passages are omitted.* Unpublished doctoral dissertation, University of Akron, Akron, Ohio.

Millman J., Bishop, C.H., & Ebel, R. (1965). An analysis of test-wiseness. *Educational and Psychological Measurement, 25,* 707-726.

Murphy, K. R. (1994). Potential effects of banding as a function of test reliability. *Personnel Psychology, 47,* 477-495.

Nobles, W. W. (1987). Psychometrics and African-American reality: A question of cultural antimony. *The Negro Educational Review, 38,* 45-55.

Officers for Justice v. Civil Service Commission, No. C-73-0657 RFP; No. C-77-2884 RFP; (Consolidated), U.S.D.C. for N.D. of Calif, 8/21/91, Order Re: Banding.

Officers for Justice v. Civil Service Commission, 979 F.2d 721 (9th Cir., 1992).

Officers for Justice v. Civil Service Commission, cert. denied, 113 S.Ct. 1645, (March 29, 1993).

Ree, M. J., Earles, J. A., & Teachout, M. S. (1994). Predicting job performance: Not much more than g. *Journal of Applied Psychology, 79*, 518-524.

Report of the Scientific Affairs Committee (July, 1994). An evaluation of banding methods in personnel selection. *The Industrial-Organizational Psychologist, 32(1)*, 80-86.

Sackett, P. R., & Roth, L. (1991). A Monte Carlo examination of banding and rank order methods of test score use in personnel selection. *Human Performance, 4*, 279-295

Schmidt, F. L. (1988). The problem of group differences in ability test scores in employment selection. *Journal of Vocational Behavior, 33*, 272-292.

Schmidt, F. L. (1991). Why all banding procedures in personnel selection are logically flawed. *Human Performance, 4*, 265-277.

Schmidt, F. L, & Hunter, J. E. (1998). The validity and utility of selection methods in personnel psychology: Practical and theoretical implications of 85 years of research findings. *Psychological Bulletin, 124*, 262-274.

Shih, M., Pittinsky, T. L., & Ambady, N. (1999). Stereotype susceptibility: Identity salience and shifts in quantitative performance. *Psychological Science, 10*, 80-83.

Steele, C. M., & Aronson, J. (1995). Stereotype threat and the intellectual test performance of African-Americans. *Journal of Personality and Social Psychology, 69*, 797-811.

Thorndike, R. L. (1986). The role of general ability in prediction. *Journal of Vocational Behavior, 29*, 332-339.

Truxillo, D. M., & Bauer, T. N. (1999). Applicant reactions to test score banding in entry-level and promotional contexts. *Journal of Applied Psychology, 84*, 322-339.

Zedeck, S., Cascio, W., Goldstein, I., & Outtz, J., (1994). Assessing fairness requires understanding the issues. *The Industrial-Organizational Psychologist, 31(3)*, 74.

Chapter 10

THE INTERNATIONAL EXPERIENCE

The primary focus of this book is on affirmative action in the United States. However, the issues discussed in this book are not necessarily limited by geography. The United States is not the only country that has instituted affirmative action programs in employment and education for minorities, women, and other groups that have suffered discrimination. The purpose of this chapter, then, is to look at the status of affirmation action related issues in other countries. Obviously, affirmative action is not a relevant concept or issue in all countries, although one could argue that it should be. Furthermore, even if it is, for variety of reasons, its saliency and the associated emphasis placed on it may not be same as in the United States. Thus, the status and relevance of affirmation action related issues is not universal.

Within this context, this chapter is composed of two sections focusing on the need for affirmative action in other countries, and national and cultural variables and their impact on reactions to affirmative action. A comprehensive search of the literature resulted in the identification of a relatively small number of non-United States or international papers on attitudes to affirmative action, with the majority of the identified articles being Canadian. One conclusion we can draw from this is that the saliency of affirmative action and equal opportunity issues is probably much higher in the United States than it is in other countries.

NEED FOR AFFIRMATIVE ACTION IN OTHER COUNTRIES

Affirmative action has been defined in this book as "policies or procedures which attempt to increase the representation of an underrepresented, protected group (primarily minority or female, but may include other groups such as the aged) in education or employment through the consideration in decision making of applicant race, sex, or protected group status." Equal opportunity has been defined here as "treating individuals in a similar fashion regardless of membership in a protected group." Thus, equal opportunity is relatively passive, whereas affirmative action is more active. In practice, of course, there are a range of procedures which can be defined as either affirmative action or equal opportunity and, at times, a specific procedure may be difficult to fit neatly into either category. The complexity of problems associated with definitions is further compounded by cultural differences and translation difficulties when studying practices across countries. As a result, what constitutes affirmative action in one country may be quite different from what constitutes affirmative action in another country.

Both affirmative action and equal opportunity share the common goal of trying to eliminate discrimination on the basis of specified demographic factors. Obviously, the social, political, and legal saliency and status of these specified demographic factors play an essential role in determining the importance, relevancy, and need for affirmative action in a given country. Consequently, anti-discrimination laws and their enforcement differ widely across countries. An excellent summary of discrimination prohibitions in a selected group of 12 countries is provided by Pincus and Belohlav (1996), and we encourage the reader to consult their article for more details.

It is commonly stated that sex discrimination in employment is a universal phenomenon (Hutchings, 1998; Pearn, 1993; Riley, 1996; Scheibal, 1995; Tougas & Beaton, 1993), and different countries have taken different approaches to counter the effects of sex discrimination. However, some countries, including Venezuela and Hong Kong, do not have any prohibitions against sex discrimination (Pincus & Belohlav, 1996). In Thailand, there are no laws restricting sex-based discrimination nor requiring "equal opportunity" language on the part of private employers (Lawler & Bae, 1998).

Race discrimination is prohibited in most countries, although again Venezuela and Hong Kong are exceptions. Similarly, many countries prohibit discrimination on the basis of national origin. A minority of countries prohibit age discrimination (Pincus & Belohlav, 1996). Other comparisons that highlight interesting discrimination prohibition differences and how they translate into different affirmative action foci is the contrast between Northern Ireland and the United Kingdom. It is unlawful in Northern Ireland to discriminate on the basis of religion, but not unlawful in the United Kingdom. However, it is not unlawful to discriminate on the grounds of race in Northern Ireland, but it is in the United Kingdom. Both Northern Ireland and the United Kingdom have comparable legislation that outlaws discrimination based on sex and marital status. Consequently, in the United Kingdom, there is anti-discrimination legislation on race, color, nationality, ethnic and national origin, sex, and marital status. There is no anti-discrimination legislation on sexual orientation, age, disability and handicap, class, and religion, except in Northern Ireland (Pearn, 1993). Thus, in the context of affirmative action in Northern Ireland, religion appears to be the primary demographic factor of interest (Donfried, 1998).

In The Netherlands, the higher unemployment rates and lower educational levels of minority workers has led to the conclusion that discrimination may play as large a role in the labor market as it does in the United States (de Vries & Pettigrew, 1994; Verheul & Terpstra, 1998). Indeed considerable research shows that when asked explicitly, Dutch employers often state that they prefer majority to minority job applicants (Becker & Kempen, 1982; Brasse & Sikking, 1986; Hooghienstra, 1991; Reubsaet & Kropman, 1985; Veenman & Vijverberg, 1982). In addition, these findings have been replicated in field experiments at temporary employment agencies where majority and minority applicants with equivalent qualifications and characteristics received differential treatment (Bovenkerk, 1978; Den Uyl, Choenni, & Bovenkerk, 1986). In the context of these findings, it is reasonable to conclude that there is a need for affirmative action in The Netherlands.

The caste system of India, in affirmative action and equal opportunity terms, would probably be described by most as being extremely discriminatory. Caste is a many-layered social hierarchy developed several millenniums ago. Although rooted in Hindu religion, caste developed a secular role as an organizing principle and framework for India life. One is born into a caste and there one stays until death. Caste not only influences what food you cook, the sari you wear, or whom you marry, but it also determines your station in life including educational and employment opportunities. Thus, in India, there certainly would appear to be a need for affirmative action. Consequently, reform of the caste system began a little over 50 years ago and despite its shortcomings and failings, most Indians agree that the lowest castes would still be powerless outcasts without affirmative action (Jonah, 1995).

Created to undo the effects of the caste system, India probably has the most extensive program of quotas in the world. For instance, more than half of all government jobs and educational slots, as well as a large number of seats in most legislatures, are permanently reserved for members of some 2,000 specific castes, more than half of India's population (Jonah, 1995).

In South Africa, apartheid entailed the segregation and differential treatment of races in all aspects of social life including political, educational, legal, and employment. Affirmative action, as promulgated by South Africa's Employment Equity Bill, is considered to be a mechanism of ensuring social justice and is beginning to be used to address some of the imbalances created by apartheid. It is considered by some to have the potential to play a pivotal role in equalizing and democratizing public and private institutions in South Africa (Human, 1990, 1993; Mallet, 1998; Reddy & Choudree, 1996).

To summarize, the preceding review demonstrates that the need for affirmative action is not restricted to the United States. However, the historical and cultural factors that shape this need, and the resulting focus on specified demographic factors (e.g., race, sex, religion) as reflected in differences in anti-discrimination laws, varies greatly from one country to the next.

NATIONAL AND CULTURAL VARIABLES AND THEIR IMPACT ON REACTIONS

A comprehensive search of the extant literature resulted in the location of attitudinal studies for only three countries, namely Canada, The Netherlands, and New Zealand. This section of the chapter reviews these studies, by country, in an attempt to compare and contrast their finding with those obtained for United States-based studies.

Canada

Although Canada has both sex- and race-based anti-discrimination legislation and affirmative action policies (Fletcher & Chalmers, 1991), all of the attitudinal studies that we identified focused on sex-based affirmative action. The Canadian experience, in terms of sex discrimination in employment, is not much different from that of other industrialized countries (Tougas & Beaton, 1993), particularly the United States. There has been a commitment to pursue efforts to ensure proportional representation of women in both the public and private sectors. In the past, private industries were encouraged to promote the situation of women on a voluntary basis. However, as it became clear that the voluntary approach did not have the expected impact, more direct measures were embraced, with the introduction of the Employment Equity Act in 1986. Consequently, as noted by Fletcher and Chalmers (1991), "affirmative action programs have today become part of the contemporary political landscape in Canada" (p. 68).

The obvious question is, what are Canadian attitudes to these programs? Fletcher and Chalmers (1991) presented the results of a field study designed to survey Canadians' attitudes toward affirmative action among both citizens and decision makers. In general, they found low levels of support for affirmative action across a variety of contexts and intended beneficiaries (e.g., women, French Canadians, vs. "native peoples"). However, they also found opinions on both sides of the issue to be rather soft, with large portions of those taking positions on the matter willing to reconsider their views when prompted.

Leck, Saunders, and Charbonneau (1996) asked 1,412 White male and female employees of a large Canadian printing and publishing firm how they would respond if female or minority employees were added to their work groups. Using a distributive justice framework, their results demonstrated that participants who believed in the equitable allocation of rewards, equal treatment of all employees, and the distribution of rewards on the basis of need were more likely to express positive attitudes and engage in more accepting behaviors.

Tougas, Crosby, Joly, and Pelchat (1995) examined factors that motivate the acceptance of, or resistance to, affirmative action when the programs stand clearly to benefit people of a different group than one's own. Specifically, using a sample of employed Canadians, Tougas et al. (1995) investigated male reactions to sex-based affirmative action seeking to determine whether they could explain male attitudes in terms of self-interest, prejudice, and/or genuine fairness concerns. Their results showed the importance of prejudice in male attitudes toward affirmative action leading them to conclude that males who rank low on neosexism supported affirmative action more strongly than did males scoring higher (see also Tougas, Brown, Beaton, & Joly, 1995). Furthermore, information had its greatest impact on males who were less sexist.

Related to the above, Bobocel, Son Hing, Davey, Stanley, and Zanna (1998) found that independent of a person's level of prejudice, Canadian college students were opposed to affirmative action policies that violate distributive and procedural justice norms as a result of genuine beliefs in the principles of fairness that the programs were perceived to violate. However, in line with the justice-as-a-rationalization hypothesis, they also found that prejudice level was positively associated with opposition to affirmative action policies that were not explicitly justice violating. Moreover, the effect of prejudice was mediated through the tendency to construe affirmative action as justice violating.

The potential harmful effects of affirmative action on beneficiaries has been extensively documented with United States samples (see Chapter 8). Specifically, it has been demonstrated that the existence of affirmative action may create or exacerbate negative perceptions of groups that benefit from these programs. Maio and Esses (1998) obtained this effect using a Canadian sample. Using a fictitious editorial describing the Surinamese, a relatively unfamiliar immigrant group in Canada, their results indicated that when affirmative action was mentioned, participants expressed less favorable perceptions of and attitudes toward the group and were less favorable toward immigration by the group. Furthermore, when affirmative action was mentioned, participants were also less favorable towards immigration in general. As with United States participants, Maio and Esses' findings clearly indicate that affirmative action can have far-reaching effects on nonbeneficiaries' attitudes toward potential beneficiary groups.

Canadian researchers, Tougas, Veilleux and associates (e.g., Tougas & Beaton, 1993; Tougas, Beaton, & Veilleux, 1991) have been particularly interested in collective relative deprivation (a broader conception of self-interest) and the role it plays in attitudes toward affirmative action. For instance, they showed that collective relative deprivation and preferential treatment for women had negative effects on males' affirmative action attitudes (Veilleux & Tougas, 1989). Likewise, Tougas and Veilleux (1988) demonstrated that women's reactions to affirmative action policies were mainly influenced by the intensity of identification with their group (i.e., women), collective relative deprivation experienced, and the procedures used to arrive at fair representation in the work force.

In summary, given the similarity between United States and Canadian cultures, one would not expect much difference in the results of research studies investigating attitudes toward affirmative action. For instance, the findings of United States-based studies generally suggest that females have more positive attitudes toward affirmative action than males (see Chapters 5 and 6; also see Goldsmith, Cordova, Dwyer, Langlois, & Crosby, 1989; Kravitz & Platania, 1993; Parker, Baltes, & Christiansen, 1997). Likewise, minorities generally have more positive attitudes toward affirmative action than Whites (see Chapter 5 and 6; also see Bell, Harrison, & McLaughlin, 1997; Fine, 1992; Kinder & Sanders, 1990; Kravitz & Platania, 1993; Parker et al., 1997).

As expected, the Canadian findings were consistent with these results. Both males and females supported measures to eliminate systematic barriers (i.e., support equal opportunity; Tougas, Dube, & Veilleux, 1987; Tougas, Joly, Beaton, & St.-Pierre, 1996; Tougas & Veilleux, 1988, 1989). However, programs that advocated preferential treatment were negatively evaluated (Tougas & Veilleux, 1989; Veilleux & Tougas, 1989), with the most negative evaluations being reported for quotas or hard preferential treatment programs (Fletcher & Chalmers, 1991). Stronger forms of affirmative action were opposed mainly because they are perceived to violate the merit principle. On the other hand, as was found in the United States-based studies, females had more positive attitudes toward sex-based affirmative action than males (Matheson, Echenberg, Taylor, Rivers & Chow, 1994; Summers, 1991, 1995; Tougas & Beaton, 1993).

The Netherlands

de Vries and Pettigrew (1994) presented a comparison of Dutch and United States attitudes to affirmative action. The Netherlands' program for minority employment is patterned after affirmative action in the United States and, as noted by de Vries and Pettigrew, a comparison of the Dutch and United States experience is instructive given the differences in intergroup relations between the two countries. Specifically, the two nations differ in their types of minorities, histories and sizes, and basic structural and policy frameworks.

For instance, the Dutch minority groups are Surinamese, Antillians/Arubans, Moroccans, and Turks (de Vries & Pettigrew, 1994). Verheul and Terpstra (1998) add people from Vietnam, former Yugoslavia, Somalia, Ethiopia, Iran, Iraq, and Indonesia to this list. What is telling from this list is that unlike African-Americans, with nearly four centuries in the United States, the vast majority of Dutch minorities immigrated during the last four decades. As noted by de Vries and Pettigrew (1994), differences in the recency of the arrival of their respective minorities contributes to the fact that in contrast to the United States, cultural differences are perceived as more critical than race by Dutch Whites (Pettigrew & Meertens, 1995).

Using the triple jeopardy framework of affirmative action, namely prejudice and discrimination, solo role status, and token role status, to study attitudes to affirmative action in the Dutch police, de Vries and Pettigrew (1994) found evidence for triple jeopardy in their data. However, their intensity and negativity were muted compared to United States police data. Similar conclusions were arrived at by de Vries (1997). Concerning differences between Dutch and United States attitudes, comparisons of the data led de Vries and Pettigrew (1994) to conclude that blatant racial bias was not as strong as the American research would suggest. The absence of this racial bias in The Netherlands appeared to contribute to an atmosphere which was more conducive to affirmative action efforts.

New Zealand

Singer (1996b) investigated the attitudes of European New Zealanders toward ethnicity-based employment selection. Her results indicated that European respondents, in general, opposed ethnicity-based selection (i.e., preferential treatment), a finding consistent with the United States-based studies demonstrating that people typically reject the idea of preferential treatment in employment selection (see Chapter 5). However, respondents having a greater scope of justice regarding the Maori (the key minority group on New Zealand) were significantly less opposed to ethnicity-based selection. Finally, respondents who had more favorable attitudes toward the Maori and also included them in their justice concerns, were not only less opposed to ethnicity-based selection, but were also less supportive of merit-based selection.

The effect of sex-based affirmative action on attitudes was similar to that observed for United States samples (Singer, 1990, 1992, 1993). Sex-based preferential treatment was perceived as unfair, with the level of perceived fairness being a negative function of the size of the male-female merit discrepancy. Females also saw preferential selection as more fair than did males.

New Zealanders also favored merit over preferential selection based upon sex (Singer, 1996a). However, the level of support for merit versus preferential selection was affected by a frame manipulation (i.e., support for preferential treatment increased when a pro-preferential treatment or pro-diversity message was presented).

CHAPTER SUMMARY

Affirmative action and equal opportunity share the common goal of trying to eliminate discrimination on the basis of specified demographic factors. However, anti-discrimination laws and their enforcement differ widely across countries. The social, political, and legal saliency and status of these demographic factors play an essential role in determining the importance, relevancy, and need for affirmative action in a given country. So, for instance, the primary affirmative action-related "demographic" variable in India is caste, religion in Northern Ireland, culture in The Netherlands, sex in Canada and Europe, and race in South Africa.

A comprehensive search of the literature resulted in the identification of a relatively small number of non-United States or international papers on attitudes to affirmative action, with the majority of the identified articles being Canadian; the other two countries were The Netherlands and New Zealand. One conclusion we can draw from this is that the saliency of affirmative action and equal opportunity issues is probably much higher in the United States than it is in other countries. In general, the results of these studies were not much different from those obtained in United States-based studies with attitudes reported in the Dutch studies being relatively more favorable.

REFERENCES

Becker, H. M., & Kempen, G. W. (1982). Vraag naar migranten op de arbeidsmarkt: Een proefonderzoek naar de faktoren die de vraag naar migranten op de arbeidsmarkt bepalen [Demand for migrants on the labor market: A pilot study of the factors determining the demand for migrants on the labor market]. Totterdam, The Netherlands: Erasmus.

Bell, M. P., Harrison, D. A., & McLaughlin, M. E. (1997). Asian American attitudes toward affirmative action in employment. Journal of Applied Behavioral Science, 33, 356-377.

Bobocel, D. R., Son Hing, L. S., Davey, L. M., Stanley, D. J., & Zanna, M. P. (1998). Justice-based opposition to social policies: Is it genuine? Journal of Personality and Social Psychology, 75, 653-669.

Bovenkerk, F. (Ed.). (1978). Omdat zij anders zijn: Patronen van discriminatie in Nederland. [Because they are different: Patterns of discrimination in The Netherlands]. Meppel, The Netherlands: Boom.

Brasse, P., & Sikking, E. (1986). Positie en kansen van etnische minderheden in nederlandse ondernemingen [The position and chances of ethnic minorities in Dutch companies]. Den Haag, The Netherlands: Ministry of Social Affairs and Employment.

de Vries, S. (1997). Ethnic diversity in organizations: A Dutch experience. In S. A. Sackmann (Ed.), Cultural complexity in organizations: Inherent contrasts and contradictions (pp. 297-314). Thousand Oaks, CA: Sage.

de Vries, S., & Pettigrew, T. F. (1994). A comparative perspective on affirmative action: Positieve Aktie in The Netherlands. Basic and Applied Social Science, 14, 179-199.

Den Uyl, R., Choenni, C. E. S., & Bovenkerk, F. (1986). "Mag het ook an buitenlander wezen?": Discriminate bij uitzendburo's [Is a foreigner allowed? Discrimination by temporary employment agencies]. Utrecht, The Netherlands: National Bureau Against Racism.

Donfried, K. (1998). Northern Ireland: Fair employment and the MacBride Principles. Locating fulling reference. In S. N. Colamery (Ed.), Affirmative Action: Catalyst or Albatross (pp. 135-145). Commack, NY: Nova.

Fine, T. S. (1992). The impact of issue framing on public opinion: Toward affirmative action programs. The Social Science Journal, 29, 323-334.

Fletcher, J. F., & Chalmers, M. C. (1991). Attitudes of Canadians toward affirmative action: Opposition, value pluralism, and nonattitudes. Political Behavior, 13, 67-95.

Goldsmith, N., Cordova, D., Dwyer, K., Langlois, B., & Crosby, F. J. (1989). Reactions to affirmative action: A case study. In F. A. Blanchard & F. J. Crosby (Eds.), Affirmative action in perspective, (pp. 139-146). New York: Springer-Verlag.

Hooghienstra, E. (1991). Gelijke kansen voor allochtonen op een baan? Wervings- en selectieprocessen op de arbeidsmarkt voor on- en laaggeschoolden [Equal chances for minorities on a job? Recruitment and selection procedures on the labor market for the un- and low educated]. Migrantenstudies, 7, 15-23.

Human, L. (1990). Empowerment through development: The role of affirmative action and management development in the demise of apartheid. Management Education and Development, 21, 272-286.

Human, L. (1993). The development of black and female managers in South Africa: Why many affirmative action programmes fail. Management Education and Development, 24, 153-166.

Hutchings, K. (1998). Good corporate citizens or perpetrators of social stratification? International business in Malaysia. In M. A. Rahim, & R. T. Golembiewski (Eds.), Current Topics in Management, 3, (pp. 345-364). Stamford, CT: JAI Press.

Jonah, B. (1995, March 27). Quotas that are case in stone: India's backlash against affirmative action. United States News and World Report, pp. 38-41.

Kinder, D. R., & Sanders, L. M. (1990). Mimicking political debate with survey questions: The case of white opinion on affirmative action for blacks. Social Cognition, 8, 73-103.

Kravitz, D. A., & Platania, J. (1993). Attitudes and beliefs about affirmative action: Effects on target and of respondent sex and ethnicity. Journal of Applied Psychology, 78, 928-938.

Lawler, J. J., & Bae, J. (1998). Overt employment discrimination by multinational firms: Cultural and economic influences in a developing country. Industrial Relations, 37, 126-152.

Leck, J. D., Saunders, D. M., & Charbonneau, M. (1996). Affirmative action programs: An organizational justice perspective. Journal of Organizational Behavior, 17, 79-89.

Maio, G. R., & Esses, V. M. (1998). The social consequence of affirmative action: Deleterious effects on perceptions of groups. Personality and Social Psychology Bulletin, 24, 65-74.

Mallet, V. (1998, Sept. 11). South Africa's "affirmative action" law meets negative responses. The Financial Times, p. 4.

Matheson, K., Echenberg, A., Taylor, D. M., Rivers, D., & Chow, I. (1994). Women's attitudes toward affirmative action: Putting actions in context. Journal of Applied Social Psychology, 24, 2075-2096.

Parker, C. P., Baltes, B. B., & Christiansen, N. D. (1997). Support for affirmative action, justice perceptions, and work attitudes: A study of gender and racial-ethnic group differences. Journal of Applied Psychology, 82, 376-389.

Pearn, M. (1993). Fairness in selection and assessment: An European perspective. In H. Schuler, & J. L. Farr (Eds.), Personnel selection and assessment: Individual and organizational perspectives (pp. 205-219). Hillsdale, NJ: LEA.

Pettigrew, T. F., & Meertens, R. W. (1995). Subtle and blatant prejudice in Western Europe. European Journal of Social Psychology, 25, 57-75.

Pincus, L. B., & Belohlav, J. A. (1996). Legal issues in multinational business strategy: To play the game, you have to know the rules. Academy of Management Executive, 10, 52-61.

Reddy, P. S., & Choudree, R. B. G. (1996). Public service transformation and affirmative action in South Africa. Public Personnel Management, 25, 25-39.

Reubsaet, T. J. M., & Kropman, J. A. (1985). Beeldvorming over etnische groepen bij de werving en selectie van personeel [The development of ethnic group images in the recruitment and selection of employees]. Nijmegen, The Netherlands: University of Nijmegen, Institute for Applied Sociology.

Riley, N. E. (1996). Holding up half the economy. The China Business Review, 23, 22-25.

Scheibal, W. (1995, Sept. - Oct.). When cultures clash: Applying Title VII abroad. Business Horizons, pp. 4-8.

Singer, M. (1996a). 'Merit', 'preferential' or 'diversity-based selection': Effect of information frame and informant gender on the public's views on preferential treatment in selection. International Journal of Selection and Assessment, 4, 1-11.

Singer, M. (1996). 'Merit', 'preferential' or 'diversity-based selection': Effect of information frame and informant gender on the public's views on preferential treatment in selection. International Journal of Selection and Assessment, 4, 1-11.

Singer, M. S. (1990). Individual differences in category width and fairness perception of selection decisions. Social Behavior and Personality, 18, 87-94.

Singer, M. S. (1992). The application of relative deprivation theory to justice perception of preferential selection. Current Psychology: Research & Reviews, 11, 128-144.

Singer, M. S. (1993). Gender-based preferential selection: Perceptions of injustice and empathy of deprivation. International Journal of Selection and Assessment, 1, 184-202.

Singer, M. S. (1996b). Effects of scope of justice, informant ethnicity, and information frame on attitudes towards ethnicity-based selection. International Journal of Psychology, 31, 191-205.

Summers, R. J. (1991). The influence of affirmative action on perceptions of a beneficiary's qualifications. Journal of Applied Social Psychology, 21, 1265-1276.

Summers, R. J. (1995). Attitudes toward different methods of affirmative action. Journal of Applied Social Psychology, 25, 1090-1104.

Tougas, F., & Beaton, A. M. (1993). Affirmative action in the work place: For better or for worse. Applied Psychology: An International Review, 42, 253-264.

Tougas, F., Beaton, A. M., & Veilleux, F. (1991). Why women approve of affirmative action: The study of a predictive model. International Journal of Psychology, 26, 761-776.

Tougas, F., Brown, R., Beaton, A. M., & Joly, S. (1995). Neosexism: Plus ca change, plus c'est pareil. Personality and Social Psychology Bulletin, 8, 842-849.

Tougas, F., Crosby, F., Joly, S., & Pelchat, D. (1995). Men's attitudes toward affirmative action: Justice and intergroup relations at the crossroads. Social Justice Research, 8, 57-71.

Tougas, F., Dube, L., & Veilleux, F. (1987). Privation relative et programmes d'action positive. Revue Canadienne des Sciences du Comportement, 19, 167-177.

Tougas, F., Joly, S., Beaton, A. M., & St.-Pierre, L. (1996). Reactions of beneficiaries to preferential treatment: A reality check. Human Relations, 49, 453-464.

Tougas, F., & Veilleux, F. (1988). The influence of identification, collective relative deprivation, and procedure of implementation of women's response to affirmative action: A causal modeling approach. Canadian Journal of Behavioral Science, 20, 15-28.

Tougas, F., & Veilleux, F. (1989). Who likes affirmative action: Attitudinal processes among men and women. In F. A. Blanchard & F. J. Crosby (Eds.), Affirmative action in perspective (pp. 111-124). New York: Springer-Verlag.

Veenman, J., & Vijverberg, C. H. T. (1982). De arbeidsmarkt-problematiek van Molukkers: Een verkennend onderzoek [The labor market problems of Moluccans: An exploratory study]. Rotterdam, The Netherlands: Erasmus University.

Veilleux, F., & Tougas, F. (1989). Male acceptance of affirmative action programs for women: The results of altruistic or egotistical motives. International Journal of Psychology, 24, 485-496.

Verheul, R. M., & Terpstra, J. J. (1998). Affirmative action in The Netherlands: Is it effective? In Kravitz, D. A.(Chair), Affirmative action: Expanding our horizons. Symposium presented at the 13th Annual Conference of the Society for Industrial and Organizational Psychology, Dallas, TX.

Chapter 11

IMPLICATIONS FOR IMPLEMENTATION

In many respects, the debate over affirmative action remains stuck in the first stage of affirmative action. In this first stage, the dominant concern is with relatively simple approaches to affirmative action which are concerned primarily with meeting numerical goals associated with affirmative action. As a result, the debate centers around issues such as the relative merits of hard versus soft preferential treatment.

Many organizations also find themselves still stuck in the first generation of affirmative action efforts (Morrison & Von Glinow, 1990). As such, organizational decision makers view themselves as forced by legislative and legal pressures into superficial and crisis-oriented actions designed to increase the numbers of Blacks and females (Morrison & Von Glinow, 1990). There is, however, some hope, in that there are organizations and individuals who have taken affirmative action beyond the first stage and are engaged in a serious debate over diversity issues and over the ethical and fair treatment of all employees and/or students.

Given the artificial nature of much of the research on fairness and affirmative action, one might question the relevance of the research to applied settings. This chapter attempts to answer the call for real-world application by developing suggestions for implementations based on the psychological research literature. In the first part of the chapter, we summarize the research on the organizational consequences, in particular the effects on organizational attractiveness, of using affirmative action procedures. In the second part of this chapter, we rely upon the research literature reviewed in the previous chapters in order to make suggestions for understanding resistence to affirmative action. In the third part of this chapter, we draw heavily on the research on justice, especially procedural and interactional justice, in order to provide a framework from which suggestions can be made for enhancing the implementation of affirmative action. In the fourth part of the chapter, we outline principles derived by others for achieving success in the implementation of affirmative action procedures in the private sector, public sector and in education.

RESEARCH ON IMPLICATIONS FOR ORGANIZATIONS

Does the presence of an affirmative action program make an organization or an educational institution more attractive to minority and female applicants? Does the presence of an affirmative action program make an organization or educational institution less attractive to White male applicants? Do employees prefer to work in an organization which has affirmative action in place and rewards managers for meeting affirmative action goals? Although fairly extensive bodies of research exist on the effects of affirmative action policies on an individual respondent's attitudes and fairness judgments (see Chapters 5 - 7), and on attitudes toward the intended beneficiary (see Chapter 8), somewhat surprisingly, much less research attention has been focused on the question of the effects of affirmative action policies on attitudes toward the organization.

On the surface, it would appear logical to assume that an organization's affirmative action policy would affect its recruiting and help to shape its image. According to signaling theory (Rynes & Miller, 1983), experiences during the initial stages of recruitment and selection are taken as representative of the norms of the organization. Thus, we would expect that the presence or absence of an affirmative action policy would have an impact on organizational attraction. After all, one of the main purposes of affirmative action is to encourage the entry and career development of women and minorities.

Unfortunately, the research on the question of effects on attraction is equivocal and may well depend upon the exact wording of the research question. Many different topics have been examined by researchers in this area, including the impact of affirmative action on beneficiaries' attraction to the organization, perceptions of organizational fairness, and satisfaction with the organization.

The first set of studies documents the way affirmative action influences applicants' attraction to organizations. Organizational decision makers may assume that stronger affirmative action policies attract members of underrepresented groups, and women and minorities have been found to respond more strongly to an advertisement when it includes an equal opportunity statement encouraging women and minorities to apply (Barber & Roehling, 1993; Williams & Bauer, 1994). In a study with Black engineers, Highhouse and associates (Highhouse, Stierwalt, Bachiochi, Elder, & Fisher, 1999) manipulated the staffing policy (i.e., identity-blind versus identity-conscious) of an organization through a job advertisement. In the identity-conscious condition, the organization was described as an aggressive, affirmative action employer. In the identity-blind condition, the organization was described as an equal opportunity employer. Respondents were more likely to apply when the staffing policy was one which considered group status. They were also more likely to see the organization as having a positive attitude toward minorities.

Affirmative action does not always result in negative reactions from beneficiaries. In a study with minority students, those students who were told that there was an affirmative action policy in place which was designed to encourage the recruitment and retention of underrepresented students on campus tended to believe that their admission into college was based on ability rather than race or ethnicity (Ponterotto, Martinez & Hayden, 1986). In a field study conducted with female carpenter apprentices (Latack, Josephs, Roach, & Levine, 1987), perceptions of organizational support for affirmative action policies were positively related to job satisfaction and support for the organization. Williams and Bauer (1994) found that a statement which suggested that the organization was interested in ensuring that women had equal access to employment opportunities and employment had the effect of increasing the attractiveness of the organizational. Thus, weaker forms of affirmative action, which emphasize retention and recruitment, may have a more positive effect on the attraction and satisfaction of minorities and women than stronger forms such as soft and hard preferential treatment.

The available research suggests that it is not always the case that the presence of an affirmative action policy will prove attractive to minorities and women. In one study (Heilman & Herlihy, 1984), male and female college students were asked to review a description of a managerial job in which the proportion of women holding the job was varied. In the low representation condition, the proportion of women in the job was identified as 8%. In the high representation condition, the proportion of women in the job was identified as 28%. In addition, subjects were either told that the women currently in the organization had attained the position because of preferential treatment, merit, or were given no information regarding how the women had been selected. Only in the merit condition was there an increase in interest in the position as a function of greater female representation (Heilman & Herlihy, 1984).

Nacoste (1987) also found a negative relationship between the use of affirmative action and organizational attraction. In his study, selection on the basis of sex, as opposed to merit, led to lower ratings of the fairness of the policy and the perceived fairness of the organization. Fairness was then related to attraction such that as the perceptions of organizational fairness decreased there was a corresponding decrease in the degree of attraction to the organization. Thus, the relative emphasis on sex versus merit in selection was associated with differing views of organizational fairness, which in turn had an impact on organizational attraction.

As part of a laboratory study on reactions to soft and hard preferential treatment, Taylor-Carter, Doverspike, and Alexander (1995) found that when the affirmative action policies were perceived to be fair and unlikely to result in harm, female respondents were more likely to describe themselves as likely to apply for a position with an organization. However, females were less willing to indicate that they would apply to a firm if they felt the affirmative action policy was unfair, regardless of the likelihood of harm. Thus, both self-interest and perceptions of justice/fairness may mediate the effect of the type of affirmative action policy on the person's degree of attraction to the organization.

In a survey study conducted with 55 female managers, Chacko (1982) examined the effects of preferential treatment. For the females in his sample, there was a significant negative relationship between overall job satisfaction and the belief that sex had been a factor in selection. Compared to females who felt that they had been hired on the basis of merit, those who viewed their hiring as a function of their sex experienced lower organizational commitment, lower overall satisfaction, and lower job satisfaction. Due to the correlational nature of the study, it was not possible to establish cause and effect. It may be that the women who were hired because of their sex really did have more negative experiences, given that research suggests that females in non-traditional fields may experience adverse working conditions and may not be treated as favorably as male coworkers (Ott, 1989; Palmer & Lee, 1990; Mansfield et al., 1991).

However, based on other research, the connection between affirmative action policies and general satisfaction is less than clear. It seems likely that the amount of variance in job or organizational satisfaction explained by affirmative action is quite small (Konrad & Linnehan 1995; Kravitz et al., 1997; Witt, 1990). Based on a survey study conducted with federal employees, Parker, Batles, and Christiansen (1997) found that White males did not associate support for affirmative action by their employer with a loss in career development opportunities, organizational justice, or negative work attitudes. For women and minorities, perceptions of organizational justice and increased career opportunities were correlated with the perception of organizational support for affirmative action.

Of course, the presence of affirmative action policies may result in negative feelings toward the organization on the part of White males, especially those who have been denied educational or employment opportunities. A real-world illustration of the potential impact of affirmative action policies on White applicants is provided by a study of 3,290 police officer applicants (Schmitt & Ryan, 1997). The presence of minority preferences was listed as the second most common reason for withdrawal from the process, with some applicants indicating that Whites had been discouraged from applying for the police officer positions. Based on procedural justice theory, equity theory, and the research previously reviewed (see Chapter 5), we would expect that resentment, hostility and resistance would be greatest under strong preferential treatment policies (Veilleux & Tougas, 1989).

LESSONS FROM THE LITERATURE - REDUCING RESISTANCE

One way to confront resistance to affirmative action is by trying to make attitudes toward the policies and toward the beneficiary groups more favorable. A second approach is to take into account the powerful effect of contextual variables in determining responses to the policies. An intervention which takes into account the full range of psychological variables influencing attitudes toward affirmative action would include consideration of both the perspective of the respondent and contextual variables, including characteristics of the message and the sender, as well as mediating variables.

A consistent finding in the research literature is that the weaker forms of affirmative action receive more support than the stronger forms of affirmative action. The greater the emphasis on protected group status as compared to merit, the more negative the reactions. Different specific policies evoke different levels of resistance. Stronger forms of affirmative action are intended to enhance the employment opportunities of females, Blacks, and other underrepresented groups. However, these policies may produce resistance when they are introduced in organizations. Before the underlying goal of equal opportunity can be achieved, more attention must be paid to dealing with resistance to the policies and the way in which these policies are implemented and communicated to organizational members.

Organizations should emphasize the merit and competency of those beneficiaries brought in under affirmative action programs (Clayton & Crosby, 1992; Loury, 1989; Turner & Pratkanis, 1993). An emphasis on the competence and merit of beneficiaries will help to decrease resistance from those whose opposition stems from negative beliefs about the competency of females and Blacks (Kravitz & Platania, 1993; Taylor-Carter, Doverspike & Alexander, 1995; Taylor-Carter, Doverspike, & Cook, 1995, 1996). The effect of negative stereotypes may be decreased by providing information on the abilities and performance of individual Black or female beneficiaries which demonstrates their competence (Heilman, 1984). By providing challenging assignments to beneficiaries, accompanied by the appropriate levels of organizational support, organizations allow the beneficiary an opportunity to demonstrate their competence, both to themselves and to others. Organizational decision makers should also ensure that those who implement policies understand the importance of beneficiary merit when they take actions to meet affirmative action goals. This may involve informally educating policy implementers about the nature of the particular policy. Given Kravitz and Platania's (1993) research, resistance to policies may stem from a belief that any minority must be selected, regardless of qualifications. Educating management in employment settings, or administrators and faculty in academic settings, may lead to a decrease in negative reactions.

Supervisor and organizational support for affirmative action policies are critical. A clear statement should be sent to all members of the organization that discrimination is not acceptable (Larwood, Szwajkowski & Rose, 1988) and that progress toward affirmative action goals will be rewarded. Selection decisions should be monitored in order to track progress toward affirmative action goals (Anderson & Wilson, 1985; Hyer, 1985). Affirmative action officers should be given the power and authority necessary to effectively implement policies and procedures (Kahn & Robbins, 1985).

What suggestions for decreasing resistance can we draw from the research on mediator variables? In order to be accepted, affirmative action procedures must be perceived as just and fair. The organization can influence fairness perceptions through the content of the communications it uses to frame its affirmative action message and by allowing organizational members a chance to voice their opinions regarding policies.

Self-interest may be the most powerful factor affecting reactions to affirmative action procedures. If individuals can be shown that a diverse workforce is in their best interest, this should increase acceptance of affirmative action. Furthermore affirmative action should be designed and implemented so as to reward organizational members for achieving diversity goals and so as to minimize the costs for both potential beneficiaries and nonbeneficiaries.

In order to establish acceptance of affirmative action, there must be a perceived need for such policies. Organizational members must see that there is a need to increase the representation of the targeted groups and must also attribute any differences in current opportunities to external rather than internal factors (Crosby & Clayton, 1990). One method of establishing the need for affirmative action policies would be to present data on past inequities, although this can sometimes be a dangerous procedure in that some organizational members may take it as a signal that the organization is admitting to past discrimination. Thus, while organizations should clarify the reasons for embarking on a policy of affirmative action, this should be part of a wider effort to educate organizational members concerning the benefits of a diverse workforce and must be handled with appropriate care especially when dealing with potentially harmful, confidential data.

ENHANCING IMPLEMENTATION -
THEORY AND POSSIBLE SOLUTIONS

The presence of soft and hard preferential treatment will result in both costs and benefits for the organization. If an organization wishes to engage in affirmative action efforts, the problem, then, becomes one of how to maximize the benefits and reduce the costs. Any remedies will have to be targeted at the individual beneficiary or nonbeneficiary and also at the level of the organization as a whole. In the following segment, based on the literature presented previously, we present what we feel are potential solutions, or areas to look toward for potential solutions (Taylor-Carter et al., 1996).

Avoid the Use of Unfair Procedures

If we closely examine the selection process, it becomes clear that organizational policies have an impact at even the initial stages of selection. These policies color the impressions applicants form of the organization. The use of selection procedures which are viewed as unfair may decrease applicants' perceptions of the fairness of both the organization and organizational decision makers (Thorton, 1993). Research by Nacoste (1985, 1987) has shown that the use of strong affirmative action procedures can have an unfavorable impact on beliefs about the organization. When using affirmative action, the organization is viewed as unfair when there is no clear need for equalizing minority representation in the firm. In turn, these negative impressions may decrease the percentage of applicants who apply and accept positions (Gilliland, 1993). The net effect of the use of unfair procedures is restriction of the applicant pool (Arvey & Sackett, 1993). Clearly, this has a direct and negative effect on the utility of selection systems and can cause public relations problems.

A second outcome of the use of unfair procedures involves individuals already in the organization. Unfair procedures may lead to negative emotional reactions including decreased organizational commitment, hostility, lack of trust, lowered satisfaction, and associated feelings of inequity (Arvey & Sackett, 1993; Gilliland, 1993; Sweeney & McFarlin, 1993; Thorton, 1993). Research shows that these affective reactions have significant consequences for the organization. Behavioral outcomes of these emotions include a broad range of counterproductive behaviors probably intended as a means to restore equity. These behaviors range from lowered task performance to an increase in hostile behaviors. Turnover intentions also increase among those who are dissatisfied with organizational policies. Finally, these feelings are also linked to an increase in discrimination charges and complaints. The presence of counterproductive behaviors has been reported by a number of researchers in procedural justice across a range of settings (Arvey & Sackett, 1993; Gilliland, 1993; Greenberg, 1990; Rutte & Messick, 1995; Tyler & Bies, 1990).

Apparently, there is great truth in the statement made by Rutte and Messick (1995) in their analysis of the end effects of unfair procedures: "Unfairness empowers." In summary, organizational decision-makers would be wise to attend to the available information in the justice literature and avoid implementing procedures which will be perceived as unfair.

Emphasize Procedural Justice

Given this evidence on the importance of fairness perceptions, how can organizations enhance procedural justice perceptions? A first step in this process is isolating the parts of the policy which carry the greatest "weight" in fairness judgments. A recurrent finding is that people weigh the procedural aspect of justice more heavily than the actual outcome (Greenberg, 1990; Folger and Greenberg, 1985). In other words, the actual content of a policy may be more influential than the outcome of using the policy. This is not meant to suggest that outcomes are irrelevant. It may be the case that outcome justice moderates procedural justice; overall perceptions of fairness of a procedure are greater when outcomes are fair (Gilliland, 1993). However, procedural justice carries weight in fairness perceptions even when the outcome is perceived as fair.

This is particularly relevant in the area of affirmative action. A wealth of research reveals that many forms of affirmative action such as hard and soft preferential treatment are viewed as unfair in terms of their outcomes, with ratings of fairness decreasing as the emphasis of the policy on nonmerit factors increases (Arthur, Doverspike & Fuentes, 1992; Heilman, McCullough & Gilbert, 1996; Nacoste & Lehman, 1987). When an organization is in a position where affirmative action policies must be implemented, it is safe to assume that either the outcomes, more opportunities for minorities or women, or the process, the reduced weight on merit, will be viewed as unfair by a significant proportion of White males.

As noted in the chapter on theories of justice and affirmative action (see Chapter 2), theories of distributive justice do not lead as easily to recommendations for applied settings as do the theories of procedural and interactional justice. Attempts to enhance fairness perceptions of affirmative action may be more successful when elements of procedural and interactional justice are closely examined. Therefore, we have chosen to focus on aspects of procedures and interactions which may increase acceptance of the policies.

This is not meant as a tutorial on how to manipulate fairness judgments. Rather, we simply wish to suggest ways to achieve the real goal of affirmative action, increased acceptance and representation of minorities and women. Several factors which impact fairness are, to some extent, under the control of the organization. The way in which a policy is presented or framed has a significant impact on fairness perceptions. A number of different factors in the implementation process influence perceptions of fairness, as suggested by the literature on procedural and interactional justice. These theories allow us to make specific recommendations for one who is implementing affirmative action. Important factors in the implementation process include the motivation of the people influenced by the policy to scrutinize it, the actual content of the message, the characteristics of the person who implements affirmative action, and the extent to which people are allowed to express their opinion of the message.

Be Aware of the Motivation to Scrutinize

The motivation of those influenced by a policy to scrutinize it is an important consideration for policy makers. Work on persuasion and social justice suggests that people may be motivated to carefully analyze policies under certain circumstances. When policies influence outcomes which are important to people, this increases the probability that the policy will be scrutinized (Thorton, 1993). Furthermore, the work in referent cognitions theory suggests that people will be most resentful of affirmative action, and more motivated to carefully consider the policies, in situations where they think the outcome would have been more positive had a fairer procedure been used (Greenberg, 1990).

It seems safe to assume that nonbeneficiaries will be highly motivated to examine affirmative action procedures and will evaluate and discuss among themselves affirmative action policies. This may be most likely to occur when an outcome is visible to organizational members (e.g., such as a promotion for a desirable position awarded to a minority or the existence of minority scholarships at a university) and when this outcome is viewed as unfair. When outcomes are valued and are viewed as unfair by organizational members, this may trigger an analysis of procedures. Thus, people may not scrutinize procedures unless an outcome perceived to be unfair motivates them to do so.

It is worth noting that employees may not always be interested in or even aware of the outcomes of affirmative action. This may explain why much of the research which reports the strongest negative impact of the policies takes place in laboratory settings, where the policy and the beneficiary are particularly salient. In organizational settings, where information on affirmative action is embedded in a much more complex background of competing information, the policies may not be scrutinized as closely.

When involvement is high, the manner in which affirmative action is implemented is particularly important. Under these conditions, those who believe they may be negatively influenced by the policy are more likely to reject weak or specious rationales for policy implementation (Taylor-Carter, Doverspike, & Cook, 1995). Assuming that people in the firm are interested in analyzing affirmative action leads us to consider specific aspects of the way in which affirmative action is framed, or presented to organizational members.

Frame the Content of Policies

A major consideration in framing the message involves the description of the content of the policy as presented in communications to organizational members. As noted, it seems quite likely that stronger forms of affirmative action will violate many standards of fair procedures. For instance, research would suggest that affirmative action violates a number of rules or distribution or procedures including consistency. Consistency refers to using the same standards for evaluating all people. The most common acceptable standard for evaluating those for employment opportunities is merit. As noted previously, affirmative action policies which emphasize other aspects such as race and gender will be viewed as unfair (Kravitz, 1995; Kravitz et al., 1997; Kravitz & Platania, 1993).

One way of overcoming the role of consistency violations is to emphasize the organizational level justification for affirmative action

(Nacoste & Lehman, 1987). This may be most persuasive when organizational level needs for affirmative action are explained. Explaining legal aspects of affirmative action and potential benefits of affirmative action may be helpful in decreasing resistance, especially when one frames affirmative action as a means to decrease discriminatory barriers and restore equity to minority members in the firm (Kossek & Zonia, 1996; Pratkanis & Turner, 1996; Tyler & Bies, 1990). For instance, providing a justification for sex-based promotion decisions can enhance fairness perceptions of the policy (Bobocel & Farrell, 1996). While White males' support of affirmative action may not be as high as that of females and minorities, it is not the case that these policies are inevitably viewed as unfair (Parker et al., 1997). Examining factors which influence fairness perceptions of majority group members can help the policy succeed in organizations.

Emphasizing the benefits of the policy rather than focusing on its potentially negative impact on majority group members may aid acceptance of affirmative action. It is probably the case that seeking acceptance for affirmative action through an appeal based on minority group needs alone will not successfully eradicate resistance especially when distributive justice rules have been violated (Gilliland, 1993). Again, affirmative action explicitly violates most merit-based rules of equity or equality, so need may not be a central consideration for those evaluating the policy. Furthermore, new and more subtle forms of discrimination against one beneficiary group, Blacks, stems from majority member beliefs that Blacks no longer need forms of economic or government-based assistance such as affirmative action (Sears, 1988). Those with this belief system are unlikely to be persuaded to accept affirmative action through need-based arguments. However, the simple process of explaining why affirmative action is implemented may be important. Justifying a decision, even to those who disagree with the nature of the decision, may enhance fairness perceptions of the policy (Bies & Shapiro, 1988; Folger & Martin, 1986).

In order to give a specific example of how to present affirmative action, one could emphasize that it is a temporary means of remedying past inequities in the firm. In addition, one should insure that the merit of beneficiaries is emphasized, since majority group members may have negative attitudes about the qualifications of women and racial or ethnic minorities and somewhat less positive attitudes toward efforts to increase diversity (Konrad & Linnehan, 1995; Kossek & Zonia, 1993). Providing a justification for affirmative action is critical, since explanations are especially important when they involve reallocating resources, when outcomes are valued, and the reasons behind the decision are not clear (Rutte & Messick, 1995).

This does not mean that the negative aspects of affirmative action should be ignored. Extreme arguments or one-sided positive arguments about the benefits of the policies should be avoided. These are more likely to anger those who initially oppose affirmative action, and may actually encourage them to generate arguments against the policies (Taylor-Carter, Doverspike, & Alexander, 1995). The implementer should anticipate negative arguments revolving around qualifications of beneficiaries and concerns about lost employment opportunities of majority group members. Again, simply manipulating the way affirmative action is presented is unlikely to eradicate feelings of injustice, but is one of the factors which should be considered in implementing policies.

Define the Role of the Policy Implementer

Very little research exists on the effect of the sender of the message. Nevertheless, common sense and the general social psychology literature tell us that the person who implements any controversial policy should have good conflict management and interpersonal skills, and should be trusted by participants. Those individuals who violate these characteristics are more likely to behave in a way which triggers perceptions of unfairness (Tyler & Bies, 1990). Similarly, the implementer should not "bully" those in the organization to accept the policy, since this increases resistance (Greenberg, 1990).

Sincere support of the policies by policy implementers and top decision makers is one of the strongest, most consistent predictors of attempts to increase organizational diversity (Hitt & Keats, 1984; Morrison & Von Glinow, 1990; Rynes & Rosen, 1995). The support of affirmative action by decision makers should not stop at the level of impression management; people in the firm will be motivated to see if the verbal support is backed by actions (Pettigrew & Martin, 1987). For example, the success of diversity training is dependent on making diversity a priority in a firm, as well as on the expression of positive attitudes toward diversity by policy makers and implementers (Rynes & Rosen, 1995). Some companies have gone so far as to make the success of diversity programs a dimension in the performance appraisal of implementers. However, this may lead others to question the reason why minority members are promoted or accepted in the organization (Pettigrew & Martin, 1987).

Allowing Voice in the Implementation of Affirmative action

The effects of voice are so persuasive that they can enhance fairness perceptions even when the outcome is negative and the speaker cannot change the outcome (Bies & Shapiro, 1988; Greenberg, 1990). Allowing organizational members to voice their opinions communicates a message of trust and respect (Folger & Greenberg, 1985) and accomplishes a number of other important goals. It satisfies the speaker's need to be heard (Greenberg, 1990), implies a consideration of the views of organizational members (Tyler & Bies, 1990), and allows people to feel a sense of participation in and control over the process.

BLUEPRINTS FOR SUCCESS

Evaluations of affirmative action interventions are rarely conducted in the field. Nevertheless, there are success stories out there from which valuable lessons can be learned and from which conclusions regarding effective implementation can be drawn. In discussing various "Blueprints for Success," we will offer suggestions culled from literature on the private sector, the public sector, and affirmative action in education.

Enhancing diversity: Morrison's (1992) five-step model

The choice of an appropriate affirmative action and diversity management program may depend, in part, on the climate of a particular organization (Ellis & Sonnenfield, 1994; Morrison, 1992). After examining the diversity management practices of 16 progressive U.S. companies, Morrison (1992) cautioned against assuming that a program which worked in one organizational environment will readily transfer into another. Morrison identified more than 52 types of diversity practices in her survey of U.S. firms. The various strategies can be described as fitting into one of the following categories: Multicultural workshops; multicultural core discussion groups; female and minority support groups, networks, and advisory panels; managerial reward systems for managing diversity; fast track programs and targeted training for minorities; mentoring programs and finally, organizational communications designed to enhance diversity (Ellis & Sonnenfeld, 1994). Based on Morrison's (1992) survey, she created a series of steps or recommendations for creating and enhancing diversity which are generalizable across a number of organizational settings. Morrison's suggestions would appear to be especially appropriate for diversity or affirmative action interventions in the private sector.

First, Morrison (1992) suggested that there is a need to discover and rediscover the problems present in the organization. This might include gathering data on turnover, promotions, and grievances from company records. Individual interviews may also be used during this initial phase of information-gathering. At this stage, majority and minority group members should be included in the process.

The second phase in creating diversity is strengthening top management commitment. This factor has been empirically related to the success of affirmative action programs (Marino, 1980) and to the success of diversity training programs (Rynes & Rosen, 1995). Commitment may be shown in different ways, but can be expressed by incorporating affirmative action efforts into performance appraisals of managers or making it clear to employees that attendance at diversity seminars is mandatory. Forcing managerial compliance is somewhat controversial, however, in that some psychologists believe that it may result in a backlash from those who are coerced into attendance (Ellis & Sonnenfield, 1994). Again, the appropriateness of this step may depend on the organizational climate. Furthermore, while top management commitment is important, it is the supervisor who often has the greatest impact on the attitudes of their subordinates (Gard, 1996).

Third, Morrison (1992) suggested that the organization should select diversity practices which are the most appropriate for the given organizational setting. The range of practices to be considered might include educational efforts such as diversity training workshops or providing mentors for minorities. In addition, accountability for the success of affirmative action steps should be shared by organizational decision-makers, and that this should be an integral part of selecting a diversity practice. As noted earlier, there are pros and cons in tying managers' performance evaluations to meeting affirmative action goals, so the decision to do so may again rest on the climate of a given firm. Again, making managers accountable for the success of the program increases the probability that the affirmative action or diversity goals will be met (Marino, 1980; Rynes & Rosen, 1995). Finally, exposing managers and employees to successful minorities is an important part of this third stage of diversity management.

Once the diversity management strategy has been chosen, an important fourth step is in demanding results and setting clear diversity goals. Organizational decision makers should gather data on the satisfaction of minorities in the firm as well as monitor their representation in different levels of the firm. This form of data-driven evaluation is a desirable way to measure the success of affirmative action and diversity efforts, yet is absent from many programs (Ellis & Sonnenfield, 1994).

Incorporating diversity goals into existing organizational practices is the fifth step in Morrison's (1992) model. This means that the diversity efforts should be organization wide and integrated with existing personnel practices.

In one of the rare field studies on diversity, Ellis and Sonnenfeld (1994) closely examined the diversity management strategies of three Fortune 500 Companies. These firms incorporated very different diversity management strategies. This is what one would expect, given the importance of the climate of the company in planning an affirmative action or diversity intervention (Morrison, 1992). The anonymity of the three firms was maintained by the authors, presumably because the diversity training implementers were more comfortable sharing information about the positive and negative aspects of their interventions under this condition.

One of the companies was described as having a conservative corporate environment. In this firm, the organization offered a one day mandatory seminar on diversity facilitated by local managers. While requiring attendance was in concert with the firm's conservative climate, Ellis and Sonnenfeld (1994) noted that this approach would be inappropriate in a less formal firm.

The seminar started with a videotaped introduction in which the CEO explained the importance of the workshop and the importance of diversity as a corporate goal. The use of top management commitment is one method of increasing the probability that a program will succeed, since top management support is consistently related to program success.

The seminar was followed by a discussion of race and gender biases led by a trained facilitator. Care was taken to ensure that the group of participants consisted of a cultural mix so that no participant would feel isolated. As noted by Ellis and Sonnenfeld (1994), the facilitator should be knowledgeable and discourage participants from relying on stereotypes of minorities, even positive stereotypes.

Unfortunately, there was no formal evaluation of the effectiveness of the program. This could have taken place by any of the techniques suggested by Morrison (1992), but the lack of formal evaluation is quite common.

In a second firm, the diversity management program differed in many respects. First, the corporate environment was much less formal and characterized by fewer rules and regulations. As one might expect, attendance at diversity workshops was not mandatory in this relatively informal firm. The diversity management program consisted of a series of seminars, discussion groups and corporate presentations on diversity issues. One specific example of this technique was the use of ten male and female employees from varied cultural backgrounds. The group met once a month to discuss their differences. An important aspect of this intervention was that participants were required to attend a two day training program to increase their sensitivity to racial- and gender-based issues and to enhance their understanding of group-level processes. This was implemented after some initial discussion groups proved to be somewhat counterproductive and hurtful to minority group members. In contrast to the first organization, which implemented a one day diversity seminar, these discussions were ongoing.

As in the first firm, top management of the second firm, demonstrated their support for the program. However, again no formal evaluation of the success of the program was gathered. While some manufacturing plants reported higher productivity as a result of the diversity maintenance efforts, this was based on subjective reports rather than a statistical analysis of productivity changes.

The discussion of these two firms hopefully demonstrates the wide range of options open to employers who wish to enhance affirmative action efforts. Ellis and Sonnenfeld's (1994) recommendations to employers echo many of Morrison's strategies for increasing diversity. In addition to Morrison's recommendations, Ellis and Sonnenfeld's (1994) emphasize the importance of carefully selecting those who will lead diversity seminars, and maintaining diverse groups of participants in the workshops.

Public Sector

In the public sector, all decisions are open to scrutiny. Policies and procedures are open to public review. Even individual personnel decisions, who will be hired and why, are publicly posted. Job applicants know who beat them out for a job and why they lost the job to another individual. As a result, affirmative action efforts in the public sector are likely to lead to contentious public debate and, all too frequently, to litigation. Recently, Trice (1999) summarized some of the factors leading to successful implementation in the public sector.

Based on public sector organizations identified as having best practices in the area, Trice (1999) concluded that formal programs should exist. By formalizing programs, and by mandating their existence, affirmative action programs are much less likely to be subject to shifting political agendas and acquire the "force of law." The formalization of procedures should emphasize processes as well as goal. In order to comply with the demands of formal programs and with the established mandates, workforce utilization analysis is necessary. Workforce utilization analysis involved compiling a database and maintaining statistics on workforce data. When, based on the statistical data, underutilization is identified, then action must be taken in order for diversity and affirmative action programs to be successful.

Successful organizations were also found to have oversight committees which were responsible for reviewing and monitoring the programs. However, the affirmative action efforts themselves were decentralized, so that individual agencies could tailor plans to their own needs and requirements. As in the private sector, both top management support and lower level ownership are critical. Thus, individual employees must also be accountable for the successful execution of affirmative action plans.

Finally, in order to achieve success, diversity and affirmative action programs should be linked to other organizational systems, including recruitment, development, and training. Training should not be limited to awareness effort, but should incorporate diversity information into all types of training programs. Affirmative action should be integrated into the organizational culture and management processes.

Education

Ethnic minorities, especially African Americans, remain underrepresented in many academic fields. In some fields and at some institutions, the proportion of Blacks and other minorities, remains near zero. The question is whether this is an acceptable situation for institutions which are supposed to be devoted to education and development.

In order to address the underrepresentation of minorities, and sometimes women, many colleges and universities have developed special minority programs aimed at increasing recruitment and retention. Unfortunately, the literature on the effectiveness of these programs is rather sparse and the psychological literature is almost nonexistent. In response, Lam, Doverspike, and Mawasha (1997) presented a framework based upon a psychological model for understanding success in implementing minority programs in academe. Their framework was then used to create a minority program for use with engineering students.

In creating the psychological model, Lam et al. (1997) found that while a substantial body of literature existed concerning the problem of how to increase the interest and enrollment of women in nontraditional occupations, relatively little attention has been paid to the question of the design of effective career interventions for African Americans. In developing the model and framework for their program, Lam et al. (1997) theorized that success would be a function of several classes of variables which could be matched to specific educational interventions, including:

1. Math and science knowledge - which could be operationalized in terms of math courses completed, math achievement, math self-efficacy, science courses completed, and science achievement.
2. Career orientation - which could be operationalized in terms of commitment to engineering as a career, reasons for pursuing engineering as a career, and the perceived opportunity to pursue a career.
3. Educational and occupational values and beliefs - which could be operationalized in terms of the value of cooperative versus individualistic approaches to learning, and the value of community versus individualism.

4. Social support - which could be operationalized in terms of number of role models, amount of family support, amount of peer support, and amount of faculty support.
5. Self-concept - which could be operationalized in terms of self-assessments of self-efficacy, instrumentality, and competence.

Based upon the psychological model, specific interventions were developed including a signed contract, financial incentives, a minority study center, peer mentoring, and various transition classes and activities. The design of the program was heavily influenced by Landis (1991, 1995), who argued that the goal of minority programs was to offer all students the opportunity to participate in a collaborative learning situation. Over a five-year period, the minority engineering program designed by Lam et al. (1997) resulted in an increase in retention rate from 31% to 73.91% and was acknowledged to be a success by important constituencies including students, administration, and the community. Thus, it is insufficient to simply admit greater numbers of minority or female students. The learning environment must also be reengineered to encourage and promote retention. The development of an appropriate academic environment should be based upon an analysis of critical psychological and learning-related variables.

CHAPTER SUMMARY

In order to progress beyond the first generation of affirmative action, organizations must make a real commitment to move past the easy fix of fads or quick, patchwork solutions. Organizations must be willing to engage in organizational change efforts which foster the recruitment, selection, development and retention of minority and female organizational members. At the same time, employers and educational institutions must consider the manner in which all organizational members are treated. In employment situations, every employee has the right to be treated in a just and fair manner. In educational institutions, every employee and every student has the right to be treated in a just and fair manner.

The organization must not simply implement change but must also educate. The need to educate extends beyond organizational members and includes the general public, legislators and the courts. Organizations must offer training or developmental activities aimed at changing the behavior and attitudes of both majority and minority group members toward affirmative action interventions. Attitudes toward affirmative action are malleable and often based on a lack of adequate information regarding affirmative action. Thus, developmental activities should be created to educate organizational members.

This development of educational activities and interventions requires the availability of an adequate knowledge base concerning the psychological effects of affirmative action programs on individuals. Fortunately, a body of research on psychological implications of affirmative action does now exist, although there are still significant holes in the literature, especially with regard to the existence of true field studies.

Any attempt to enhance the perceived fairness of organizational policies is complicated by a number of variables, some of which may be unique in any given organizational setting. However, a consideration of the factors which consistently influence justice perceptions is well worth the time of policy implementers. Based on the research reviewed, the way a policy is implemented, framed, and communicated can determine reactions to the policy and to the organization as well. The perceived justice or fairness of the policies certainly impacts upon views of organizational fairness and it is logical to expect that the presence of fairer policies would have a positive impact on reactions to the employing organization or educational institution (Nacoste, 1990, 1992; Taylor-Carter, Doverspike, & Cook, 1996).

There is a clear need for research on the effects of implementations in industrial and educational settings. Greater attention needs to be paid to conducting research which explores the extent of resistance in "real world" settings and factors which can decrease this resistance. In addition, it seems clear that the most negative reactions to the beneficiaries of affirmative action stem from laboratory research. Some field studies do not find that beneficiaries suffer as a result of affirmative action. Perhaps the negative impact of affirmative action is most likely to occur in situations where little is known about the beneficiary, such as in initial hiring. If this is the case, then longitudinal studies of the impact of affirmative action on beneficiaries would greatly increase our understanding of the policies and help resolve some of the discrepancies in the research.

Another possibility is that affirmative action has the strongest impact when the beneficiary has "solo status" in the organization. Negative attitudes toward minorities are exaggerated in situations where other information is minimal and when only one minority is hired (Lott, 1985; Pettigrew & Martin, 1987). Again, lab studies generally isolate the race or gender of the beneficiary, thus making it a very strong cue to raters. If one were judging the beneficiary in a context where other minorities were already hired and performing successfully in the firm, the negative impact may not be as strong. Thus, the number of minorities in a firm may be an important determinant of reactions to beneficiaries and the impact of negative stereotypes on treatment of minorities (Taylor, 1981). However, the existing racial or gender mix of firms is typically not reported in field research.

REFERENCES

Anderson, M. R., & Wilson, G. N. (1985) Faculty women's association: An instrument for change. *Journal of Social Issues, 41,* 73-83.

Arthur, W., Doverspike, D., & Fuentes, R. (1992). Recipients' affective responses to affirmative action interventions: A cross-cultural perspective. *Behavioral Sciences and the Law, 10,* 229-243.

Arvey, R. D., & Sackett, P. R. (1993). Fairness in selection: Current developments and perspectives. In N. Schmitt & W. Borman (Eds.), *Personnel selection in organizations* (pp. 171-202). San Francisco: Jossey-Bass.

Barber, A. E., & Roehling, M. V. (1993). Job posting and the decision to interview: A verbal protocol analysis. *Journal of Applied Psychology, 78,* 845-856.

Bies, R. J., & Shapiro, D. L. (1988). Voice and justification: Their influence on procedural fairness judgments. *Academy of Management Journal, 31,* 676-685.

Bobocel, D. R., & Farrell, A. C. (1996). Sex-based promotion decisions and interactional fairness: Investigating the influence of managerial accounts. *Journal of Applied Psychology, 81,* 22-35.

Chacko, T. I. (1982). Women and equal employment opportunity: Some unintended effects. *Journal of Applied Psychology, 67,* 119-123.

Clayton, S. D., & Crosby, F. J. (1992). *Justice, gender, and affirmative action.* Ann Arbor, MI: University of Michigan Press.

Crosby, F., & Clayton, S. (1990). Affirmative action and the issue of expectancies. *Journal of Social Issues, 26,* 61-79.

Ellis, C., & Sonnenfeld, J. A. (1994). Diverse approaches to managing diversity. *Human Resource Management, 33,* 79-109.

Folger, R., & Greenberg, J. (1985). Procedural Justice: An interpretive analysis of personnel systems. In K. M. Rowland and G. R. Ferris (Eds.), *Research in personnel and human resource management: A research annual* (Vol. 3, pp. 141-183). Greenwich, CN: JAI Press.

Folger, R., & Martin, C. (1986). Relative deprivation and referent cognitions: Distributive and procedural justice effects. *Journal of Experimental Social Psychology, 22,* 531-546.

Gard, J. (1996). *Valuing diversity as a prosocial organizational behavior.* Unpublished doctoral dissertation, University of Akron, Akron, Ohio.

Gilliland, S. W. (1993). The perceived fairness of selection systems: An organizational justice perspective. *Academy of Management Review, 18,* 694-734.

Greenberg, J. (1990). Organizational justice: Yesterday, today and tomorrow. *Journal of Management, 16,* 399-432.

Heilman, M. E. (1984). Information as a deterrent against sex discrimination: The effects of applicant sex and information type on preliminary employment decisions. *Organizational Behavior and Human Decision Processes, 33,* 174-186.

Heilman, M. E., & Herlihy, J. M. (1984). Affirmative action, negative reaction? Some moderating conditions. *Organizational Behavior_and Human Performance,* 33, 204-213.

Heilman, M. E., McCullough, W.F., & Gilbert, D. (1996). The other side of affirmative action: Reactions of nonbeneficiaries to sex-based preferential selection. *Journal of Applied Psychology,* 81, 346-357.

Highhouse, S., Stierwalt, S. L., Bachiochi, P., Elder, A. E., & Fisher, G. (1999). Effects of advertised human resource management practices on attraction of African American applicants. *Personnel Psychology, 52,* 425-442.

Hitt, M. A., & Keats, B. W. (1984). Empirical identification of the criteria for effective affirmative action programs. *Journal of Applied Behavioral Science, 20,* 203-222.

Hyer, P. B. (1985). Affirmative action for women faculty: Case studies of three successful institutions. *Journal of Higher Education, 56,* 282-299.

Kahn, E. D., & Robbins, L. (1985). Social-psychological issues in sex discrimination. *Journal of Social Issues, 41,* 35-154.

Konrad, A. M., & Linnehan, F. (1995). Race and sex differences in line managers' reactions to equal employment opportunity and affirmative action interventions. *Group and Organization Management, 20,* 409-439.

Kossek, E. E., & Zonia, S. (1993). Assessing diversity climate: A field study of reactions to employer efforts to promote diversity. *Journal of Organizational Behavior, 14,* 61-81.

Kravitz, D.A. (1995). Attitudes toward affirmative action plans directed at Blacks: Effects of plan and individual differences. *Journal of Applied Social Psychology, 25,*2192-2220.

Kravitz, D. A., Harrison, D. A., Turner, M. A., Levine, E. L. Chaves, W., Brannick, M. T., Denning, D. L., Russell, C. J., & Conrad, M. A. (1997). *Affirmative action: A review of psychological and behavioral research.* Bowling Green, OH: Society for Industrial and Organizational Psychology.

Kravitz, D. A. & Platania, J. (1993). Attitudes and beliefs about affirmative action: Effects of target and respondent sex and ethnicity. *Journal of Applied Psychology, 78,* 928-938.

Lam, P.C., Doverspike, D., & Mawasha, R. P. (1997). Increasing diversity in engineering academics (IDEAs): Development of a program for improving African American representation. *Journal of Career Development, 24,* 55-70.

Landis, R. B. (1991). *Retention by design: Achieving excellence in minority engineering education.* New York, NY: National Action Council for Minorities in Engineering.

Landis, R. B. (1995). *Studying engineering: A road map to a rewarding career.* Burbank, CA: Discovery Publishing.

Larwood, L., Szwajkowski, E., & Rose, S. (1988). Sex and race discrimination resulting from manager-client relationships: Applying the Rational Bias theory of managerial discrimination. *Sex Roles, 18,* 9-29.

Latack, J. C., Josephs, S. L., Roach, B. L., & Levine, M. D. (1987). Carpenter apprentices: Comparison of career transitions for men and women. *Journal of Applied Psychology, 72,* 393-400.

Lott, B. (1985). The devaluation of women's competence. *Journal of Social Issues, 41,* 43-60.

Loury, G. C. (1989). Why should we care about inequality? In *The Question of Discrimination* (pp. 268-290). Middletown Court: Wesleyan University Press.

Mansfield, P. K., Koch, P. B., Henderson, J., Vicary, J. R., Cohn, M., & Young, E. W. (1991). The job climate for women in traditionally male blue-collar occupations. *Sex Roles, 25,* 63-79.

Marino, K. E. (1980). A preliminary investigation into the behavioral dimensions of affirmative action compliance. *Journal of Applied Psychology, 65,* 346-350.

Morrison, A. (1992, Summer). Developing diversity in organizations. *Business Quarterly,* pp. 42-48.

Morrison, A. M., & Von Glinow, M. A. (1990). Women and minorities in management. American Psychologist, 45, 200-208.

Nacoste, R. W. (1985). Selection procedure and responses to affirmative action: The case of favorable treatment. *Law and Human Behavior. 9,* 225-242.

Nacoste, R. W. (1987). But do they care about fairness? The dynamics of preferential treatment and minority interest. *Basic and Applied Social Psychology, 8,* 177-191.

Nacoste, R. W. (1990). Sources of stigma: Analyzing the psychology of affirmative action. *Law and Policy, 12,* 2, 175-195.

Nacoste, R. W. (1992). Toward a psychological ecology of affirmative action. *Social Justice Research, 5,* 269-289.

Nacoste, R. W., & Lehman, D. (1987). Procedural stigma. *Representative Research in Social Psychology, 17,* 25-38.

Ott, E. M. (1989). Effects of the male-female ratio at work: Policewomen and male nurses. *Psychology of Women Quarterly, 13,* 41-57.

Palmer, H. T., & Lee, J. A. (1990). Female workers' acceptance in traditionally male-dominated blue-collar jobs. *Sex Roles, 22,* 607-626.

Parker, C. P., Baltes, B.B., & Christiansen, N.D. (1997). Support for affirmative action, justice perceptions, and work attitudes: A study of gender and racial-ethnic group differences. *Journal of Applied Psychology, 82,* 376-389.

Pettigrew, T. F., & Martin, J. (1987). Shaping the organizational context for black American inclusion. *Journal of Social Issues, 43,* 41-78.

Ponterotto, J. G., Martinez, F. M., & Hayden, D. C. (1986, July). Student affirmative action programs: A help or hindrance to development of minority graduate students? *Journal of College Student Personnel*, pp. 318-325.

Pratkanis, A. R., & Turner, M. E. (1996). The proactive removal of discriminatory barriers: Affirmative action as effective help. *Journal of Social Issues, 52,* 111-132.

Rutte, C. G., & Messick, D. M. (1995). An integrated model of perceived unfairness in organizations. *Social Justice Research, 8,* 239-261.

Rynes, S. L., & Miller, H. E. (1983). Recruiter and job influences on candidates for employment. *Journal of Applied Psychology, 68,* 147-154.

Rynes, S.L., & Rosen, B. (1995). A field survey of factors affecting the adoption and perceived success of diversity training. *Personnel Psychology, 48,* 247-270.

Sears, D. O. (1988). Symbolic racism. In P. A. Katz & D. A. Taylor (Eds.), *Eliminating racism: Profiles in controversy* (pp. 53-84). New York: Plenum Press.

Schmitt, M. J., & Ryan, A. M. (1997). Applicant Withdrawal: The role of test-taking attitudes and racial differences. *Personnel Psychology, 50,* 855-876.

Sweeney, P.D., & McFarlin, D. B. (1993). Workers' evaluations of the "ends" and "means:" An examination of four models of distributive and procedural justice. *Organizational Behavior and Human Decision Processes, 55,* 23-40.

Taylor, S. E. (1981). A categorization approach to stereotyping. In D. L. Hamilton (Ed.), *Cognitive processes in stereotyping and intergroup behavior* (pp. 83-115). Hillsdale, NJ: Lawrence Erlbaum.

Taylor-Carter, M. A., Doverspike, D., & Alexander, R. (1995). Message effects on the perceptions of the fairness of gender-based affirmative action: A cognitive response theory-based analysis. *Social Justice Research, 8,* 285-303.

Taylor-Carter, M., Doverspike, D., & Cook, K. (1995). Understanding resistance to sex and race-based affirmative action: A review of research findings. *Human Resource Management Review, 5,* 129-157.

Taylor-Carter, M. A., Doverspike, D., & Cook, K. D. (1996). The effects of affirmative action on the female beneficiary. *Human Resource Development Quarterly, 7,* 31-54.

Thorton, G. C., III. (1993). The effects of selection practices on applicants' perceptions of organizational characteristics. In H. Schuler, J. L. Farr and M.. Smith (Eds.), *Personnel selection and assessment: Individual and organizational perspectives* (pp. 57-69). Hillsdale,NJ: Lawrence Erlbaum.

Trice, E. (1999, July). Diversity best practices. *IPMA News*, pp. 1,5.

Turner, M. E., & Pratkanis, A. R. (1993). Effects of preferential and meritorious selection on performance: An examination of intuitive and self-handicapping perspectives. *Personality and Social Psychology Bulletin, 19,* 47-58.

Tyler, T. R., & Bies, R. J. (1990). Beyond formal procedures: The interpersonal context of procedural justice. In J.S. Carroll (Ed.), *Applied Social Psychology and Organizational Settings.* Hillsdale, NJ: Lawrence Erlbaum.

Veilleux, F., & Tougas, F. (1989). Male acceptance of affirmative action programs for women: The results of altruistic or egotistical motives. *International Journal of Psychology, 24,* 485-496.

Williams, M. L., & Bauer, T. B. (1994). The effect of a managing diversity policy on organizational attractiveness. *Group and Organization Management, 19,* 295-308.

Witt, S. L. (1990). Affirmative action and job satisfaction: Self-interested v. public spirited perspectives on social equity -- Some sobering findings from the academic workplace. *Review of Public Personnel Administration, 10,* 73-93.

Chapter 12

CONCLUSION

In the beginning of this book, we raised the question of the applicability of psychological research to the affirmative action debate (i.e., should organizations engage in affirmative action based on protected group status in the awarding of opportunities). The paradox of affirmative action is that a procedure where the intent is the elimination of decision making based upon race and sex often leads to or requires decision making based upon race and sex.

This leads to strong arguments on both sides with the proponents arguing that affirmative action corrects and remediates the effects of past discrimination, while also promoting diversity, inclusion, and greater representation in a variety of occupations and organizations where minorities and women have been traditionally underrepresented. On the other hand, the opponents argue that affirmative action violates the basic rule of distributing opportunities on the basis of merit without regard to race and sex, and results in awards being made on the basis of race and sex. It is argued then that the violation of the rule of merit leads to anger, hostility and resistance on the part of nonbeneficiaries (i.e., primarily White males) and may also cause psychological harm to the intended beneficiaries due to the negative effects on self-assessments and evaluations by others.

In this book, we sought to show that attitudes toward affirmative action are malleable and can be changed by simple communications. After a discussion of the basic theories and methods used in psychological studies, we reviewed the major findings based on a general model of the psychological processes involved in reactions to affirmative action.

Hopefully, we were able to demonstrate that the psychological research is relevant to issues raised in the debate over affirmative action. However, we are still left with the question as to why it is that the psychological literature has not had more of an influence on the participants in the debate nor on the general public.

This final chapter begins with a brief summary of some of the important findings from the review of the literature. Next, we present suggestions for future research. Finally, we offer some closing comments on the critical question as to why it is that psychological research has not had more of an influence on the affirmative action debate and whether research on affirmative action has a future.

RESEARCH FINDINGS

In psychology, it is actually somewhat rare to find results that are reproducible from study to study. The inconsistency in results across studies can be explained by a number of factors, including the use of small sample sizes, the relatively weakness of many effects, and the unreliability of measurement. In this section, we briefly summarize the research results in an order which reflects the overall strength and reproducibility of the effects.

If fairness is treated as a mediator rather than as a dependent variable, then it is highly correlated with attitudes toward affirmative action. After controlling for unreliability due to measurement error, the correlation is probably close to one. Thus, fairness or justice perceptions are a major predictor of attitudes and mediate the effects of most other variables upon attitudes. However, treating fairness as a mediator leads to a number of troublesome measurement and definitional problems. In future research, we would recommend distinguishing between fairness and justice, and argue that the two should be measured separately with justice being treated as a mediator and fairness as one type of attitude.

One of the most consistent and strongest effects is that the relative emphasis on merit as compared to protected class status is a major factor in determining reactions toward affirmative action policies. As the weight accorded to merit increases, ratings of fairness and positive affect also increase. This finding appears to be reproducible in studies using a variety of methods (i.e., opinion survey, correlational study, paper-person scenario, and assigned leader paradigm). It is also consistent with psychological theories, including equity, procedural justice, and reasoned action theory. Not only does the manipulation of the tradeoff between merit and protected class status affect attitudinal ratings, but the relative qualifications of the candidates also has a consistent effect on attitudes and fairness ratings. Respondents tend to believe that the candidate with the highest merit should be selected and, when a decision violates this norm, it results in dissatisfaction or in feelings of inequity. As a result, the type of affirmative action is an important variable in acceptance. Harder forms of preferential treatment result in negative reactions and are unlikely to be seen as fair. Support for more general policies, such as equal opportunity or training, are much more prevalent. On the other hand, soft forms of preferential treatment, where the exact weighting of merit and protected group status may be ambiguous, are likely to result in the greatest variance in attitudinal reactions.

Affirmative action policies are viewed more positively by the potential beneficiaries than by those experiencing no benefit or likely to experience a loss, and this effect is relatively consistent across the various research methods. Blacks are more likely to react positively to affirmative action than are Whites. Females are more likely to react positively to affirmative action than are males. Given the strong effects obtained for beneficiary status, sex, and race, it is then logical that self-interest emerges as a major mediator. The self-interest effect is consistent with a number of theories including reasoned action theory and equity theory.

Although potential beneficiaries view affirmative action as being in their best interest, affirmative action policies may also result in social psychological costs for the intended beneficiaries. Consistent with the predictions of attribution theory, nonbeneficiaries perceive beneficiaries as being less competent. In addition, affirmative action has a negative effect on beneficiary's self-assessments of competence. The negative effects of affirmative action on ratings of competence can be reduced by providing information on the merit or qualifications of the beneficiaries.

Affirmative action does have costs for its potential beneficiaries. Not only is there the potential for resistance and hostility from nonbeneficiaries, but beneficiaries may question their own competence and engage in self-blame. Thus, there are psychological costs, both self- and other-imposed, on the intended beneficiary. However, these effects may be of relatively short duration and providing information on the qualifications of the beneficiary reduces the negative effects. Any costs to minorities and women would appear to be offset by the long-term benefits resulting from the increase in opportunities.

By definition, this book has dealt with the psychological literature on affirmative action. We have purposely excluded the legal literature and the economic literature. There is a large body of research attempting to measure the economic effects of affirmative action and we will not attempt to do this literature justice. The President's Report on Affirmative Action (White House, 1995) reached what might be described as ambivalent and ambiguous conclusions regarding the results of economic studies. According to the report, while anti-discrimination programs, including affirmative action, appeared to have produced an improved standard of living for African Americans and led to gains in education and employment (Bowen & Bok, 1998; Murrell & Jones, 1996), it was difficult to link any improvements to specific anti-discrimination programs or to even say that individual programs, by themselves, had been effective. There was also a great improvement in educational and employment opportunities for women, which was accompanied by a growth in income. However, again it was difficult to link any increase to specific affirmative action programs.

When the organization defines what affirmative action means, including information on the type of policy, or when it offers compensatory explanations, such as a history of past discrimination, the organization is framing its message. The framing of the message affects the interpretation and acceptance of the information in the message, a finding which is consistent with both Nacoste's (1996) theory of procedural-interdependence and interactional justice-communication theories. However, the recipient of the message is an active processor of information and, therefore, the final effect of the message on attitude change will depend upon how the recipient interprets the message. Support from organizational members (e.g., administrators, managers, supervisors, faculty, coworker, other students) is also a critical factor in shaping reactions to the message.

The history of previous discrimination by the organization does not appear to have a major effect on attitudes. However, individual differences in beliefs concerning the causes of the distribution of educational and employment opportunities does appear to be an important predictor, and thus a major mediator, of reactions to affirmative action. Simply believing that differences in opportunities exist is not sufficient. The difference in opportunity must be attributed to past discrimination rather than to characteristics of the members of the protected class.

Both racism and sexism are correlated with resistence to affirmative action policies. Again, the caution can be offered that this does not imply that everyone who opposes affirmative action is a racist or a sexist. Surprisingly, relatively little research has been conducted on personality dimensions, although personality would appear to be related to both racism and sexism. Political beliefs, including the individual difference variables of individualism-collectivism and liberalism-conservatism, also appear to be related to reactions to affirmative action.

The group targeted by the affirmative action effort does appear to affect fairness and attitude ratings with race-based affirmative action receiving less support than sex-based affirmative action and remedial efforts aimed at other groups. It would seem likely that this effect could be mediated by both self-interest and beliefs concerning the causes for the relative imbalance in the distribution of educational and employment opportunities.

The type of opportunity (i.e., educational or employment, public or private sector) appears to have a small effect, if any. Relatively little research has been conducted on the question of public sector versus private sector. Opinion survey research would suggest that more favorable attitudes are expressed toward affirmative action in education than in employment.

SUGGESTIONS FOR FUTURE RESEARCH

We have resisted the temptation to include a section in the conclusion dealing with criticisms of the existing research. Rather than fixating on problems, we have tried to take a positive attitude and move right to suggestions for future research. The suggestions for future research are organized around our model of the psychological processes involved in affirmative action (see Figure 1, Chapter 1).

There is a clear need for research on characteristics of the sender of the message. Two sender variables which should affect reactions are the expertise of the sender and the degree of trust the respondent has in the sender. Research using correlational methods and paper-person scenarios could easily be modified to include measurement or manipulation of characteristics of the sender.

In organizations, affirmative action is a very complex procedure involving many component parts, which cannot be easily reduced to one simple sentence. An affirmative action plan for a typical organization may easily run one hundred pages and involve complex statistical and legal issues. In research, affirmative action policies are often presented without any reference to a need or a rationale for a policy. As both Nacoste (1996) and Kravitz et al. (1997) have suggested, researchers should begin to include more realistic and more detailed descriptions of affirmative action policies. Kravitz et al. (1997) have also noted that an alternative way to operationalize past history of discrimination would be by offering data on economic indicators and utilization ratios.

In answering the call for more realistic research, there is also a clear need for research on the effects of actual implementations of affirmative action policies in real organizations. Research is needed on the extent of resistance and the factors which effect resistence. Consideration should also be given to conducting more longitudinal studies. Most of the research on affirmative action has involved short time intervals. Studies should be conducted which include longitudinal designs of multiple measures over an extended period of time.

Especially in the laboratory, it is easier to do research on sex than on race. As a result, there seems to have been an overemphasis on sex-based affirmative action. While it may be difficult to attract sufficient sample sizes, empirical research is needed on ethnic groups such as Native Americans, Asians, and Hispanics. Much of the research on beneficiary's self-assessments has been based on sex-based affirmative action involving White females, although in our research we have tried to investigate more thoroughly the question of race-based affirmative action. Additional research is needed on the effects of race-based affirmative action on beneficiary's self-assessments and on the effects of race or ethnicity on sex-based affirmative action.

Advances in our understanding of the role of individual differences in reactions to affirmative action would appear to require major improvements in our ability to measure personal traits, especially racism and sexism. Modern variations of racism and sexism seem to cause more problems than they solve, in that they often assess support for affirmative action. Measures of racism and sexism could be developed which avoid this overlap in content.

A major question which research should ask is whether it is possible to change racist and sexist attitudes. Racist attitudes among college students appear to be fairly malleable and can be changed by simple messages (Blanchard, Lilly, & Vaughn, 1991; Blanchard, Crandall, Brigham, and Vaughn, 1994).

The effects of personality on reactions to affirmative action is an area in need of research. Correlational survey studies based on five-factor theory could be conducted in order to collect some basic data. We have also speculated upon the existence of a cosmopolitan personality, which is based on an open personality type combined with multicultural knowledge. Research could be directed toward testing for the presence of such a personality type.

We have identified three variables which we consider to be likely mediators of the effects of independent variables on reactions to affirmative action. However, only a few studies have directly tested for the presence of mediators. In designing research studies, consideration should be given to incorporating elements which allow for the appropriate statistical tests for the presence of mediating variables.

Researchers should consider using a wider range of dependent variables. Fairness and affect have been researched quite extensively. Studies are needed which measure the effects of affirmative action on performance, attraction to the organization, and on other organizational outcomes. Most of the research on social psychological costs to beneficiaries has used competence as the dependent variable. Studies are needed using other dependent variables including motivation, satisfaction with the organization, and effects on actual task, school or job performance.

In research on self-assessments, consideration should be given to including measures assessing whether negative evaluations also generalize to one's group (Kravitz et al., 1997). Pinel's (1999) recent work on group identity, group consciousness and stigma consciousness would appear to represent a theoretical foundation upon which to base future research. A simple hypothesis which could be tested is whether negative self-evaluations are more likely to be generalized to the group when group identity is high.

Psychological research should be guided by theory. However, as Nacoste (1996) points out, it is too easy to become enthralled with the magic allure of theory. Nevertheless, we believe that justice theories, particularly Nacoste's (1996) theory of procedural-interdependence and interactional justice-communication theories provide a foundation upon which programs of research on affirmative action can be built. Although attribution theory has proven useful in explaining the effects of affirmative action on evaluations of beneficiary competence, another theory which may prove useful in explaining assessments of beneficiary competence is Turner and Pratkanis' (1993, 1994, Turner, Pratkanis, & Hardaway, 1991) conceptualization of affirmative action as a type of helping behavior.

DOES AFFIRMATIVE ACTION RESEARCH HAVE A FUTURE?

Having just discussed future research possibilities, it may seem strange that we now ask and attempt to answer the question as to whether research on affirmative action does have a future. However, there are several good reasons for asking whether affirmative action research does have a future. First, an argument could be made that given the current political and legal environment existing in the United States, affirmative action is a dead issue. Second, it could be argued that organizations now emphasize diversity rather than affirmative action (Jackson, 1992). Third, the contribution of psychology research to the affirmative action debate could be questioned (Nacoste, 1996).

Even if we accept the argument that the current political trend is anti-affirmative action, the pendulum will swing back. The problem is that without affirmative action policies, and even with affirmative action policies, the representation of minorities and women in many occupations and organizations remains very low. The question which must be asked is whether society is willing to accept a situation in which a university may have no Black engineering students, or a city may have no female firefighters, or a company may have no female executives. If the answer to the above question is no, then some type of program must be initiated in order to boost the representation of minorities and women in underrepresented areas, and the most likely solution is affirmative action procedures including soft preferential action. Thus, at least in the short term, it would appear that underrepresentation of women and minorities will continue and that some method of increasing representation will be sought.

Diversity has replaced affirmative action as the term used to describe procedures intended to increase representation and integrate underrepresented groups into organizations (Jackson, 1994; Riccucci, 1997).

However, "diversity" is a difficult term to define and when we do try to operationalize it in research, it ends up looking a lot like affirmative action. Thus, our opinion would be that the trend toward diversity programs will only lead to an intensification of the debate over affirmative action issues, even if it is under a new nom de plume. It is difficult to see how the psychological ramifications of being a "diversity hire" would be much different from the effects of being an "affirmative action hire." Research on affirmative action is also extremely relevant to the diversity debate; indeed, we do not think that the two can really be separated. Many of the factors which predict resistance to affirmative action should also predict opposition to diversity efforts.

Nacoste (1996) provided an excellent summary of some of the reasons why psychology has not contributed more to the affirmative action debate. In addition to the usual culprits, including too great a concentration at the individual level and the tendency to become trapped by one's political beliefs, Nacoste (1996) criticized the inappropriate use and applications of theory to affirmative action issues and the limited definition and operationalization of affirmative action used in many studies. While agreeing with Nacoste's (1996) criticisms, it also seems that psychology often asks the wrong questions or the easy questions. Examples would include the limited number of laboratory studies dealing with Blacks and other minority groups and the lack of research on attitude change. This does not mean that psychological research should always be driven by popular trends, but more attention should be paid to the types of questions which are asked. There is also a real need to develop integrated programs of research which lead to the design of more effective implementation efforts.

The debate over affirmative action will continue, but can psychology contribute to the debate? The answer is yes, if psychology can ask the right questions and communicate the answers in a manner which the public can understand. Psychologists must also return to their roots and remember that affirmative action is controversial because it does have the potential to affect people's lives. The debate over affirmative action is not just about profits or politics but also about people's hopes for a better education, a better job, and a better life for themselves and their children. Unfortunately, many of the issues dealt with in the psychological literature seem rather trivial when compared to the potential impact of affirmative action policies on people's lives.

Affirmative action issues are unlikely to go away. It is likely that we will see the affirmative action debate resurface and intensify. Affirmative action attempts to atone for past discrimination. However, the remnants of past discrimination remain, and prejudice, in its many forms, is still an unfortunate reality. American society seems trapped in its own equity-equality debate; although people believe in the distribution of opportunities based upon merit, they are unwilling to accept large inequities in representation as a function of race or sex. Affirmative action, including the use of preferential treatment, remains one of the few effective methods available for increasing representation.

REFERENCES

Blanchard, F., Lilly, T., & Vaughn, L. A. (1991). Reducing the expression of racial prejudice. *Psychological Science, 2,* 101-105.

Blanchard, F., Crandall, C. S., Brigham, J. C., & Vaughn, L. A. (1994). Condemning and condoning racism: A social context approach to interracial settings. *Journal of Applied Psychology, 79,* 993-997.

Bowen, W. & Bok, D. (1998). *The shape of the river: Long-term consequences of considering race in college and university admissions.* Princeton, NJ: Princeton University Press.

Jackson, S. & Associates (Eds.). (1992). *Diversity in the workplace: Human resource initiatives.* New York, NY: Guilford.

Kravitz, D. A., Harrison, D. A., Turner, M. A., Levine, E. L. Chaves, W., Brannick, M. T., Denning, D. L., Russell, C. J., & Conrad, M. A. (1997). *Affirmative action: A review of psychological and behavioral research.* Bowling Green, OH: Society for Industrial and Organizational Psychology.

Murrell, A. J. & Jones, R. (1996). Assessing affirmative action: Past, present and future. *Journal of Social Issues, 52,* 133-144.

Nacoste, R. W. (1996). Social psychology and the affirmative action debate. *Journal of Social and Clinical Psychology, 15,* 261-282.

Pinel, E. C. (1999). Stigma consciousness: The psychological legacy of social stereotypes. *Journal of Personality and Social Psychology, 76,* 114-128.

Riccucci, N. M.. (1997). Cultural diversity programs to prepare for work force 2000: What's gone wrong? *Public Personnel Management, 26,* 35-41.

Turner, M. E., & Pratkanis, A. R. (1993). Effects of preferential and meritorious selection on performance: An examination of intuitive and self-handicapping perspectives. *Personality and Social Psychology Bulletin, 19,* 47-58.

Turner, M. E., & Pratkanis, A. R. (1994). Affirmative action as help: A review of recipient reactions to preferential selection and affirmative action. *Basic and Applied Social Psychology, 15,* 43-69.

Turner, M. E., Pratkanis, A. R., & Hardaway, T. (1991). Sex differences in reactions to preferential selection: Towards a model of preferential selection as help. *Journal of Social Behavior and Personality, 6,* 797-814.

White House (1995). *Affirmative action review: Report to the President.* [On-line], Available: www.whitehouse.gov /WH /EOP /OP /html /aa/aa-index.

INDEX